TEACHING AI

CW00373620

A selection of other How To Books

Applying for a Job
Applying for a US Visa
Career Networking
Career Planning for Women
Doing Voluntary Work Abroad
Finding a Job in Canada
Finding a Job in New Zealand
Finding a Job with a Future
Finding Work Overseas
Freelance Teaching & Tutoring
Getting a Job After University
Getting a Job in America
Getting a Job in Australia
Getting That Job
Getting Your First Job
How to Communicate at Work
How to Emigrate
How to Find Temporary Work Abroad
How to Get a Job Abroad
How to Get a Job in Europe
How to Get a Job in France
How to Get a Job in Germany
How to Live & Work in Germany
How to Live & Work in Greece
How to Live & Work in Italy
How to Live & Work in New Zealand
How to Live & Work in the Gulf
How to Manage Your Career
How to Market Yourself
How to Master Languages
How to Return to Work
How to Start a New Career
How to Study & Learn
How to Study Abroad

How to Teach Adults
How to Travel Round the World
Improving Your Written English
Know Your Rights at Work
Know Your Rights: Students
Know Your Rights: Teachers
Learning New Job Skills
Living & Working in America
Living & Working in Australia
Living & Working in Britain
Living & Working in China
Living & Working in France
Living & Working in Hong Kong
Living & Working in Israel
Living & Working in Saudi Arabia
Living & Working in Spain
Living & Working in the Netherlands
Managing Your Personal Finances
Mastering Business English
Migrating to Canada
Obtaining Visas & Work Permits
Passing That Interview
Planning Your Gap Year
Rent & Buy Property in France
Rent & Buy Property in Italy
Securing a Rewarding Retirement
Selling Your House
Spending a Year Abroad
Working Abroad
Working in Japan
Working in the Gulf
Working on Contracts Worldwide
Working with Children
Writing a CV that Works

The How To series now contains more than 250 titles in the following categories:

Business & Management
Computer Basics
General Reference
Jobs & Careers
Living & Working Abroad

Personal Finance
Self-Development
Small Business
Student Handbooks
Successful Writing

Please send for a free copy of the latest catalogue for full details (see back cover for address).

JOBS & CAREERS

TEACHING ABROAD

How and where to find world-wide opportunities and contacts

Roger Jones

3rd edition

How To Books

By the same author

Getting a Job Abroad
Getting a Job in America
How to Emigrate
How to Get a Job Abroad
How to Manage Your Career
How to Master Languages
How to Retire Abroad
Obtaining Visas & Work Permits

British Library Cataloguing in Publication Data
A catalogue record for this book is available from the British Library.

© Copyright 1998 by Roger Jones.

First published in 1989 by How To Books Ltd, 3 Newtec Place, Magdalen Road, Oxford OX4 1RE, United Kingdom. Tel: (01865) 793806. Fax: (01865) 248780.

First edition 1989
Second edition 1994
Third edition 1998

All rights reserved. No part of this work may be reproduced or stored in an information retrieval system (other than for purposes of review) without the express permission of the Publisher in writing.

Roger Alan Jones has asserted his moral right to be identified as the author of this book.

Note: The material contained in this book is set out in good faith for general guidance and no liability can be accepted for loss or expense incurred as a result of relying in particular circumstances on statements made in the book. The laws and regulations are complex and liable to change, and readers should check the current position with the relevant authorities before making personal arrangements.

Produced for How To Books by Deer Park Productions.

Typeset by Concept Communications Ltd, Crayford, Kent.
Printed and bound by Cromwell Press, Trowbridge, Wilthsire.

Contents

Preface
to the Third Edition

Ten years ago I conceived the idea of a handbook for people planning to work in education overseas, which would deal with the range of opportunities available and offer advice on how to achieve one's aims. It was eventually published under the title *How to Teach Abroad*.

Now the handbook has reached its third edition sporting a different cover and a (slightly) different title. However, the differences are more than superficial. The world of teaching has not stood still in the intervening decade, so it has been necessary to revise the original text comprehensively in order to reflect current realities. More countries than ever — over 180 — have been included in this edition.

Ensuring that the advice in these pages is appropriate is a particularly difficult task, since circumstances differ so widely from post to post. If you are taking up a post in an Australian university, for instance, you could be less prone to culture shock than if you are sent to a rural school in the middle of the jungle.

I also realise that readers of this book will represent a wide spectrum of experience. Some will be 18 year olds about to spend the gap year between school and university working as teaching assistants simply for the sake of the experience. At the other end of the spectrum there may be senior educationalists who are anxious to deploy their skills in the Third World.

I have endeavoured to write a book which will suit both ends of the scale and also the majority of readers who will fall between these two extremes. For this reason I must crave the understanding of those who have spent many years at the chalkface, so to speak. If at times I appear to be stating the obvious, please remember that what is obvious to some will be a revelation to others.

In some cases I include countries which are not recruiting teachers and lecturers at the present time. More often than not this is because the country is engulfed in conflict and the educational system is hardly functioning. A number of African countries are currently suffering from such a fate. Yet I am optimistic enough to believe that such situations can only get better, and that one day recruitment will resume.

I apologise for any factual errors. While I have spent a good deal of time updating and correcting, information has a nasty habit of going out of date. Recruitment policies change, organisations move to new addresses, educational priorities are modified. However, I hope that in these pages you will find useful contacts and the information you need to make an informed choice. If you find mistakes, please let me know of them (c/o How To Books), and I will rectify them in a future edition.

The world of education is becoming increasingly cosmopolitan and this book will doubtless find readers living outside the British Isles. In order to facilitate international communication I have included websites, e-mail addresses and fax numbers, where possible. People living outside Britain wishing to ring or fax UK based organisations have simply to dial the international dialling code (usually 00), then 44 and finally the number indicated omitting the initial 0. Wherever you live, please note that in the year 2000 a number of area dialling codes (notably London) are to be changed — again.

Let me also address a matter of terminology. Teaching English to people whose native tongue is not English is known by a number of acronyms (including TEFL, TOEFL, TESOL and TESL) to differentiate it from teaching English to those whose mother tongue is English. I realise there is some debate in teaching circles as to whether TEFL is the same as TESL, but for the purposes of this book I use the acronym TEFL (teaching English as a foreign language) and sometimes EFL (English as a foreign language) to refer to all of these.

Finally, may I thank those people who have helped me in the compilation of this book and extend my good wishes to all of you who are either teaching abroad already or hope to do so in the future. May your assignments be successful, stimulating and trouble-free.

Roger Jones

1
Opening Doors of Opportunity

THE ATTRACTIONS OF TEACHING ABROAD

Judging from the millions of people who take their holidays abroad each year foreign climes have their attractions. Sometimes it is the warmer climate which entices people away from their native shores; sometimes it is the scenery, or the cultural treasures, or the atmosphere of the place.

Some people become so enamoured with the place that they look into the possibility of staying there for an extended period of time. Unless you have a private income, such a plan usually entails looking round for a job. Teachers and lecturers are particularly well placed when it comes to finding employment, although the availability of jobs tends to vary according to your subject.

There are other attractions, too. There is the opportunity to gain valuable experience, and a certain amount of overseas work experience on your CV might well impress discerning selectors at some future date. There is also the opportunity — in certain countries — to earn a substantial salary which could have the added attraction of being tax-free.

THE RANGE OF OPPORTUNITIES
Short-term

How short-term is short-term? It could be a matter of just a month or two teaching on a vacation course. Or it could be half a year. Sometimes schools and colleges need to replace staff who have left or fallen ill, and are ready to employ someone on a short-term basis.

At the senior level there may be an opportunity to do short consultancies — perhaps on secondment from your employer.

One year

A number of organisations offer one year renewable contracts. There may be a number of reasons for this. The place may be somewhat uncongenial so that employers doubt whether they will attract people on a

9

long-term basis or there may be legal reasons, as would be the case if you have to obtain a work permit every year.

Two to three years
Many contracts tend to be two or three year ones, especially public sector appointments. In many cases such contracts are renewable.

A long-term career
For anyone thinking in terms of teaching abroad as a long-term commitment, there is a snag. It is comparatively rare to find a post offering security of tenure. Virtually all posts are contract posts of up to a maximum of three years. You live from one contract to another, and can miss out on perks such as in-service training and pension schemes.

There are several reasons for this. First, in the Third World especially, you are really filling in until a suitable local person can take over your position. Secondly, political upheavals can occur which may render it impossible for you to continue with your work. Thirdly, your employability rating may decline if you stay in one place too long (see Chapter 9).

WEIGHING UP THE PROS AND CONS

Before you embark on a contract of a year or more, consider the social and professional implications at the outset. A lot will depend on the stage you have reached in your teaching career, but for the sake of convenience I have divided people into three categories:

● **young teachers:** teachers in their twenties who are at the beginning of their careers

● **mid-term teachers:** teachers in their thirties and early forties who may well have family commitments

● **mature teachers:** teachers in their mid-forties onwards.

As a *young teacher* you need to get plenty of experience, and so it doesn't make sense to stay too long at a particular post. If you are planning to settle down to a career in the UK it is advisable not to stay abroad too long, or you may find it more difficult to land a post commensurate with your experience when you eventually return.

Mid-term teachers with families are often in a dilemma when their offspring reach secondary level, particularly if there are no suitable schools locally for them. Professionally this is a time when decisions have to be made which will affect your long-term future. If you opt for overseas service, is there a chance you'll miss a promotion at home? If you stay overseas too long, will you be able to get back into the system?

As a *mature teacher* you probably know how you want your career to develop and may no longer be encumbered with youthful dependants. You are able to please yourself and may think of teaching overseas as a second career offering challenges you are unlikely to get at home. Opportunities may arise which will take you out of the classroom or lecture room into management or advisory positions.

Other Categories

There are two other categories of teacher who deserve a mention.

- **Students**: young people doing a gap year before going on to university; undergraduates doing a year abroad as part of their course; or recent graduates who want to take a year off before getting down seriously to their chosen career.

- **Retired people**: older people who are keen to spend their time usefully in a foreign environment, passing on their skills to others.

If you fall into either category your principal aim is to gain useful experience and perhaps add a new dimension to your life. However, even if you do not consider teaching or training as your chosen profession, this does not mean that you should not take your duties any less seriously.

ARE YOU THE TYPE?

What qualities and qualifications are required in anyone venturing abroad?

- adapability
- open-mindedness
- stability
- good health
- tact
- curiosity
- patience
- resourcefulness
- a sense of humour
- good qualifications.

Adaptability

This is obviously the first thing that springs to mind. The kind of person who expects life to be exactly the same as back home is in for a shock. A capacity to adapt may be required on a number of fronts, the most crucial being:

- Professional adaptability. You could find that syllabuses and teaching methods are strictly regulated by the government. Or you may find that you are constrained by poor textbooks and enormous classes.

● Environmental adaptability. You could find yourself in a place where you are surrounded by abject poverty, or where the differences between rich and poor are very pronounced. You may find that your social life is restricted to a very small, inward-looking community.

● Cultural adaptability. There are national differences in temperament, outlook and behaviour to be aware of and to accept. For instance, it is quite customary for men to kiss each other in parts of Southern Europe and the Arab World, while in parts of Asia such physical demonstrations of affection tend to be avoided — even between the sexes.

Open-mindedness

Although there is more than one way of solving a problem, expatriates are sometimes bewildered by the way other nationals set about their tasks. Yet foreign methods may be just as valid as your own, and you need to be prepared to accept them and even adopt them.

Personal stability

If you are prone to nervous breakdowns or have problems in coming to terms with life, a foreign posting will rarely provide the relatively sheltered environment which you may think you need to exist. Indeed, people living abroad are frequently exposed to much greater stresses and strains than at home, so if you believe that a spell abroad will help you through a bad patch — forget it!

Good health

Certain climates can prove trying for people who are not in the best of health. Some people find it difficult to withstand excessive heat or high altitudes; nasty infections can lay you low, particularly in tropical areas. However, if you are reasonably healthy and take sensible precautions, you have very little to worry about.

Tact

In a sense every expatriate is a representative of his or her country, and this means you need to act diplomatically. If you are adept at the ready retort, you may find this does not go down particularly well with the locals. They may misunderstand, and equate your down-to-earth bluntness with rudeness.

Curiosity

Your natural curiosity could stand you in good stead, provided you don't take it to extremes — to understand a country and its people, and make the most of the experience, you need to be keen to find out all you can about the place.

Patience
You may have to deal with inefficient bureaucracies; you may find that your students are less alert and slower to learn than you have been led to believe. If you are impatient to succeed at the job, the chances are that you won't!

Resourcefulness
There will probably be occasions where you have to rely on yourself to solve problems, particularly if you are in a fairly isolated spot. This could range from making teaching aids out of nothing to repairing the plumbing.

A sense of humour
Many agencies I talked to mentioned this as a desirable quality. Unless you are able to laugh at yourself and the situations in which you find yourself from time to time, you could find life quite unbearable.

Good qualifications
Good qualifications are also important. Most countries hold qualified people in high regard. The more experience you have and the more impressive your qualifications, the higher your status will be within the academic community. Indeed, you will not get a job abroad unless your qualifications are adequate. This applies to volunteer posts as much as to fully-paid contract posts.

However, exceptionally well-qualified people are not necessarily the most successful in a foreign environment. There have been instances of overseas institutions recruiting PhDs for quite low level teaching. If you are an intellectual powerhouse you may become frustrated if there are few, if any, facilities for pursuing your research.

Not all posts, however, require teaching qualifications. A number of gap year and other exchange programmes offer teaching assistantships for the non-qualified, and there are language schools — not necessarily the most reputable ones — that will appoint people solely on their ability to speak English. In some cases appointees are expected to attend an introductory teaching course.

WHERE CAN I TEACH?

It is tempting to believe that the world is your oyster, but in fact it never is. Even so, there are British teachers in virtually every country of the world teaching all manner of subjects.

If your particular specialisation is very much in demand, like **Teaching English as a Foreign Language (TEFL)**, then you have a wide choice, though this will probably exclude English-speaking countries. There is also a high demand for science and maths specialists. If your speciality is in the arts or social sciences, there are fewer openings. However, occasional posts do arise, in Commonwealth universities for example, and in Commonwealth countries on teacher exchanges. There are also schools in foreign localities which cater largely for expatriates. If you are prepared to venture outside your specialism — into TEFL, for instance — the range of opportunities will widen. Some TEFL employers will accept people on the strength of their teacher's certificate and proven ability to teach.

Not all positions involve teaching. Developing countries may need curriculum advisers, teacher trainers and other educational experts.

THE REWARDS

The teaching profession in Britain has not produced many millionaires and this also holds true for the teaching fraternity in other countries, despite reports of astronomical tax-free salaries in the oil-rich countries of the Middle East.

When you look at salaries offered you need to see what the total package entails. It could include free accommodation, free medical insurance, and free education for your children. On the other hand, there may be no accommodation element at all, and this could make the salary less attractive than it seems.

At the other end of the scale come the volunteer and missionary posts. These are for people for whom income is not an important consideration. Their attraction lies in the type of experience they offer and the opportunity to serve one's fellow men. You will have enough to live on, certainly, but this may not be enough to service whatever financial commitments you have at home.

Other rewards are less tangible. You have an opportunity to travel, to extend your circle of friends, to become acquainted with different cultures, to enjoy pleasanter climates (perhaps), and experience a different lifestyle. Much will depend on what benefits you are looking for.

One warning: you must dispel any idea that working abroad is one long holiday. Indeed, it involves at least the same responsibilities, frustrations, pressures and sense of commitment that you would experience in your work at home. In one sense it can be disarmingly different; in another it is more of the same.

WHAT TYPE OF INSTITUTION?

So far we have been considering the option of teaching abroad in very general terms. Of course, no-one teaches in a vacuum, and your experiences will be shaped by the type of institution to which you are attached. The range of teaching institutions which recruit expatriates is extremely varied. Some will be similar to schools and colleges which you have worked in at home. Others will be very strange and unfamiliar — both in their appearance and their practices. This section attempts to classify them.

THE SCHOOLS SECTOR

There are three different types of school or college in this sector:

● Those which cater for children from the expatriate community (**expatriate schools**), some of which open their doors to local children.

● Those which cater solely for the nationals of the country in question (**indigenous schools**).

● Those which cater for both.

Expatriate schools

Most of these schools will be organised along familiar lines. The curriculum will usually be British or American, and your colleagues will be largely expatriate. Some teachers will be birds of passage on two- or three-year contracts like yourself, though you may find some old hands, notably wives who are married to nationals of the country in question.

Vacancies occur for teachers of most subjects and at most levels in nursery schools, primary schools and secondary schools

Service schools

These schools are exclusively for the children of army, navy or air force personnel and are usually on a base. They are financed by the Ministry of Defence and are run along exactly the same lines as a school in Britain. Such schools exist in Belgium, Brunei, Cyprus, Denmark, Germany, Gibraltar, Italy, Nepal, Norway and Sardinia. The majority cater for the primary age range, but there are some secondary schools, too.

International schools
These schools provide an education for children from the expatriate com-
munity, and in many cases local children also attend. The curriculum of
English medium schools usually follows the British or American pattern.

Some are private ventures, others may have official backing, while
others are run by a foundation. In certain countries they are limited to
the children of embassy staff and other expatriates in official positions;
in others over 50% of the clientele could be locals.

Among the most prestigious of these schools are those run by United
World Colleges (of which Atlantic College is one). The European Union
Schools are also highly regarded — there is one such school at Culham
in Oxfordshire which caters, like the others, for the children of EU officials and offers the type of education children would receive in their
respective countries.

There are also schools which serve the expatriate communities of
other countries — French and German schools, for example. Generally
speaking such schools employ teachers trained in France or Germany
and provide a French or German style education. In the Middle East
there are a number of bilingual Arabic/English schools primarily for the
expatriate Arab community.

Other opportunities
Vacancies occasionally occur for private tutors — usually for the children of very rich and aristocratic families.

Indigenous schools
Teaching in a school catering for the nationals of your adoptive country
is likely to contrast strikingly with your experience in the UK.

- You may find you are the only foreigner on the staff.
- The operation of the school may be quite different from what you
  are used to.
- The pupils you have to deal with may respond differently to your
  teaching methods. Pupils in the Far East, for example, may seem
  unduly passive, while those in some Middle Eastern countries,
  though eager, may lack self-control.

Any teacher planning to work in such a school will need to be adapt-
able. Don't assume you will be able to teach and behave just as you did
back home, but make sure you know in advance what will be expected
of you. In schools where expatriates are thin on the ground you may be
regarded as something of a novelty.

Teachers of English are in great demand in non-English speaking countries. In European countries this need is catered for principally by exchange assistantships and teaching posts operated by the **Central Bureau for Educational Visits and Exchanges**. Certain governments (Hong Kong, Singapore and Malaysia) have recruited substantial numbers of English teachers on a short-term basis in a bid to improve standards.

There are opportunities for teachers of other subjects in English- and non-English-speaking countries. However, they are not usually required (except on an exchange basis) where there is a sufficient pool of indigenous teachers. In certain Third World countries there is a shortage of qualified teachers in most subjects, but since such countries are usually short of cash, most openings for teachers are on volunteer or missionary terms.

State schools
The majority of openings for teachers are in the secondary sector — or intermediate and secondary sector, where this distinction exists. There is a considerable variation in standards between countries and regions within countries, even within Western Europe.

Some schools will be highly selective, particularly in certain developing countries where secondary education is by no means universal. Some will be progressive in their teaching methods and have plenty of equipment. At the other end of the spectrum, a good many state schools can be grim places housed in inadequate buildings and with few, if any, resources. Generally speaking, the poorer the country, the poorer the facilities.

In the attempt to provide universal education, quality tends to suffer, and schools are starved of cash. In such situations teachers are poorly motivated and poorly paid. Many of them 'moonlight', and have little time or inclination to develop themselves professionally. Not all are properly qualified.

Private schools
Private schools flourish in most countries and cater for all age groups. In some cases they are felt to offer a superior education to schools in the state sector. In others they have been set up to cope with a demand for education that the state itself is unable to satisfy. Quite a number are English medium or teach certain subjects (eg maths, science) in English. There are three main types:

● **Church or Mission schools.** These are often well established schools with a good academic reputation. They tend to be fee-paying, but many offer scholarships. In former British possessions many such schools are state aided, and may offer free schooling.

- **Schools run by a foundation**. These schools are usually insulated from commercial pressures, but even so most tend to be fee-paying. They usually take in a certain proportion of scholarship pupils.

- **Private ventures**. These schools tend to be the most variable of all. Some are very good, while others, particularly in places where the government does not exert strict controls, can be mediocre.

In some countries private schools operate quite independently of the state, and may therefore differ quite markedly from schools in the state sector. This is the case in Greece, for example, where there are British-type schools, American-type schools, etc.

Elsewhere, in neighbouring Turkey for instance, the situation is quite different. All schools are expected to adhere to a centrally controlled curriculum, which means that books, teachers, school buildings and courses have to be approved and inspected by the Ministry of Education.

THE HIGHER EDUCATION SECTOR

This sector embraces universities, colleges of education, technical institutes and the like.

Many establishments have openings for English teachers (see Chapter 2), and several — particularly in the Commonwealth — have opportunities in other fields as well, usually on a contract basis. If you are working in a higher education establishment in the UK, it may well have a link with an overseas institution of learning, and you may have the chance of being seconded to a teaching post there.

There are also opportunities in international and regional institutes, such as those operated by the South East Asian Ministers of Education Organisation. At this level much of the teaching is done through the medium of English.

It is difficult to generalise about higher education, since every university or polytechnic is likely to be different. Some of the more venerable institutions are still very traditional in their approach, with syllabuses which seem to hark back to the beginning of the century. Others turn out to be very forward-looking.

OTHER OPPORTUNITIES

This category covers educational activities which fall outside the formal system of education.

Adult institutes

These institutions, usually publicly funded, offer part-time courses, normally in the evening, for people who wish to extend their knowledge either for professional reasons or as a leisure activity. They are particularly well developed in Scandinavia and German-speaking countries. The main requirement is for teachers of English.

Language schools

The demand for English seems to be insatiable these days, and in virtually every country there are institutes which offer English tuition on a part-time or a full-time basis. The clientele tends to be adult, with a preponderance of students in their late teens and early twenties. Some take younger age groups, particularly in countries where the quality of language tuition in schools is poor.

The British Council, like other cultural institutes, is involved with language courses in many countries, either through its own teaching operations or in collaboration with a local foundation. However, many language schools are private ventures, some affiliated to organisations in the UK or US (such as International House) or are branches of large language training companies (such as Berlitz). Native English speakers are much in demand as teachers in these institutes.

In-house training programmes

In-house training is a growing field, and many large companies and government organisations have their own in-house facilities for updating and developing the expertise of their staff. In most cases the lecturers will be nationals of the country in question, but this is not always true in the developing world and on language training programmes.

Companies operating overseas are often required to provide a training package in addition to supplying equipment. British Aerospace, for instance, not only provides Saudi Arabia with jets, but it also trains pilots and ground staff in such fields as navigation, maintenance and English. Oil, health care and engineering companies are among the others that operate training programmes.

Vacation courses

There are short term opportunities mainly for English (TEFL) teachers and sports teachers at summer camps and holiday resorts for young people. For further details consult *Working Holidays* published by the Central Bureau for Educational Visits and Exchanges.

2
Teaching English as a Foreign Language

THE TEFL CHALLENGE

One of your greatest assets is your mother-tongue — English. English is the international *lingua franca* par excellence, and anyone involved in international commerce, politics and travel who does not possess at least a rudimentary knowledge of the language is at a tremendous disadvantage professionally.

The upshot of this is that people are eager to learn English, and there is a huge demand for teachers of the subject. In some places people are so desperate to learn that they will turn to any English speaker for help, whether that person is a trained teacher or not. People like this have probably picked up the rudiments of English at school, but they lack practice, particularly in speaking English. A person has much more chance to practise oral skills in an informal one-to-one situation — whether the informant is a qualified teacher or not — than in the more formal atmosphere of a classroom containing perhaps thirty, forty or fifty pupils.

WHAT QUALIFICATIONS DO I NEED?

Although most organisations and schools stress the need for TEFL qualifications, they are not always needed. For instance, if you possess university entrance qualifications, voluntary organisations like Teaching Abroad and other organisations specialising in gap year students will be interested in you, though you will have to make a contribution to your costs. The Central Bureau administers a well-established assistantship scheme to certain countries in Europe, Africa, South America and Canada, which is ideal for undergraduates and recent graduates, and usually provides an induction course. A few private training organisations, such as Callan and Linguarama, arrange intensive courses for prospective teachers lasting a week or so and will offer them teaching posts provided they reach an acceptable standard.

Qualifications likely to be required

In most cases, however, employers will expect applicants to have a qualification and preferably some experience in teaching English as a foreign or second language. The minimum qualification is likely to be either:

- the new **Cambridge/RSA Certificate in English Language Teaching for Adults (CELTA)** administered by the University of Cambridge Local Examinations Syndicate (UCLES). This supersedes the Certificate in Teaching English as a Foreign Language to Adults (Cert TEFLA) - often referred to as the RSA Certificate.

- the **Trinity College Certificate in Teaching English to Speakers of Other Languages (Cert TESOL)**

Other organisations will be looking for applicants with a degree and one of the above-mentioned certificates. A **Postgraduate Certificate in Education (PGCE)** or the equivalent, or a **BEd** with a TEFL component would be particularly useful if you are planning to work in the public sector or in a primary/secondary school.

More advanced qualifications

For positions with reponsibility a more advanced qualification is usually required, though in most cases you need a few years' experience behind you. Examples are:

- The **Cambridge/RSA Diploma in English Language to Adults (DELTA)** which supersedes the Diploma in Teaching English to Adults (Dip TEFLA) — also known as the RSA Diploma.

- The **Trinity College Licentiate in TESOL**

- An **advanced degree** or **diploma in TEFL or Applied Linguistics.**

Other qualifications

If you are a teacher whose mother tongue is not English other qualifications may be acceptable. Cambridge/RSA, for instance, currently offer a **Certificate for Overseas Teachers of English (COTE)** which tests both language competence and teaching methodology.

TEFL training

A generation ago there were only a handful of courses to prepare teachers for teaching English to foreigners. Now there are courses in all shapes and sizes at universities, colleges and private language institutes.

Full-time courses
- One year courses leading to a Postgraduate Certificate in Education, many of which are recognised by the Department for Education and Employment.
- Advanced courses for experienced teachers leading to a Diploma or Master's Degree.
- BEd courses which include a TEFL component.

Part-time courses
Many of these prepare people for the Cambridge RSA or Trinity College TEFL or TESOL certificates and diplomas mentioned above and can take up to a year. International House runs a distance learning programme.

Intensive courses
These take various forms:
- A one week introductory course. Some may be induction courses for particular schools.
- A four/five week course leading to a recognised certificate.
- A 10-14 week course leading to a diploma.

For further information on the Trinity College and Cambridge RSA examinations and a list of centres which run recognised courses you should contact:

University of Cambridge Local Examination Syndicate (TEFL).

Trinity College, External Examinations Department. (See Useful Addresses section.)

The EFL Guide published by *The EL Gazette* lists a wide range of courses for EFL teachers in the British Isles and elsewhere, including higher degrees.

The British Council English Language Courses Information Service (ELCTIS) has details of courses throughout the UK. It is also accessible on the ECCTIS 2000 network.

THE RANGE OF TEFL POSTS ABROAD

Primary level opportunities

There has been a big expansion in recent years in teaching English in primary schools of all kinds. Often pupils are hoping to enter English medium or bilingual secondary schools for which competition may be very keen. In some cases the tuition is provided by specialist language schools. Junior departments of some international schools employ TEFL staff too, and there may be opportunities in countries (in Africa, for instance) where English is the second language.

Secondary level opportunities
Working in state schools
Most of the assistantships handled by the Central Bureau are in government schools. In the developing world many of the teaching posts in government schools are for volunteers.

Opportunities exist for experienced teachers in countries which do not have enough English teachers of their own or are anxious to raise standards. This is particularly the case at present in parts of the Middle East and South East Asia, notably in relatively prosperous countries.

Working in private secondary schools
Well established English medium schools with a substantial expatriate clientele will probably have no need for TEFL teachers at all.

Others will have, and they range from church or missionary schools and schools belonging to foundations to private enterprise establishments. Middle class parents in many countries believe that a thorough grounding in English is the passport to a good job, and the presence of a native English speaker on the staff of a school often acts as a considerable incentive for them to enrol their children there.

Opportunities in Higher Education
English has become a medium of instruction for many subjects at university now, and a large proportion of undergraduates and most postgraduates will need to read and consult textbooks written in English.

As a consequence there are three types of English teaching activities:

● **Traditional courses** in English departments including literature, composition, linguistics, English life and institutions for students studying for an English degree.

● **Teacher training courses** designed to turn out people who are able to teach effectively in secondary schools and sometimes at university level.

● **Service English courses** for students of other subjects for whom English is the key to the proper understanding of their chosen subject, eg science, economics, engineering. Service courses may be run concurrently with the study programme, or be intensive programmes which take place before the study programme begins. Often acceptance on the study programme is dependent on a student acquiring proficiency in English first.

Working in government language institutes

In several countries there are language institutes for training civil servants or the military, sometimes independent, sometimes attached to ministries, such as the Foreign Ministry or Ministry of Defence, and sometimes attached to universities. Possible clientele will be diplomats, officials going on courses abroad, or officials who need to deal with foreigners in the course of their work.

Large international organisations, such as the UN in New York, also have language training programmes for their staff.

Working in private language institutes

These are usually commercial organisations which take all comers. The age range can be considerable, but the majority cater especially for students in their teens and twenties. Many prepare their students either for national examinations or international tests such as Cambridge Proficiency and First Certificate. Some may provide in-company language training outside the institute.

While most tend to be independent organisations, others may be members of a national chain (eg the British School in Italy). Alternatively they may be part of, or affiliated to, an international group (Inlingua, International House, or Linguarama).

Courses can vary considerably, even within one school — some may be full-time and intensive, with anything from one to 25 students per class, but the majority will probably be part-time, for those who come along in their spare time. As a consequence many schools operate in the evening and even at weekends in some countries. The 9 to 5 day is the exception rather than the rule for teachers in this sector.

The quality of the premises and the teaching can also vary. Some organisations pay badly and as a consequence lack properly qualified teachers. Others offer first-rate facilities.

On the whole, private language schools are for the single and unencumbered, though some organisations are able to accommodate teaching couples. Senior positions in these organisations offer better salaries and sometimes a few perks.

Working for cultural associations

Other language schools are operated by cultural organisations such as the British Council, which has 120 direct teaching operations in over 50 countries.

Elsewhere, there are non-profitmaking cultural associations, such as the Turco-British Association, which run similar operations. These generally have a link with the local British Council office and may well be housed in the same building.

Courses like these are generally highly regarded locally, and the staff are likely to be a mix of locally recruited teachers and those recruited from Britain and other English-speaking countries.

Working for companies

Large companies may well have language training programmes for their staff, with both full-time and part-time vacancies. Companies with large contracts overseas often have to provide a training package for local staff which contains a substantial EFL component.

Private tuition

This is another option. Teachers often take on private students to supplement their earnings at a language institute. It is possible, once you have established a reputation for yourself in a locality, to concentrate entirely on private students or tuition in companies. Care must be taken, however, that you do not fall foul of the residence laws.

Other opportunities

For experienced TEFL practitioners there are advisory posts, generally within ministries of education but sometimes in HE institutions. Other opportunities may occur within the educational inspectorate educational broadcasting and training organisations.

POTENTIAL PITFALLS FOR A TEFL TEACHER

Linguistic chauvinism

Enthusiastic but inexperienced English teachers often see their subject as the most important on the curriculum but it never is (except in the case of language schools). If you come in that category you may be somewhat chastened to find that your students, particularly the younger ones, do not show much enthusiasm for your native tongue, and seem to be irritatingly slow at picking it up. Bear in mind that language learning is a chore which does not yield immediate returns. As a language specialist you should make an effort to come to grips with the mother tongue of your students — often a very sobering exercise.

'I'm the expert' attitude

Your English may be more fluent than that of your native-born colleagues, but it does not follow that you are a more capable teacher than they are. After all, most of them have had to learn English from scratch and are consequently more aware of the problems their pupils face.

Don't be patronising. They will resent you for it. Don't presume to teach them how to teach, unless you are employed as a teacher trainer.

And don't push the type of methodology which you used with great success at a summer school at home, since it could prove to be completely inappropriate.

Inflexibility

The most successful TEFL teachers tend to be those who can adapt to local circumstances and expectations. No matter how keen you are about a certain method of training or a particular textbook, you may have to accept that it doesn't work with your students.

This is particularly true in primary and secondary schools. Indeed, some of the most successful teachers of TEFL at this level turn out to be those with several years' experience in schools back home specialising in subjects other than TEFL, and with no axes to grind.

Losing touch

If you are in a fairly isolated area it is easy to lose touch with developments in your professional field. Fortunately a number of British Council offices overseas have teaching resource centres which you will be able to use, and there may be professional associations locally which serve the TEFL profession. The International Association of Teachers of English as a Foreign Language (IATEFL) based in Kent holds conferences and publishes a newsletter. A subscription to *EL Gazette* and other TEFL publications is another good way of keeping in touch.

✳ IT WOULD HELP IF YOU SPOKE A LITTLE JAPANESE

3
Opportunities in other Subjects

Although TEFL teachers may appear to have all the advantages teachers in other subject areas can have the best of both worlds — they can find a ready market for their skills in any school or university where English is the medium of instruction.

Such institutions are not confined to the British Isles, North America and Australasia. English is also the main language of many Commonwealth countries in Africa, the Caribbean and the Pacific. Moreover it is widely used in higher education institutions, in the Middle East and Far East, for example. And finally it is the medium of instruction for many of the international schools to be found all over the world.

PRE-SCHOOL, PRIMARY AND SECONDARY EDUCATION

Service schools
Service Children's Education handles these posts. Service schools require teachers in all subjects, especially primary school teachers in Germany, Cyprus and Gibraltar. The SCEA recruits some 200 primary teachers annually and 100 secondary teachers. The majority of the latter are required for British military bases in Northern Germany.

Applicants need to have two years' recent experience in UK schools and be below the age of 47. Salaries are based on the Baker scale plus London weighting and certain allowances which vary according to the size of one's family and the location. You may also have access to duty free goods. The first two tours are of three years each; subsequent ones last five years.

While teaching duties will not differ markedly from those in a school in the UK, there is a far greater turnover of pupils, just as you would find in a school based in a garrison town. Amenities may be poor and some pupils may have adjustment problems. Some schools are boarding establishments which will involve teachers in extra duties.

A teacher's social life will be different, too. You will be mixing a lot with service personnel and their families and must therefore be able to

27

accept the values of military life. Professional commitment and an out-going personality are important.

International schools

Recruitment for these schools is handled either by the schools them-selves through advertisements and personal contacts or by agencies such as the **European Council of International Schools (ECIS), Gabbitas Educational Consultants** and **Search Associates**.

It is impossible to describe a typical international school. Some may have thousands of pupils, others less than a hundred. A single nationality may predominate or more than 60 different nationalities may be repre-sented. There are schools for expatriates only, while others take in a size-able proportion of pupils from the country in which they are located. Some are highly selective; others — particularly the American International Schools — are designed to serve children with a wide range of abilities. *The World Yearbook of Education 1991* is recommended reading.

Some of the main features of an international school with a high pro-portion of expatriate pupils are:

● **High pupil turnover**. Parents move on after finishing their contracts, and take their children with them, so there may be a lack of continuity.

● **High staff turnover.** Teachers are usually on two-year or three-year contracts. Younger ones like to move on to other countries; older ones may decide to return home before it is too late for them to resume a career there.

● **Heterogeneous clientele**. Pupils come from a variety of educational backgrounds and may return to their own educational system at a later date. The curriculum has to take into account these differing needs.

● **Varied teaching staff**. The teaching staff could well be drawn from different countries, and so misunderstandings can arise. Locally-recruited staff are often on lower salaries than staff recruited from abroad and this can give rise to tensions.

● **Disorientated pupils**. Not all children settle down easily in differ-ent schools in different environments, so teachers may need some expertise in counselling.

● **Strong parent involvement**. International schools often have strong links with the local expatriate community. Expatriate mothers with no job to occupy their attention may become very closely involved.

- **Good pupil-teacher ratios**. Compared with other schools in the country this is more than likely to be the case. It is perhaps just as well considering the heterogeneous nature of the classes.

- **Above average intelligence**. Generally speaking, people who work abroad are drawn from the higher social echelons — businessmen, diplomats, aid officials, teachers. Children often inherit their parents' traits.

- **Enhanced opportunities for education**. There are opportunities for experiencing multicultural education and for studying a new environment.

The *ECIS Directory* provides details on more than 750 primary and secondary international schools in around 140 different countries.

For international school staff there is a professional association — the **International Educator's Institute** — based in the USA but with a branch in the UK. The Institute publishes a quarterly newspaper which includes vacancy listings, and offers certain perks such as insurance cover. (For address see Further Reading section.)

The International Baccalaureate

A growing number of international schools — some 250 at present — prepare their pupils for the International Baccalaureate examination. This is a two year pre-university course designed to facilitate the mobility of students and promote international understanding. It leads to either a Diploma which is recognised by tertiary institutions in several countries, or certificates in separate subjects.

For the Diploma pupils choose one subject from each of six groups:

- Language A — usually the pupil's native tongue
- Language B — a modern foreign language or pupil's second language
- Social sciences
- Experimental sciences
- Mathematics and computing
- Art, design, music, another language, various other options.

Three of the subjects must be offered at Higher Level and three at Subsidiary Level. For example:

Higher: Mathematics, Physics, Chemistry
Subsidiary: English (A), German (B), History

For further information contact the IB Office in Geneva. (See Useful Addresses.)

Other schools

Opportunities exist for teachers in most subjects in state and church supported schools, not only in English-speaking countries but in secondary schools in countries where the second language is English.

Recruitment tends to be done by the schools themselves, the volunteer organisations, missionary societies, the British Council, and a number of private recruitment agencies. There are also teacher exchange schemes operated by the Central Bureau and the League for the Exchange of Commonwealth Teachers.

Understanding different systems

The important thing to bear in mind is that you are entering a different system which may be founded on **different principles** from the one you have grown up with. Your duties — in the classroom and outside it — may be different. The aims of the school may be at variance with your own. Some education systems set out to teach pupils how to think and reason. Others place greater stress on learning facts. Some encourage specialisation; others go for an extremely broad curriculum. Whatever your personal views, you will need to **adapt** to the system in use.

State schools in many countries are underfunded. They have classrooms with blackboards, but there are often few, if any, facilities for practical work. This can pose problems for science and craft teachers. Even modest audio-visual aids may be hard to come by. The teacher in the state sector has to be resourceful, if nothing else.

Many educational systems and their protegés are obsessed by grades, not necessarily because there is a form of continuous assessment in operation. Education is seen primarily as a path to advancement where grades, certificates and diplomas are the key to future success.

The **motivation** of the pupils cannot be taken for granted. In parts of Africa where secondary education is the privilege of a few, you may well find yourself teaching bright and keen pupils. In other places there may be fewer incentives to learn.

Communicating

In bilingual schools and countries where English is the second language there can be problems of **communication**, which may be puzzling to teachers who have only taught English native speakers. The onus is on the teacher to express himself more clearly and check at regular intervals that the pupils have fully understood the points made.

Coping with different cultures

Another problem to contend with is **cultural differences**. In parts of Asia, for instance, it is regarded as rude to contradict the teacher, and pupils may seem irritatingly quiet and passive. Children from other cultures may expect a teacher to be authoritarian, and become disruptive if any sign of friendliness is shown. Religious custom can also affect the way pupils behave.

It is naive to envisage teaching abroad as being exactly the same as it is at home. You will have to learn a lot about the educational system and country you will be working in if you want your pupils to learn a lot from you!

WORKING IN HIGHER EDUCATION

Higher education is very much an international business, and always has been ever since the Middle Ages when the first universities came into existence. The Association of Commonwealth Universities (ACU), for instance, handles over 1,200 staff vacancies for its members each year.

Universities abroad recruit staff from Britain and elsewhere for one of two reasons.

- **By choice** — This is true, for instance, in the developed countries of the English speaking world, such as the US, Australia and New Zealand. There is no shortage of academics in these countries but universities like to have outsiders on their staff in order to stimulate an exchange of ideas and methods. They also like to recruit from a wider pool of talents than exists in their own countries. This can be achieved by the implementation of staff exchange agreements with universities in the UK and elsewhere, under which a lecturer would be seconded to a foreign institution for up to a year. More usually, though, universities actively recruit people for the long term, even to the extent of offering security of tenure.

- **Out of necessity** — Not all countries are self-sufficient in professors and lecturers, and this is particularly true of the Third World. But for many developing nations foreign expertise comes expensive — unless lecturers are employed on volunteer terms or provided free by donor governments. This means that higher education managers are keen to replace foreign staff by less expensive indigenous lecturers at the earliest possible opportunity. As a consequence, contracts tend to be fixed term only.

DEMANDS AND CONSTRAINTS IN HIGHER EDUCATION

Any idea that service abroad is an option for lacklustre academics needs to be firmly scotched. **Competition for posts** in universities abroad has become very keen indeed. This is particularly true in the case of institutes in the developed world which can offer ample research facilities, good salaries and often security of tenure.

Third World universities, on the other hand, operate under **financial constraints,** so that both library and research facilities may prove inadequate. However, if your area of interest is connected with the environment in which you will find yourself — tropical agriculture, the flora and fauna of the region, for example — this need not be a handicap.

Research is, of course, vital if you intend to progress in your chosen field, particularly if you are at the beginning of your career, since the profession demands that you publish on a regular basis in order to keep your name to the fore. If you are successful in doing this you should not experience difficulty in returning later to British academic life.

As for the **teaching environment,** all Commonwealth universities have grown out of the same tradition and are surprisingly homogeneous in their methods and outlook. Most new appointees are therefore able to adapt easily.

Communicating effectively

Difficulties may be experienced in other countries outside the English-speaking world, where English is used as a medium of instruction in higher education although many students lack fluency in the language. To overcome the problem lecturers there may need to develop more **effective communication skills.** Foreign academics, whose native language is not English, often cope better in this area since they feel they have to try harder to overcome their linguistic handicap.

Subjects in demand

Currently there is a high demand for specialists in medicine, computer science, the natural sciences and engineering. With the growing popularity of high level business schools there could be also possibilities here. There are very few openings for specialists in arts subjects and architecture.

4
Finding a Vacancy

Once you have made the decision to work abroad, you have to start looking round for institutions that might employ you.

You could try **visiting** foreign countries on spec. Some teachers have a knack of being in the right place at the right time and manage to land first-class job offers. Or, if you have an extensive network of colleagues abroad, you could make use of the **grapevine**. Teaching contacts may be able to suggest establishments that you could apply to on a speculative basis. Names and addresses can easily be obtained from other sources as well. Alternatively, you may decide to approach **UK based agencies** which recruit for positions abroad.

The main way of learning about a teaching job abroad is through scanning the **advertisement columns** of specialist education periodicals, like the *Times Educational Supplement* and the *Times Higher Education Supplement*, certain national newspapers like the *Guardian* (Tuesday edition), or *The Times* (Monday edition). Periodicals related to your own particular discipline (such as the *Economist* or *New Scientist*) could prove a fruitful source of opportunities. Certain Church journals also carry details of vacancies abroad including *Opportunities Abroad* from Christians Abroad, and for TEFL teachers there is the *EL Gazette*. If you have access to the Internet, you will find some vacancies are advertised there too.

MAKING VISITS ON SPEC

The advantage of actually visiting a country to find a job is that you can gain a first-hand impression of the place. You can see the educational institution and its working methods, and get an idea of the living conditions you can expect, before signing any contract.

However, while this may be a feasible option in the case of countries close to home, it can be a costly undertaking where more distant places are concerned. And there are countries that are difficult to enter unless you have specific business to undertake or are on an organised tour.

Visiting European Economic Area countries

If you are a British or Irish citizen planning to go to a country within the European Economic Area (Austria, Belgium, Denmark, France, Finland, Germany, Greece, Iceland, Italy, Liechtenstein, Luxembourg, Norway, Netherlands, Portugal, Spain, Sweden), you do not need a special visa in order to enter the country and look around for employment, though there will be other regulations you need to comply with. (Note that Iceland, Liechtenstein and Norway are not EU members.)

The European Commission (Directorate General 15) produces a number of factsheets on living in other EU countries available on the Internet: http://citizens.eu.int or by phoning 0800 581591.

Visiting other countries

For most other countries you need a work visa/permit in order to take up employment, and as a general rule this has to be applied for before you arrive in the country. If you enter as a tourist you may be prevented from taking up employment in the country. You will probably need a work permit, and may have to leave the country in order to obtain the required documentation.

The **penalties** for working illegally in a country can be severe if you are caught, so it is important to check immigration regulations carefully first of all.

Tips

● If you are visiting a place 'on spec' remember to take evidence of your background and qualifications as well as copies of your CV.

● Before accepting a post, ask whether you are to be employed on expatriate terms or as a locally recruited staff member. Expatriate terms are usually more generous with return air fares paid to your country of origin, accommodation and other allowances.

MAKING SPECULATIVE APPLICATIONS

These may be sent either direct to an overseas educational institution or to a representative or agency in the UK.

Applying direct

There are a number of ways of finding the names and addresses of schools and colleges who might be interested in you.

- **Personal contacts**. Friends and colleagues overseas may be able to recommend establishments.

- **Diplomatic missions**. The Information Officer or Cultural Attaché of the appropriate High Commission, Embassy or Consulate General may be able to advise. Some missions may be able to supply you with a list of the principal educational institutions in the country concerned; others may let you consult books of reference.

- **Libraries**. Some large public reference libraries will have reference books, such as yearbooks and telephone directories from foreign countries. There are international education yearbooks such as *The World of Learning, The Commonwealth Universities Yearbook, The ECIS Directory, Learning Languages: Where and How* and *The EARLS Guide to Language Schools in Europe*.

- **Education Departments** of universities and colleges. Many of these have links with schools and colleges in other countries and may know of vacancies. Or they may have foreign educationists teaching or attending courses there who can advise you.

- **Language schools.** These often have links with schools and teachers abroad who may contact them about staffing needs.

Tips
- Don't bank on getting a reply. Popular institutions are often overwhelmed by speculative applications and do not have the manpower to cope with unsolicited applications.

- You are more likely to receive a reply if you enclose an international reply coupon with your letter, fax number or e-mail address.

Applying to agencies and representatives

Very few agencies recruit for posts in *every* country of the world or every type of post, so it makes sense to find out which country or countries and what positions they specialise in. The reference section of this book offers some guidance. Either send for details of their service or write enclosing an up-to-date CV, stating the countries and the type of work you are interested in, and asking if they know of any vacancies. They may not have vacancies then and there, but they may be willing to put your name on file, send you a vacancy list, or alert you as to when posts are likely to crop up.

While some agencies operate a teacher's register and welcome unsolicited letters others, such as the **Association of Commonwealth**

Universities (ACU) recruit solely through advertisement, and such an approach can be counterproductive.

APPLYING FOR ADVERTISED VACANCIES

Advertisements for jobs appear all the year round, and the starting dates vary considerably, according to the academic year, which differs from continent to continent, hemisphere to hemisphere. **Gabbitas Educational Consultants**, for example, recruits between July and October for posts in the southern hemisphere, which tend to start between January and March, while their main period of recruitment for the northern hemisphere is January to May.

Don't limit yourself to newspapers and journals published in the UK. Diplomatic missions often have reading rooms where you can peruse local newspapers and so widen your choice.

Making an application

There are two ways of obtaining a position

- applying direct to an educational institution
- applying through an intermediary, eg a recruitment agency, an affiliated school, an embassy or high commission.

Countless schools, colleges and universities abroad place advertisements in British newspapers and educational journals. Often they will send a staff member to interview applicants in the UK or other handy locations. Others will be prepared to make an appointment on the basis of a letter or a telephone call.

Using an agency

While many of the institutions which advertise are highly reputable establishments, it is not always possible to judge this on the strength of an advertisement and a brief description. For this reason, if this is your first foray abroad, it would be more prudent to apply for an overseas position through a reputable **agency** (public or private).

A specialist agency should be experienced in recruiting people like yourself and able to offer an unbiased view of the establishment in which you are interested. It does not make sense for them to place unsuitable people in unsuitable posts. Should things go disastrously wrong they may be in a position to mediate between you and your employer.

AGENCIES RECRUITING TEACHERS

The most common method of finding a job overseas is through an agency, and you need to be aware of the various organisations working in this field, their scope, and the various schemes they operate.

Exchange schemes

The Central Bureau for Educational Visits and Exchanges and the League for the Exchange of Commonwealth Teachers should be mentioned in the context of opportunities to work abroad, although they are not in the business of *recruiting* teachers for long-term engagements. Teachers undertake **exchanges** for reasons of professional development and return to teaching within the UK at the end of their term.

The **Central Bureau** offers educational exchanges of up to a year to Europe and the USA for experienced and qualified teachers. In addition, it administers a large foreign assistantship exchange scheme for modern languages undergraduates and recent graduates. There are opportunities not only in Europe, but in French-speaking Canada, Latin America, and a few countries in Africa.

The **League** sends about 250 teachers overseas each year, mostly to Australia, Canada and New Zealand. The preferred age range is 25-45.

The **Japan Exchange and Teaching Programme (JET)** more or less fits into this category though there is no reciprocal exchange. Administered by the Council on International Educational Exchange (CIEE) and the Japanese Embassy it sends around 150 would-be TEFL teachers a year to work in Japanese schools and with local educational authorities.

Work experience organisations

A number of organisations have grown up in recent years which offer experience of living and teaching in foreign countries. These schemes are best regarded as work experience and participants are usually required to make a contribution to the costs. They are especially popular with gap year students who are waiting to start a higher education course. The organisations include i to i, Teaching Abroad and SPW.

Public agencies

The British Council which has offices throughout the world recruits a substantial number of contract staff every year particularly in the area of English Language Teaching. The two departments involved in recruitment are:

● **Central Management of Direct Teaching** (London) which recruits about 300 EFL teachers and supervisory staff a year to work at its 120 or so English Language Centres in over 50 countries.

- **Overseas Appointments Services** (Manchester) which recruits teachers and specialists mainly for public sector posts and projects, many of which form part of the UK's aid programme. The Division advertises posts and also operates a candidate database.

British Council offices abroad, even if they are not directly involved with teaching, can often advise on teaching opportunities in their locality. For addresses see the relevant country section.

The Department for International Development maintains a register of qualified people interested in working for the aid programme and also advertises for specific posts which fall into three categories:

- a teaching co-operation officer is employed by DFID and works 'on loan' to the overseas government;

- a supplemented officer works under contract to the overseas government and his salary is 'topped up' by DFID;

- a consultant is either self-employed or works for a consultancy company and DFID pays the fee.

Generally most of the vacancies are for people in advisory roles.

Service Children's Education (SCE) recruits for service schools all over the world and operates in the same way as a local education authority in the UK, except that positions are offered on a contract basis.

The **Department for Education and Employment** also recruits for jobs abroad through

- **The European Schools Team**. They recruit teachers for the prestigious European Schools, set up to provide educational facilities for the children of European Union officials.

- **Job Centres**. Most Job Centres can conduct a search for overseas teaching vacancies (as well as other jobs abroad) on the database of the Overseas Placing Unit (OPU) in Sheffield. A recent search uncovered teaching and lecturing posts in Germany, Hong Kong, Russia, Thailand and Turkey.

Volunteer agencies

The largest of these agencies is **Voluntary Service Overseas** which operates in more than 40 Third World countries and recruits more than 400 teachers annually. The average age of a volunteer is 30 and some are in their sixties. There are posts in most subjects in all educational sectors, including special education.

Accommodation and payment based on local rates are provided by the community, organisation or government requesting volunteers. VSO for its part provides training and pays for air fares, national insurance, medical insurance and equipment grants. 'Every volunteer. . . often leaves secure employment in the UK with little anticipation of any real material reward for the two years' tough and unpredictable experience ahead', says a VSO brochure. The organisation recruits for posts in Africa, the Caribbean, China, SE Asia and the Pacific, and has an associate agency EEP which recruits for Eastern Europe and Russia.

VSO recruits on behalf of **United Nations Volunteers**. Other agencies are **Skillshare Africa** and the **United Nations Association International Service (UNAIS)**. Other countries have similar organisations, eg **APSO** — Ireland, **CUSO** — Canada, **Peace Corps** — USA.

Private sector agencies

Perhaps the oldest established agency of its kind is **Gabbitas Educational Consultants** which recruits mainly primary and secondary school teachers for private English-medium schools in most parts of the world.

The Centre for British Teachers (CFBT), on the other hand, recruits teachers for its own projects and employs them directly. Most of the posts on offer are in state secondary schools in Germany, Brunei, Malaysia and Oman. In most cases a few years' experience is required. The leading recruitment agencies are listed in the reference section of this book.

Language school recruitment agencies

There are a number of these. Some actually own the schools for which they recruit, while others are just acting as recruitment agencies, so when approaching such an agency find out what the precise relationship is. The following are two typical examples.

International House recruits world-wide for 70 independent language schools and teacher training institutes affiliated to the International House Trust, especially in Spain, Portugal and Italy. Teaching posts within the organisation are suitable for single people and married couples with no dependants. The minimum qualification is the RSA Preparatory Certificate with a Pass A or Pass B (which can be studied at IH's Teacher Training Institute), though preference is always given to people with teaching experience as well. There are also opportunities at a more senior level for suitably experienced and qualified people.

Inlingua is a Swiss owned organisation of independent private language schools, most of which operate in Germany, Italy and Spain. Graduates in all specialisms are considered, and those without TEFL qualifications may be expected to enrol on a short training course in the Inlingua method.

Other agencies in this category are **ELT** and **Linguarama**.

Church and missionary agencies

Christians Abroad is an organisation funded largely by aid agencies and mission agencies to provide information, counselling and general support for people seeking work abroad. It also recruits teachers in its own right — not necessarily to mission establishments — and publishes on a regular basis an extensive bulletin of vacancies abroad for which its member agencies (all 37 of them) are recruiting.

It also organises half day 'New Eyes' workshops for people who are interested in the idea of working overseas, and operates a Professional Development Worker Register for people with several years' experience overseas who are looking for another contract.

In general, missionary societies are not looking for teachers but lay missionaries with teaching qualifications. Their purpose is to proclaim the gospel, but some have an extensive teacher recruitment programme.

Applying
When applying for a position you need to establish whether the posting is on

● **volunteer terms**: salary/allowance normally sufficient for an individual only.

● **missionary terms**: salary/allowance variable but generally sufficient to support a family.

● **contract terms**: salary comparable with professional salaries in educational institutions in the UK and other industrialised countries.

Some of the older established agencies operate through a system of recommendation, and the first point of contact for a lay missionary is likely to be a parish priest or chaplain.

However, some, like the **Volunteer Missionary Movement**, advertise their vacancies in journals from time to time, and many use the vacancies bulletin put out by Christians Abroad.

Other agencies

The Association of Commonwealth Universities
The Association (which does not deal with unsolicited applications) advertises posts on behalf of its 400 member universities in the press and specialist journals, and also circulates vacancies to university registrars and careers advisory services. The largest number of vacancies are for institutions in Australia, Botswana, Brunei, Hong Kong, Lesotho, New Zealand, Papua New Guinea, Fiji, Swaziland, West Indies, Zimbabwe and Malaysia. The ACU interviews candidates on behalf of its member institutions if asked to do so, and sends off individual reports which are designed to help the institution in question come to an informed decision. The Association has no hand in either the shortlisting or the final outcome, and does not act as a mediator between its members and their appointees. The ACU publishes a useful source of reference, *The Commonwealth Universities Handbook.*

The European Council of International Schools
The ECIS operates a teachers' register and recruits for primary and secondary schools throughout the world which, generally speaking, offer a British style or American style curriculum. The number of teaching opportunities outside Europe is currently on the increase. One feature of the ECIS programme is a two-day recruitment fair held in London every February and May which brings together candidates and representatives of 90 schools throughout the world. Recruitment continues throughout the year, the busy period being from February to May. Among the other organisations which recruit for International Schools are **PACES**, **Search Associates** and **WES**.

Embassies
Teacher recruitment is also conducted by embassies, high commissions and other diplomatic missions based in London, usually for posts in the state secondary and tertiary sector. Among the countries which have used this method of recruitment in recent years are the UAE, Ghana, Nigeria, Singapore and Sudan.

Companies operating overseas
British Aerospace is one of a number of companies which has a contract to supply both hardware and a training package. In Saudi Arabia, for example, the company employs personnel to train pilots and ground staff, and this includes English language tuition. A number of other companies, in the oil and hospital sectors particularly, are also heavily involved in

training. In some cases the company does its own recruitment, but more often than not a recruitment agency is asked to do the work.

The Internet

It is likely that more recruitment will be conducted via the Internet in future and there are already a number of websites devoted to overseas jobs vacancies. They include:

● www.overseasjobs.com

● www.infoseek.com

● www.careerpath.com (for jobs in the USA).

The reference section of this book includes the websites and e-mail addresses of around 60 organisations which recruit for educational posts.

5
Securing a Job

UNDERSTANDING THE APPLICATION PROCEDURE

The fact that you have discovered a job vacancy does not mean that it is automatically yours. Competition can be very keen for some of the more attractive posts, and the successful candidate is the one who can give a good account of him or herself.

Remember that the application process itself is time-consuming. True, there are cases where a person finds himself jetting towards his destination within days of the interview, but they are very much the exception.

How the overseas recruitment process works

This is a typical example of recruitment procedures when a third party (ie a recruitment agency) is involved. When you are dealing direct with prospective employers some of the stages do not apply.

1. Agency receives request to fill a vacancy from institution abroad.
2. Agency advertises the position or circulates information about it.
3. Candidate sees advertisement and sends off for details.
4. Agency sends the candidate a job description and an application form.
5. Candidate sends in application.
6. Agency selects suitable candidates for interview.
7. Agency contacts referees. (This may occur either before or after the interview.)
8. Candidate receives invitation to an interview.
9. Candidate confirms that he can attend for interview.
10. Agency interviews candidate (in some cases there may be two interviews: a preliminary interview followed by an in-depth one, perhaps with the prospective employer, at a later date).
11. Candidate receives letter from agency to say whether he has been successful. If so, his name will be passed on to the institution for approval.
12. Candidate confirms that he is still interested in the post.

13. Agency sends off candidate's details for approval by the institution.
14. Institution considers candidate's details. (In some cases the institution has to submit the candidate's particulars for government approval, otherwise it may be difficult to get an entry visa or work permit.)
15. Agency receives go-ahead from institution to appoint the candidate.
16. Agency contacts candidate to confirm appointment.
17. Candidate visits agency for briefing and to sign contract.

As you will see, this is quite an involved procedure, and hiccups can occur anywhere along the line. If the advertisement fails to attract a reasonable number of candidates, the post may well be re-advertised (stage 2). Interviews may have to be delayed for the sake of candidates from overseas (stage 10). There may be delay in getting official approval (stage 14). Even if things go smoothly, the whole process could take two to three months, and even at the end of it all, you may not be appointed.

MAKING YOUR APPLICATION

Drafting your letter of application

This is your first point of contact with the agency or employer and since first impressions count, you have got to impress. In these competitive times it has to amount to more than just a covering letter. You need to convey:

● I'm interested . . . in the post.
● I can do the job . . . I have the right qualifications and just the experience you are looking for.
● I'm available . . . to attend for interview/to start . . .

The letter has to be

● **Neat**— on A4 paper, preferably typed, unless your handwriting is impeccable.
● **Concise** — don't write more than five crisp paragraphs.
● **Relevant** — mention aspects of your experience which make you well-suited to the post in question.
● **Enthusiastic** — show that you really want the job.

Think of those wonderful blurbs that you see on the jackets of books. Your letter in its modest way serves the same purpose. It has got to make you wanted (see p.45). A speculative letter of application needs to be in a similar vein, but instead of targeting on a particular job you will need to mention a broader range of experience (see p.46).

Tel................   82 Cawdor Place
                                                 Dundee
                                                 Scotland

                                                 30 May 199 -

Director of Recruitment
Macduff International
12 Duncan Road
Dunsinane
DU5 9ZQ

Dear Sir

I wish to apply for the post of Teacher of Science at St Andrew's
International School in Bulawayo, as advertised in this week's *Scottish
International Review.*

I am most interested in this post, firstly — because it sounds varied and
challenging, secondly — because I wish to extend my experience, and
thirdly — because I am a fervent believer in the idea of international
education.

Since graduation I have worked in the state sector of education, teaching
physics and chemistry up to 'A' level standard. I am happy to say that
during this period we achieved 90% pass rate in all subjects.

Last year I started a pilot scheme designed to establish closer links
between my school and local industry by means of factory visits. The
project has been so successful that sixth formers will have a chance to gain
practical experience in company laboratories during the next 12 months.

I am Secretary of the regional branch of the Association of Science
Teachers, and am currently working on an elementary science workbook
for Africa.

I would welcome a chance to meet you to discuss the post in depth.

Yours faithfully

Banquo MacBeth

Model Letter of Application

Tel................   P.O. Box 100
Mandalay
Burma

24 September 199 -

Principal
Atlantic University
Funchal
Madeira

Dear Sir

I am writing to enquire whether you have any vacancies in your English Department, preferably with effect from the beginning of next year when my contract at Kipling Teacher Training Institute comes to an end.

I have an MA in English and Linguistics from Tara University in the USA, and have spent some 15 years overseas in the field of English language teaching, and teacher training. During that time I have written a number of learned papers as well as a textbook, *Speak English like a Native*, which has been approved for use in schools by the Ministry of Education of Vanuatu.

Having worked in Brazil over a number of years I am familiar with the language learning problems of Portuguese speakers. I am also a fluent Portuguese speaker myself, and have visited Lisbon on two occasions to address teacher training conferences. I have also taught in Mauritania, Liechtenstein and Ecuador.

I do so hope you will be able to give me a positive reply. I enclose an international reply coupon.

Yours sincerely

Sean O'Hara

Model Speculative Letter

Curriculum Vitae
HELEN TROY

Address: 2 Paris Close, Priamsville, Hectorshire HS12 3ZY
Telephone: 10 234 5678 (daytime); 9087 654321 (evenings and weekends)
Date of Birth: 1st January 1966
Nationality: British   *Marital Status:* Single

EDUCATION AND QUALIFICATIONS

1977-1984   Dido Park Comprehensive, Minervathorpe, London W29 9XV
            GCE 'O' Level 1982:
            English Language (A); History (B); Mathematics (B);
            Sociology (B); Greek (C); Biology (C)
            GCE 'A' Level 1984:
            Latin (A); Russian (A); Sociology (C)

1984-1987   University of Carthage
            BA Hons in Linguistics and Philosophy (Lower Second) 1987

1987-1988   Hades Polytechnic
            Postgraduate Certificate of Education (Latin and TEFL)

WORK EXPERIENCE

Summer 1985   Organiser, YMCA Holiday Camp for the Disabled, Lake
              Tarquin
Summer 1986   Relief Manageress, Juno Ladies' Wear, Spartaham
Summer 1987   Social organiser, Lethe Summer School for Foreign Students,
              Styx
August 1988   Supply Teacher with Cassandrashire Education Authority. I
onwards   have undertaken a number of assignments with the authority
              notably teaching remedial English to immigrants, French to 'O'
              Level standard, and General Studies.

INTERESTS AND ACTIVITIES

Hang Gliding: I was Treasurer of the Hades Poly Hang Gliding Club
Amateur Dramatics: While at university I acted in several productions, including
                     'Charley's Aunt' and 'Cat on a Hot Tin Roof', and directed
                     'Oedipus Rex'
Mountaineering
Music: I play the French Horn

OTHER INFORMATION

I have a clean driving licence
I am currently attending evening classes in Italian and hope to take 'O' Level this
    coming summer
In addition to speaking Russian, I know some Spanish and Bulgarian.

A Model CV

John C. Falstaff — Career History

Home Address: 16 Bardolph Court, Windsor, Berks
Address for correspondence: P.O. Box 2, Ulan Bator, Outer Mongolia
Date of Birth: 31st December 1938
Nationality: Australian   *Family Status:* Married with 6 children

Educational Record

1949-1957	Arden Forest Grammar School
	5 'O' Levels; 'A' Level in Biology, Physics and Anatomy
1960-1964	Warwick University, NSW, Australia
	BSc Hons in Comparative Botany (First Class)
1964-1969	Agincourt University, Hotspur, USA
	PhD in Botanical Studies

Professional Experience

TEACHING AND LECTURING

I have taught Botany and Applied Biology to Master's Degree level and supervised research and graduates in these fields.

RESEARCH

I have conducted research studies on three continents, and have been published in numerous journals over the years. My 800 page study on the Tanzanian lesser spotted orchid is regarded as a milestone in botanical research. (A list of my publications is appended to this document).

ADMINISTRATION

As a former assistant head of a botanical research establishment I have plenty of experience of managing people and coping with red tape.

Career details

1957-1958	Management Trainee, Boar's Head Hotels, Sydney
1958-1960	Quality Control Manager, Boar's Head Hotels
1969-1975	Lecturer in Botany, Eastcheap Polytechnic
1975-1976	Adviser to the Ministry of Agriculture, Republic of Ruritania
1976-1979	Senior Lecturer in Biology, Eastcheap Polytechnic
1983-1985	Deputy Director, Botanical Research Establishment, Alice Springs
1985-1990	Acting Head of Botany Department, Eastcheap Polytechnic
1990-	Currently doing research into the flora of Outer Mongolia on a fellowship awarded by the Mongolian Institute of Sciences

Interests and Hobbies

Croquet, Billiards, Sailing and Jazz

Additional Information

During recent years I have also held a number of part-time and honorary positions:
Member of Crumhorn Commission on the Countryside (UK)
Consultant to the Irish Universities Board
Chairman of the Orchid Development Board in Australia

Preparing your Curriculum Vitae

A good CV takes time to prepare whether you are at the beginning of your teaching career or have many years' experience behind you. Take time over it. Make copious notes of your achievements and then start to whittle them down so that you can accommodate everything on a sheet of A4. Pages 47 and 48 show examples of typical CVs.

A CV needs to be typed and to look good. If you can't type yourself, ask a professional to do the job for you, preferably on a word-processor so that it can be edited and looks smart.

Although it is a factual document, it offers you a chance to blow your own trumpet. Draw attention to your successes, but not your failures.

● **Personal details**. Name, address, telephone number, age, nationality. You don't necessarily have to put in items like marital status, dependants or religion. If you have a fax number or e-mail address, include these.

● **Education**. Educational institutions, dates attended, examinations passed. You don't need to go into detail about your O Level results if you left school decades ago.

● **Summary of work experience**. This is optional, but it gives you an opportunity to list your strengths and accomplishments.

● **Employment record (or career)**. List posts held and organisations worked for with approximate dates. There is no need to disclose reasons for leaving or the salary you earned. Give a concise description of your responsibilities for each post. Go into more detail if you have opted to leave out the summary of work experience. Use words which are likely to impress like 'initiate', 'expand', 'introduce', 'achieve', 'exceed'. Every selector appreciates dynamism. If you have recently graduated, remember to include vacation employment.

● **Interests and activities**. List memberships of clubs, societies, professional bodies, including any posts of responsibility you hold or have held in them. Don't list too many, otherwise you may give the impression that you won't have enough time to cope with a job!

● **Other information**. This is where you include other skills not yet mentioned such as language ability, possession of a driving licence, or other information, such as your DES number (if you have one).

Filling in the application form

'Is the application form really necessary?' is a question that passes through the minds of many candidates. If you have sent in a comprehensive CV, filling in another form seems a waste of time. Besides, it may be difficult to accommodate your details on it.

If the agency/employer considers it necessary, then you have no option but to fill it in. It the vacancy attracts a large number of candidates it is much easier for the selectors to compare them if their details are in a standardised format. To complete only half the form may suggest that you are half-hearted about the post.

An application form needs to be approached with respect, otherwise the completed article may turn out to be a mess. So:

- **Read it through** to find out what information is wanted.
- **Make notes** on how you will fill in each section.
- **Fill it in** slowly and clearly following the instructions carefully.

The **personal details** section is fairly straightforward. Don't forget to include a telephone number (that of a neighbour, friend or relative will do if you don't have one of your own), the selectors may need to contact you urgently during office hours.

When filling in your **educational details** don't put in bogus information — it may be checked. Include details of any short courses you may have done recently to show that you like to keep on top of your subject.

Your record of **work experience** should include all jobs even if they have nothing to do with teaching. This applies particularly if you are near the beginning of your career.

If your work experience is extensive devote more space to jobs you have held in recent years. If you are required to mention your reasons for leaving a job, and you are uneasy about disclosing information, write 'To be discussed at interview'. Don't do this too often, though — the selectors might become suspicious.

When selecting your **referees** make sure you choose people who know you well and can give a good account of you, and keep them informed of your career developments. Check that they are willing to do the chore. There are three types of referee which could be required:

- **Academic:** If you have completed a course within the last five years or so this will be your tutor or Head of Department. If you haven't, ignore this requirement, unless you happen to have kept in very close touch with your *alma mater*.

- **Personal:** This is someone who has known you for several years, and who can vouch for your honesty and integrity. A friend, but not a relative, is quite acceptable. Don't go in for an eminent person for the sake of effect, unless he or she knows you well enough to give a convincing reference.

● **Professional:** This will normally be your present employer or head of department. If you don't want them to be contacted, choose someone you have worked for or under in the past. If you have worked abroad in a government subsidised post, someone in the British Council or Embassy who knows your work may be an acceptable substitute.

Good general advice would be: Try to answer every question honestly. If it doesn't apply to you write N/A (not applicable) in the space. Do follow instructions to the letter. If BLOCK LETTERS are specified, write in block letters. Some forms specify black ink or typescript, for example, to facilitate photocopying. If you are sending an application abroad make sure that it will arrive quickly and safely. Consider using fax or e-mail.

MANAGING YOUR INTERVIEW

Your endeavours so far have been pitched at securing an interview. The purpose of the interview is to secure the job, and having reached this stage you are in with a chance. However, many people regard the interview as a nerve-racking affair, where their fate hangs in the balance.

Remember, you are going to be in the spotlight, and so, like any performer, you need to prepare yourself for the ordeal:

● read up about the job, country and organisation you will be working for
● list the qualities and experience you could bring to the job
● try to envisage what kind of person the organisation wants
● note down the type of questions you expect the selectors to ask
● decide how you might answer the questions, particularly the tricky ones
● think up some questions that you would like to ask about the job
● get in some interview practice.

In a word you have to **sell yourself.** This means being knowledgeable about the product (yourself), your client and his needs, and being able to handle the interview effectively, always drawing attention to your eminent suitability for the post. This is a tall order. Don't worry though. No interviewee is perfect.

Dos and don'ts at the interview

- arrive in good time
- endeavour to create a favourable impression right from the start
- try to establish some rapport with the interviewer
- be positive about your achievements
- display enthusiasm
- keep calm
- ask the interviewer to repeat a question if you haven't understood it
- be as natural as you can in the circumstances.

On the other hand:

- don't sit down until invited to
- don't make exaggerated claims
- don't argue with the interviewer or interrupt him
- don't draw attention to your weaknesses by trying to justify yourself
- don't make jokes
- don't run down your present or past employers
- don't ramble on.

After some time you may be invited to ask some questions. Don't assume that the interview is over at that moment. You are still in the business of making an impact, so don't spoil your chances by mounting a detailed investigation into salary and conditions unless this crops up during the course of the interview.

Suggested questions to ask

When do you hope to make an appointment?
To whom will I be responsible?
When will I be expected to start?
What sort of textbooks does the institution use?
What educational aids will be available at post?
Who actually issues the contract and can I see a copy?
What facilities do you offer in the way of briefing?

Don't expect to get precise answers, particularly if the organisation is acting merely as an agent.

A final word — don't forget that you are likely to be competing with a goodly number of well qualified and keen candidates. And don't make the mistake of underestimating the standard of application which the better candidates will undoubtedly be making.

6
Making up Your Mind

When you receive a firm offer of a job overseas, you need to make up your mind fairly quickly. However, a number of teachers and lecturers come to grief every year because they make up their mind *too* quickly. Going to work abroad is a much bigger step than going to work in an adjacent county, and you must take nothing for granted. Working conditions and living conditions aren't going to be precisely as they are back home. Even if you only venture as far as Calais, you will find yourself in a different environment, and this can bother some people if they come unprepared.

The onus is on you — and you alone — to find out in advance what you are letting yourself in for *before* you sign your contract. There is little point in taking up a post unless it satisfies at least some of your aspirations — in areas such as remuneration, experience, job satisfaction, status, for instance.

SOURCES OF INFORMATION AND ADVICE

The employer or recruitment agency
When you apply for a position, many organisations will provide you with a detailed job description and notes on living conditions in the country. The interview is another opportunity to learn about what is on offer so make a list of relevant questions in advance. The final opportunity to gather information will be when you are actually offered the job, when you may have cause to query certain aspects of your contract — and perhaps negotiate changes.

Using libraries
The reference sections of most larger public libraries will have handbooks on different countries or regions of the world, ranging from guidebooks to briefings for businessmen. An encyclopedia might be a good starting point.

Lending libraries will usually have a number of books dealing with specific countries but for information on education in different countries it might be better to consult a specialist educational library belonging to a university or institute of higher education, such as the London University Institute of Education's Library at 20 Bedford Way, London WC1H 0AL. Tel: 0171-580 1122.

Foreign embassies, high commissions and consulates
A number of embassies, high commissions and consulates (particularly those of western countries) have information packs on living conditions. If not, there may be an information officer who is willing to answer your questions or supply you with some information on the country. Many will be able to supply you with tourist brochures, usually issued free, or even perhaps maps. Bear in mind, though, that these are designed to show the country in the best possible light rather than to provide a down-to-earth assessment of the living conditions you will experience. If the diplomatic mission does not have any literature of this nature, there may well be a national tourist office or national airline office in London (or in other cities) that does.

The British Council and FCO
The British Council has an extensive network of representatives throughout the world who keep in touch with educational developments in their respective countries and are therefore useful sources of advice. Country desk officers at the British Council and Foreign and Commonwealth Office should also be able to put you in the picture.

Specialist organisations
- The Centre for International Briefing at Farnham Castle organises a regular programme of briefings on different parts of the world for people due to take up postings abroad. The courses are residential and usually of four days' duration. Some employers (notably DFID) offer their recruits an option to attend such a course, but the majority do not. The Centre has an extensive library of books, videos, cassettes, reports and other material on virtually every country in the world, including many personal accounts. Non-course members may use it on a fee-paying basis. There is also a well stocked book-shop in the building which offers a mail order service for customers who cannot make a personal visit.

- Christians Abroad produces short information sheets on a number of countries and can put you in touch with people who have recent experience of a particular country.

- Corona International (the Women's Corona Society) publishes *Notes for Newcomers*, short booklets on a number of countries giving details of accommodation, educational facilities, employment opportunities for spouses, prices, etc. It also organises face to face briefings and telephone briefings.

- Employment Conditions Abroad produces briefing notes on a number of countries entitled *Outlines for Expatriates* and also organises briefings for couples and groups.

- Expats International, an expatriate support organisation, can offer advice on various matters including working conditions.

- Expat Network produces a series of briefing notes on different countries.

- *Working Abroad* (Kogan Page) contains living reports on around 40 countries.

- A series of Overseas Placing Unit fact sheets on working in different countries of the European Union is available for consultation at Job Centres.

If you belong to a teacher's union it may be able to advise you on contracts. If you are working for the British Council or DFID, you are eligible to join the Overseas Contract Teachers & Advisers Branch (OCTAB) of the Institution of Professional Managers and Specialists.

Making a personal inspection
The best way to find out about the position is to have a look at the establishment and the country first of all. Very few organisations will actually be prepared to fund a personal reconnaissance, but if it is not too far away, it could be worth making a brief trip at your own expense. By talking to people on the spot you will be in a much better position to assess the situation than if you rely on second-hand or third-hand reports.

PRACTICAL CONSIDERATIONS
Your accommodation
Teaching abroad is not without its frustrations, and sometimes at the end of the day you will need a shell in which to curl up and recuperate. Adequate accommodation should therefore rank high on your list of priorities. And it is important to be clear what provision is to be made

before you sign the contract. Generally speaking the higher the salary, the better the standard of accommodation — and *vice versa*. But this does not always follow.

Accommodation provided can vary enormously. You could find yourself housed in a modern villa with a communal swimming pool, or in spartan quarters consisting of only one room. If you are teaching at a boarding establishment, you may find that you also have supervisory responsibilities.

You will need to ask:

● What standard of accommodation can I expect?
● Do I have any choice in the matter?
● Is it furnished, and if not, do I get a furniture allowance?
● Are any deductions made from my salary as a contribution to the cost?
● What services do I have to pay for? (electricity, concierge, etc)
● How adequately furnished will the accommodation be?
● Will I move in immediately on arrival?

A **rent allowance** is advantageous from one point of view in that you have some choice in the matter of accommodation, but you need to ensure that it will be adequate. And remember you are talking about rented **furnished** accommodation. Unfurnished accommodation is out of the question unless you are also receiving a furniture allowance. There is no point in taking your Chesterfield sofa to the other side of the world. The important questions in this case will be:

● What type of accommodation will the allowance provide?
● How easy is it to find?
● Will the rent allowance cover any premium/deposit I may have to pay?
● Will I receive any assistance in finding accommodation?
● Will the contract be signed with me or my employer? (the latter is preferable)
● What accommodation provision is there for me on arrival?

There may be **no accommodation provision** or **allowance**. This is particularly likely in Europe. You will need to make sure that your salary will be adequate to pay for reasonable accommodation. Bear in mind that it could be expensive and scarce in capital cities and university towns. Try to find out the likely cost of accommodation, whether you can get help in finding it and whether a salary advance might be made to cover any deposit.

Your financial and contractual situation

Your contract should set out details of your remuneration, but the implications should be checked carefully. A fairly modest salary can look much more attractive if it is free of tax and is likely to be supplemented by bonuses and payments made for extra duties. On the other hand, what looks like a first-class salary may work out less attractive where you have to pay for your own accommodation and the cost of living is astronomical. Have the following questions in mind when considering financial and contractual matters:

- How does the salary compare with that of local teachers and other expatriates?
- Is the salary taxable? If so, how much tax must I pay?
- Are there any allowances payable? (eg for dependants)
- Is any provision made for contributions to pension funds or national insurance contributions?
- Is my salary paid in local currency and, if so, is it transferable into other currencies?
- What deductions are made, and can they be reclaimed?
- What penalties are there for premature termination of contract?
- Is there a terminal gratuity or any other form of bonus?
- What provision is made for health care and sick pay?
- What are the travel arrangements to the post? Do I have any choice in the matter?

Some contracts tend to be vague and brief, and can lead to misunderstandings, particularly if verbal promises are made which arc not incorporated into the text. A detailed contract which lays down the obligations of both employee and employer is therefore preferable, unless you have a longstanding relationship with a particular organisation and know it to be trustworthy.

Teachers sometimes find that they are expected to sign one contract with the recruitment agency and a second contract on arrival at post which may contain different conditions. This is not necessarily due to malevolence on the employer's part, but could be merely to satisfy local employment laws. You should, however, ask for clarification on this matter and an outline of the terms of the local contract.

If you have any reservations as to what you are signing, consult a solicitor, your union or the Overseas Contract Teacher's Association Branch (in the case of British Council or government contracts).

Living conditions

Apart from financial and professional considerations you need to investigate whether life is going to be worth living. If you place great value on your lifestyle or have dependants who will accompany you, amenities are going to be important.

Not only do you want an idea as to what is available, you also need to know whether you can afford it. If you are a keen golfer, for example, you will not be able to play golf in Japan on a teacher's salary. Use the following list of questions as a guide to the sort of things you need to find out about your future lifestyle:

- How does the cost of living compare with that of the UK?
- What is the inflation rate?
- What are the shopping facilities like?
- What items, if any, are in short supply?
- Are imports freely available?
- Do I have any duty free import privileges?
- What recreational facilities are there?
- What is service like?
- Is domestic help readily available?
- What is public transport like?
- How vital is it to have your own car?
- How many expatriates live in the area?
- What kind of a social life do people have?
- What cultural amenities (libraries, cinemas, theatre) are there?

Social and political climate

All other countries are foreign but some are more foreign than others. People can feel uneasy in their new environment, and the unease may increase with the passing of time. You may find the regime autocratic and oppressive, or be alarmed at the gross disparity between rich and poor. You may find that religious taboos are restricting your social life.

The proportion of genuine democracies in the world is relatively small and, much as you may wish to increase that number, as a foreigner you shouldn't attempt to influence political events within your host country. You'll need to turn a blind eye to certain matters and exercise discretion in your pronouncements.

Teachers generally have much more contact with local people than other expatriates, diplomats, for example, and are less insulated from the world outside. Some have difficulty in coming to terms with their new environment, while others are born survivors who never make a false step.

You may find in time that — as at home — some people are sensitive to criticism, unwilling to mix with foreigners, just plain dishonest, or whatever. While I have found most foreign nationals both considerate and accommodating to foreigners, it is as well to note these possibilities in advance.

In seeking to understand the culture, bear in mind, too, that the status of women will vary from country to country. Try to ascertain from the start what subjects are taboo and how cautious you need to be in expressing opinions.

You will also, of course, want to find out what the government of the country is like and what effect the political situation has on people's lives.

YOUR WORKING CONDITIONS

It is just as well to know exactly what will be expected of you. Don't assume that the same conditions apply in education throughout the world. In some cases you just need to turn up for your lessons or lectures. In other establishments you are expected to be in position from before the beginning of the school day till after the end of it. You may find that you are expected to be involved in out of school activities, like parents' meetings or students' clubs.

Be clear in your mind as to your obligations to your employers and their obligations to you. This will avoid disappointment and potential disputes when you arrive.

Many detailed questions will need to be answered, including the following:

- How many class contact hours will I have per week?
- Will I receive payment for extra hours worked?
- Will I have other responsibilities, for instance, for administration, testing or counselling?
- What are the dates of the academic year?
- Which hours and days will I be expected to be on site?
- What is my leave entitlement and will holiday pay be due in advance or in arrears?
- Are there any restrictions on outside activities, such as private teaching or consultancy?
- Are there any published guidelines for teachers?

FAMILY CONSIDERATIONS

Even if you are quite happy to go off to some distant clime, if you have dependants then family considerations will loom large. You have three options:

- Take them with you.
- Take your spouse with you and leave the children at home either in the care of a relative or friend, or in a boarding school.
- Leave the whole family at home and strike out on your own.

Option 1

There is a lot to be said for having your family about you. They will offer you moral support and comfort and help overcome any sense of strangeness that you feel. If your children are young, there is usually no problem with their education but once they reach secondary level there may be no suitable school for them in your overseas location. The *ECIS Directory* can provide information as to whether there is.

Option 2

This is a solution followed by a number of families, particularly diplomats. Your children will be able to join you on holiday, or you can arrange for your home leave to coincide with theirs. Which of the two options you choose will depend on your children. If they have reached a critical point in their school career, it might be unwise to move them, and you will want to look into ways of keeping them at home, perhaps with a relation or close family friend who will keep an eye on their progress. A boarding school education may be a very good solution for the right kind of child but, unless you are offered an allowance towards the cost of their education, the cost could prove prohibitive.

Option 3

In some cases this is the only option. Bachelor status posts are quite normal in the Middle East, and separation is often compensated for by generous leave entitlements and high tax-free salaries. However, if you are a closely knit family lengthy absences can cause problems at home, and you should discuss the implications with your family before signing the contract.

Considering the implications

It has to be admitted that overseas postings, whether accompanied or unaccompanied, can put considerable strain on marriages. In a foreign location your partner could be bored to death with having nothing to do, or fail to adapt readily to the new surroundings. Partners who are used to pursuing an active career may become frustrated if they are prevented from taking up employment by local labour laws.

According to Expats International (see p.55) prolonged separation is a frequent cause of marital break up. Posts offering bachelor-status terms are therefore more appropriate for single people and divorcees than for married people, unless the marital relationship happens to be exceptionally resilient.

The family pet
One final matter is what to do with family pets? In some cases you may be able to take them with you, but on return to this country they will need to go into quarantine. In any case, pets tend to be reluctant expatriates. The RSPCA or a similar animal welfare society should be able to advise.

CHECKLIST

This is a summary of the main points you need to be clear about when you sign your contract.

☐ What is the name and address of your employer?
☐ Where exactly will I be employed?
☐ What is my job title?
☐ What exactly does the job involve?
☐ What is the normal period of notice if either side wishes to terminate the contract?
☐ Is the contract renewable?
☐ Is there a probationary period, and if so, for how long?
☐ What will my net earnings be and what is my tax liability at post?
☐ What are the arrangements for absence due to sickness?
☐ If I have to leave before completion of contract will the return fare be paid?
☐ Are my qualifications acceptable in the country where I shall be working?
☐ What is the procedure for acquiring a visa or work permit?
☐ What help can I count on in the event of a contractual disagreement?
☐ What perks are there? (eg free transport, pension fund, commissary privileges, duty free privileges)

7
Preparing to Go

DEALING WITH PRACTICAL MATTERS

Happy the man or woman who can traverse the world living out of a suitcase! If you are someone with few possessions, no ties and no responsibilities, moving to a distant clime can be a very simple matter. If you have a house, a family and a few trappings of wealth, a move can prove much more traumatic.

Banking arrangements
You will probably want to visit your bank before you leave to:

- Inform them of your move and leave a contact address.

- Obtain foreign exchange, travellers' cheques etc, for your journey and to tide you over the initial stages of your stay abroad.

- Check if you can use your cash cards and credit cards easily at your destination.

- Arrange for a transfer of money to a bank abroad. (This may not be necessary if you are assured of an advance of salary on arrival.)

- Obtain a letter of introduction to a bank in the town where you will be working. (This is not always vital, as your employer may be able to do this for you. In any case, you may have no need to, or may not wish to, use a bank abroad.)

- Arrange to have your various financial commitments (council tax, mortgage etc) paid by standing order to reduce paperwork. (If you do not plan to remit your salary to the account, you need to arrange for the account to be topped up. Bear in mind that international bank transfers are not always speedy).

- Avail yourself of your bank's advisory services (see p.66).

62

Your car

Some employers will assist teachers in the purchase and shipping of a car, and this is a perk that you should take advantage of, since you can order a duty free car in Britain at a considerable saving on the normal show-room price. Do check, however, that it will not be subject to a heavy duty at the other end. It is best to go for a model which is fairly common in the country where you will be working and for which there is a local agent, otherwise you may have problems with spares and servicing.

Heavy duty suspension and perhaps a low compression engine are advisable for many Third World countries. Remember, too, that countries expect cars to comply with certain national standards, for example on exhaust emissions. Car distributors that specialise in export sales should be able to advise you on this score.

If you don't want to splash out too much, you could rely on your own car, but subject it to a thorough overhaul first of all, and check that it will comply with local regulations. Although certain developed countries may have a reasonable second-hand car market, you cannot always count on it.

Children of school age

If you are leaving your children in the UK with a relative or friend, you will need to leave contact addresses and make proper financial provision. If they are to attend a boarding school there is the matter of finding a suitable school. Some local education authorities have schools of this type. (See *Directory of Maintained Boarding Schools*, DFEE). Otherwise, you will have to find a private establishment.

A number of agencies can advise you on suitable schools. The leading ones are:

- Gabbitas Educational Consultants
- Independent Schools Information Service (ISIS)
- Dean Associates (See Useful Addresses).

If you are taking your children with you make sure there is some educational provision for them at your destination, and that there will be a place for them in a school when they arrive. It is wise to check with your employer, the Embassy or the *ECIS Directory*.

If there is no suitable provision at all, correspondence tuition could be considered, and for advice on this you should approach World-wide Education Service. Under the Service's Home School System, parents teach their own children with the guidance of WES tutors. The programme has been endorsed by the DFEE.

For children of secondary school age Mercers College offers corre-spondence courses.

Your health

In some places the health facilities may be expensive or of a low stan-dard, so make full use of NHS facilities before you leave, including

- a dental check
- a sight test
- a chest X-ray.

Several employers insist that you have a medical check-up before you are confirmed in the post. Even if they do not, it may be wise to con-sult your GP as to your general state of fitness.

Your employer may provide health insurance while you are at post, or you may be expected to contribute to the state social security scheme, where it exists. However, it is worthwhile bearing in mind that in many countries state health care provision is much less extensive than in the UK.

Medical matters

You need to investigate whether you need to take any precautionary measures before you leave Britain, and it is sensible to visit those who have looked after your health in recent years. You will find plenty of useful advice on going abroad in the Department of Health booklet *Health advice for travellers* obtainable free of charge from chemists, doctors, DSS offices or by phoning 0800-555777. HMSO publishes a book *Health Information for Overseas Travel*.

If you are moving to Europe, North America, Australia or Japan no special vaccinations are required. For other countries vaccinations are often necessary or advisable and your course of treatment may need to start as much as two months before your departure.

There are vaccinations against polio, typhoid, hepatitis, yellow fever, cholera, rabies, encephalitis and meningococcal meningitis, but it is highly unlikely that you will require jabs against all of these unless you are planning to live in the heart of the jungle.

Health advice for travellers should tell you what you need to know, but if you are unsure you should contact Medical Advisory Services for Travellers Abroad (MASTA), London School of Hygiene and Tropical Medicine, Keppel Street, London WC1E 7HT. Tel: 0171-631 4408. MASTA application forms are also obtainable from some chemists.

Your doctor or local health centre may be able to vaccinate you, but you may find it more convenient to use one of the British Airways Travel Clinics in Birmingham, Edinburgh, Glasgow, Leicester, Manchester, Newport Pagnell, Nottingham, Purley, Reading, Stratford on Avon and London. These are linked to the MASTA database. Telephone 0171-831 5333 for further details.

There are many good books on the market on how to keep healthy. If you don't have leanings towards hypochondria, try *Traveller's Health* by Dr Richard Dawood (OUP). For anyone going to the tropics the Ross Institute (at the Bureau of Hygiene & Tropical Diseases address above) publishes a useful handbook called *Preservation of Personal Health in Warm Climates*, and there is also John Hatt's *The Tropical Traveller* (Pan).

Getting insured

There are four types of insurance that you need to consider.

- Health and accident insurance — this is particularly vital if there is little social security provision in the country and your employer does not provide it. If you will be living in the EU you should obtain Form 121 from the DSS.
- Personal effects insurance. Loss or damage to personal effects.
- Car insurance, if you happen to be taking a car.
- Life insurance, if you have dependants. The basic 'no frills' type is quite adequate.

For all of these it pays to consult a good broker who specialises in insurance for expatriates. (See Useful Addresses).

Your house

If you have property, you need to decide what to do with it in your absence. Generally speaking, it is not advisable to leave houses and flats unattended and just hope for the best. You could either let it during your absence — perhaps enlisting the services of a letting agent — or ask someone to keep an eye on it for you (a relation, a friend or an organisation, such as Homesitters). If you are planning to be abroad for a long time, the best idea might be to sell it.

If you have a mortgage you will need to check with the building society or bank that they have no restrictions on letting. In any case you will need to notify them of your new address and make provision for repayments. At present UK tax-payers receive some tax relief on the mortgage repayments, and you will need to check whether this provision will still apply when you are abroad.

Managing your investments

If you reckon that you are going to show a surplus on your earnings, it makes sense to look into ways in which you can invest your money before you leave.

Short-term investments

You need to have some reserves in ready cash in case of emergencies, and this means a savings account with a building society, bank or other reputable financial institution. Go for the account which offers a high rate of interest and withdrawal facilities on demand. If your salary is tax-free, go for an expatriate account where interest is paid free of tax. Banks in offshore tax havens, such as the Isle of Man and the Channel Islands, are well equipped to deal with this sort of thing, but your own bank or building society may well have the facilities you require.

Long-term investments

If you are likely to have cash that you will not need for a few years, it will probably be worth your while to invest it in equities. This is, of course, riskier — but the rewards are much greater, and this holds true the longer you keep your investment.

If surplus earnings are a relatively new phenomenon for you, tread carefully. Contact a few stockbrokers or investment advisers before you leave and describe your needs. Many will recommend unit trusts or investment trusts in order to spread the risk.

Investing in property, commodities, and individual companies is riskier for a beginner. The exception, of course, is buying your own home, but you need to make sure that it is fully insured and looked after in your absence.

The ins and outs of investment for expatriates are explained in *Working Abroad* by Jonathan Golding and a number of other handbooks. Magazines for expatriates will have useful investment articles as well as information on other matters relating to life overseas:

Home and Away
Resident Abroad.

Your luggage and personal effects

If you are travelling by air you won't be able to take everything with you unless your employer happens to be remarkably indulgent. Some luggage can be sent air-freight — which is much cheaper than the excess baggage rate — while the rest may have to be sent by sea or overland, which works out even cheaper.

To avoid undue worry and hassle contact a freight forwarding agent who can arrange for all aspects of transport from the packing stage onwards. If you are going to Europe and have a car, take as much luggage as possible with you.

Your passport

Make certain that your passport is still valid and renew it, if necessary, through your local post office. If time is pressing, visit your regional Passport Office in person:

Personal callers only
Clive House, 70 Petty France, London SW1H 9HD. Tel: 0171-279 3434.

Postal and personal applications:
5th Floor, India Buildings, Water Street, Liverpool L2 0QZ. Tel: 0151-237 3010. (North of England and North Wales)
Olympia House, Upper Dock Street, Newport, Gwent NP9 1XA. Tel: 01633-244500/244292 (South Wales, South and West).
Aragon Court, Northminster Road, Peterborough PE1 1QG. Tel: 01733-895555 (Midlands, East Anglia and Kent).
3 Northgate, 96 Milton Street, Cowcaddens, Glasgow G4 0BT. Tel: 0141-332 0271 (Scotland, London and Middlesex).
Hampton House, 47-53 High Street, Belfast BT1 2QS. Tel: 01232-232371 (Northern Ireland).

Your pension

Is your job abroad pensionable? It may not be. In the case of some publicly funded posts you may receive a gratuity at the end of your term in lieu of a pension contribution, or you may be able to persuade your employer to contribute to your occupational pension.

As for your state pension at home, you can continue to make contributions on a voluntary basis. If you don't, you will not be eligible for the full entitlement when you retire. Since the state pension is index-linked, it makes good sense to keep up your payments.

If you haven't already done so, look into taking out a private pension scheme which you can continue when you return to the UK. Teachers and lecturers on British Council contracts are eligible to join the International Teachers Pension Portfolio (contact Bone & Co, Les Brehauts, St Peter, Guernsey). This is also available to any others who are eligible to invest in offshore funds.

Shopping

There are only three reasons for going on a big shopping spree before you leave, if you are to avoid a baggage problem:

- certain items are unavailable or in short supply in your adoptive country
- certain items are much more expensive there than at home
- certain items are going to be needed immediately upon arrival.

Try to find out about the availability and price of goods before you spend anything. Country profiles from Employment Conditions Abroad, Expat Network, the Women's Corona Society, the British Council, DFID and some embassies will usually include such information.

If you are buying expensive items, you will probably be able to get them free of VAT provided you deal with a store which is au fait with the tax-free export scheme. Certain portable items — cameras, radios, cassette players — could be purchased en route at an airport duty-free shop.

A radio capable of receiving short-wave broadcasts is a must if you plan to keep in touch with what is happening back home. However you may be able to receive English broadcasts by satellite TV.

Social Security

The DSS Overseas Branch, Newcastle-upon-Tyne NE98 1YX, publishes a series of booklets on all matters relating to social security, and it would be wise to write to them explaining where you are going and asking for advice. Leaflet NI38 *Social Security Abroad* is particularly useful. Your local DSS office may not have these leaflets, but should certainly be able to tell you what leaflets are available from the Overseas Branch. Northern Ireland residents should consult the Social Security Agency in Belfast.

Paying tax

It is just as well to understand your tax liability both in the UK and abroad. Your employer or his agent ought to give you some idea on these matters, and you should not assume that similar organisations offer similar terms. British Council contract staff, for instance usually get tax-free salaries, while those employed by the Department of International Development do not.

You can obtain the information from a variety of sources:

- **The Inland Revenue** — either your local office or the Claims Branch, Foreign Division, Merton Road, Bootle L69 9BL. *Booklet IR25* sets out the rules governing the taxation of income from jobs overseas. The Inland Revenue publishes a number of leaflets, eg *The Taxation of Foreign Earnings and Pensions, Income Liable to UK Income Tax, Double Taxation Relief.*

- Handbooks, such as *Working Abroad* by J Golding.
- Tax consultants with international expertise.
- Banks, particularly those in tax havens such as the Channel Islands.

If your tax affairs are complicated and there is a lot of money at stake, you could seek professional advice. Make sure that the consultant you engage is familiar with the tax problems of expatriates. Some are listed in the Useful Addresses section. Your bank may be able to advise you.

Organising your travel

Most overseas employers will provide you with an economy class air ticket. Many will also provide tickets for your dependants. If there is some reluctance to do this ask for the fare equivalent in cash and contact an agency which sells low cost fares.

Other modes of travel — by sea or overland — can be discounted, except in the case of Europe and perhaps North Africa, unless you have plenty of time at your disposal. Should you be worried about security in the country you are heading for or those you are passing through en route, advice is available on BBC Ceefax pages 564-567. Alternatively, you could ring the enquiry line of the Foreign and Commonwealth Office (FCO): 0171 270 4129.

If you have a car, car travel is a very sensible option within Europe and parts of the Middle East. Locations such as Turkey can be reached easily in a few days. But if your insurance policy is limited to the British Isles, inform your insurance company that you will need a 'green card'' before you go. You may have to make further insurance arrangements on arrival.

Arranging visas

Almost invariably you will need to obtain a visa if you are planning to work in a foreign country (the exceptions being the EU countries). To obtain a visa you will need to produce proof that you have a job offer and perhaps a statement from the authorities of the country concerned that the appointment has been approved.

Don't leave your visa application till the last minute. In some cases, the USA for example, it can take weeks or months for your application to be approved. This is less of a problem, however, in the case of exchange teaching schemes.

If you are travelling overland or plan to stop en route, check whether you will also need visas for the countries you pass through.

Miscellaneous points

● Will you need an international driving licence? Outside the European Union you probably will. Contact the AA or RAC for details.

● Make a will, just in case the unexpected happens — we are all mortal!

● Don't forget to make arrangements for the redirection of mail and make sure that your next of kin and other interested parties in the UK have an address for you.

● Electricity, water, council tax, gas, telephone, water, newspaper and milk deliveries — remember to inform those concerned that you are leaving.

● Get at least twelve passport photos of yourself and each member of your family travelling with you.

● Confirm arrival arrangements and ask for contact telephone numbers at your destination in case of emergency.

● If you are planning to travel extensively purchase a copy of *The Traveller's Handbook (WEXAS)*. The reference section deals with such matters as visa requirements, customs offices, duty free allowances, airport departure taxes, currency restrictions, hospitals with English speaking staff, driving requirements worldwide, public holidays, business hours, freight forwarders, and so on.

● To keep your right to vote inform your local electoral registration office and ask for a change of address form. For subsequent years you will need to obtain a form from your nearest British consulate.

PREPARING YOURSELF PROFESSIONALLY

If you have very little time between appointment and departure you could be so preoccupied with the business of moving that you overlook the need for professional preparation. Yet if you are to get off to a good start professionally this shouldn't be skimped as there may be little opportunity for such preliminaries once you are on the job.

Preparation should not be confined to the subject(s) that you will be teaching. In order to be effective you need to have some understanding of the people you will be teaching, since their background — cultural and economic — may well affect their learning process and their attitudes towards education.

Appreciating the culture

During your period of preparation remember that you will not just be teaching your subject, you will be teaching people. And it makes sense to learn just what makes them tick.

One of the most pleasurable ways of doing this is to read travel books or novels about the country. Go to a public library with an extensive travel section and browse. If you have something of a wanderlust, you might consider buying a guide book produced by Fodor, Baedeker or Lonely Planet, as well as a large scale map. In certain parts of the world good maps and guidebooks can be hard to come by. There are now some excellent introductions to specific countries published in the How To series, the Culture Shock series (Kuperard) and from other publishers such as Grant Dawson, Robert Hale and Vacation Work. Most of them are packed with practical advice on matters ranging from banking hours to social etiquette.

Try to find out something about the history of the country both past and recent, since the past tends to shape attitudes and practices. You may not get a chance once you are in the country itself, since some of the more candid accounts could well be unavailable or banned.

Understanding values

Each nation has its own system of values: they may be different from your own but that doesn't mean they are inferior so it's important to understand these values. Learn to respect them, and perhaps to modify your own behaviour in deference to them, and you'll become more acceptable to your hosts, more at ease with your surroundings and more successful in your work.

Riding the Waves of Culture by Fons Trompenaars is a sobering introduction to cultural differences, and there are several books listed in the Bibliography that deal with specific national cultures.

Understanding the educational background

Familiarisation with the educational system and traditions of the country is important, even though you may be teaching in an organisation that stands outside the national educational system — an international school or a regional institute, for instance.

If you are teaching within the national system then you really should make an effort to understand it — how it has developed, what the government's educational policy is, how the education provision is structured, what subjects are taught and to whom, and so on. Without this knowledge some of the educational practices you come up against may strike you as bizarre or even irrational.

Above all, you need to understand something of the learning methods your students will be used to. In the Middle East, for instance, the old Koranic tradition of learning by rote is by no means extinct, and students can learn long passages by rote for reproduction during examinations, and yet not really understand what they have learned.

In other cultures too, knowledge is there to be assimilated, never applied. Students regard the teacher as a fount of wisdom, whose ideas should never be contradicted. The idea of thinking for oneself is alien to them, perhaps because their society favours conformism rather than originality.

Understanding the teacher's role
The teacher's position needs to be understood, too. For example, is he or she a person who is respected or merely taken for granted? In many countries educational institutions and their teachers enjoy much less autonomy than they do in the UK. The ground rules are laid down by a centralist ministry and you are expected to adhere to these. As a consequence, your principal may turn out to be less of a decision-maker and professional leader than one might expect in Anglo-Saxon countries. Instead, he is largely an administrator with the unenviable task of ensuring that government directives are complied with.

Educational traditions
Some educational systems are highly selective and elitist; others subscribe to the comprehensive ideal. Some have a strongly clerical atmosphere; others are decidedly anti-clerical. The educational traditions of a country often have a strong bearing on what happens in its schools and colleges, and concepts which may seem strange to a newcomer can sometimes only be explained by reference to the past.

Useful reading
Useful reference books are:

● *International Handbook of Education Systems*, John Wiley & Sons (in three volumes)
● *The UNESCO Statistical Yearbook.*

Then there are books on individual countries and regions, and here the best idea is to browse through the comparative education section of a university or college of education library. Certain embassies (or their cultural centres) may be able to provide booklets on education in their countries, and there are surveys on various educational systems by the

Council of Europe, OECD, UNESCO and Britain's DfEE.

The following series may well have a title dealing with the country you are planning to teach in, but make sure the edition you consult is up to date:

- *World Education Series*, David & Charles
- *Society, Schools and Progress Series*, Pergamon
- *Reviews of National Policies for Education*, OECD
- The *World Education Series* of the American Association of Collegiate Registrars and Admissions Officers.

More books on specific regions and countries are listed in the **Further Reading** appendix. Education in many countries has changed very rapidly in the last decade or so, and it is important to consult books that are up-to-date, as well as recent issues of journals such as the *Comparative Education*.

LEARNING THE LANGUAGE

If you are going to a country where English is not the mother-tongue, you may find it frustrating that so few people understand you. It will be helpful to have at least a smattering of the language on arrival, and there are many methods available for learning the rudiments of a language:

- Language learning manuals. The Teach Yourself Books and Routledge's Colloquial series are the best known ones and have the advantage of being widely available. An academic bookshop which has an extensive language section, such as Foyles, Dillons and Blackwells, or a specialist language course bookseller such as Grant & Cutler and LCL, will show what else is on offer.

- Audio and video courses. The emphasis here is on the spoken language, which is going to be of immense importance to you. The following organisations distribute and/or publish courses of this nature: Linguaphone, Audio Forum, BBC Publications.

- Part-time courses. Many local colleges provide part-time courses in the more common languages, and in London and other large centres the range of languages taught can be quite considerable. Certain universities and polytechnics have their own language centres which offer facilities for casual students. Some countries, like France and Germany, have their own cultural institutes which offer language tuition, and there are many private language schools which offer courses as well. Consult your local *Yellow Pages* for details of the nearest.

● Intensive courses. If your departure is imminent there is a lot to be said for learning as much as you can in the short time available. Some universities, polytechnics, local colleges and private language schools run intensive courses. The Association of Language Excellence Centres and National Business Language Information Service can provide you with details.

● Private tuition. Many colleges can put you in touch with private tutors. Private schools, like those mentioned above, will often be prepared to provide one-to-one tuition for you. The Association for Language Learning and the Institute of Linguists can also put you in touch with tutors.

For a more thorough discussion of study possibilities you should refer to the handbook *How to Master Languages*.

TEACHING YOUR OWN SUBJECT

When you arrive at your posting you will be expected not only to be knowledgeable in your subject but also to be able to adapt that knowledge to the local environment. For example, if you are an economist going to teach in the Third World some knowledge of development economics will be useful.

Some form of preparation is vital, but in order to avoid wasting time on what will prove to be irrelevant, you need to ask for guidance. Try to track down your predecessor in the job or someone who has worked in the area before, and question them in detail along the following lines:

● What are educational standards like?
● What does the syllabus consist of and what textbooks are used?
● What books/equipment/materials do you suggest I take?
● To what extent is it possible to produce my own teaching materials (ie are there photocopiers, duplicators, typewriters, word processors, an adequate supply of paper in the school/college)?
● What are library and bookshop facilities like?
● What facilities are there for research?
● What facilities are there for practical work (laboratories, computers, tape recorders, etc)?

- Are there any locally produced studies in my subject of which I ought to be aware?
- Are there any induction courses available?
- What type of professional support can I expect (advisers, teachers' centres, etc)?

Choosing what to take

The choice of which books to take can be a problem. If you have an extensive library of your own, resign yourself to the thought that you'll have to leave most of it behind. Not even the most generous baggage allowance will allow you to ship hundreds of treasured volumes. You'll have to be selective, and again some kind of guidance will be needed on which volumes to take. If you are going to a country which has a rich assortment of libraries, the dilemma may not be so acute.

If there is some doubt as to how easy it is to obtain books at your new posting, it may well be worthwhile to open an account with an academic bookseller who offers a reliable mail order service.

8
Meeting the Cultural Challenge

No matter how well you have prepared yourself for the experience of living and working in a foreign environment, you will not be able to judge whether you have made the right decision until you actually arrive. Even then, first impressions may not be the correct ones, since it takes time to settle in.

The sort of person who is enthusiastic about their new location right from the start may find that the novelty begins to pall after a time. Another type may find the first few days or weeks the most anxious of their life and come to the speedy conclusion that they have made a terrible mistake. Yet after a time they begin to appreciate both their new home and their job.

The initial period is an absolutely crucial time when you have to be at your most alert. For in addition to coming to grips with new professional challenges you are also involved in making suitable domestic arrangements for yourself in unfamiliar surroundings.

This section touches on some of the problems that you may encounter at first and suggests ways in which you might cope with them.

YOUR ARRIVAL

Your arrival at a strange airport (or station or port) after a long journey can be a bewildering experience when a helping hand can be very useful. With luck there will be someone there to meet you and put you right, but don't count on it.

It is sensible to prepare yourself in advance in case of misadventure:

● Arm yourself with one or two contact addresses or telephone numbers.
● Try to have some local currency by you in case the *bureaux de change* are shut.
● Carry a decent guide book with you which lists accommodation addresses.

You may have to deal with immigration and customs yourself. This is a fairly simple procedure in most of Europe, but in other areas of the world it can be a wearisome and time-consuming experience. You may be required to show a letter from your employer, for example, and fill in copious forms.

When all is completed, if you look at the stamp that has been put in your passport and find that it is valid for only seven days, don't despair. You will probably need to register within this period in order to obtain your residence permit.

If someone has come to meet you and you have doubts about your documentation, check with him that you have acted correctly before you leave your port of arrival. If, on the other hand, the expected welcoming party has failed to materialise, again don't despair.

● Check with the information desk for any messages
● Telephone one of your contacts
● Mention your problem to a representative of the airline you have arrived by
● If everything else fails, leave a message and look round for an accommodation booking service and transport into town.

FINDING ACCOMMODATION

Short-term

It is quite usual for new teachers to spend their initial period in a hotel, and this is a sensible idea. The first 24 hours need to be a period of acclimatisation when you sleep off the journey, if it has been a lengthy one, and are free of domestic concerns.

After a time the novelty of living in a hotel begins to wear off, particularly if you have a family. As quickly as possible you need to find a place of residence for the long term. You won't feel truly at home and able to concentrate fully on your professional duties until you have taken this step.

Hotel accommodation, in any case, can work out expensive, and it is advisable to check with your employer, if you have not already done so, what elements — if any — you have to pay for. The initial period is likely to be an expensive time anyway, and you don't want to have to spend vast amounts of cash on hotel bills.

In some cases, however, new arrivals are put into permanent accommodation right away.

Long-term

Comfortable accommodation can play an important part in making your life palatable. Teaching abroad is not without its frustrations and you need to be able to escape from it all at the end of the day in order to relax. The question is: can you?

Accommodation arrangements differ and this should have been made clear to you before you signed the contract. The employing institution may provide accommodation for you; it may give you a rent allowance; or alternatively — and this is particularly the case within Europe — paying for accommodation may be your own responsibility entirely.

Accommodation provided by your employer

Accommodation **provided by the employer** can be first class or downright mediocre. Before you signed the contract you should have been given some indication as to what to expect, but the moment of truth does not come until you arrive.

For teachers accommodated in a boarding establishment there may be disadvantages which you failed to anticipate. Instead of being able to escape from your duties at the end of the day, you may find that you are permanently on call or surrounded by the noise of children from early in the morning till late at night. If it is in an isolated location you may find your social horizon is excessively limited.

It is as well to recall that in signing the contract you signify your agreement to certain conditions. If the accommodation differs considerably from what you were led to believe at your interview or briefing, you have grounds for complaint. If it does not, you really have to accept it.

Finding your own accommodation

Generally speaking, teachers feel happier if they can **find their own accommodation**. Yet this can present problems, particularly when rented accommodation is scarce. In a sense, you have enough on your plate coming to grips with your new job, and trailing around to find suitable accommodation can be a chore.

Don't be afraid to seek advice. Find out which areas expatriates prefer — where the transport and shopping are good, for instance. While you may have a fairly good idea of the kind of accommodation you would like, remember that an old hand will have useful knowledge about matters that are less apparent to the newcomer. Some areas may be prone to flooding, power cuts and water shortages. In others security may be a problem.

If you have been recruited by an organisation such as the British Council or an international company, the local office staff should be able to put you right and render you invaluable assistance. If you are dealing with an organisation with little experience of coping with expatriates, you may not be quite so lucky.

Teachers recruited in Europe will often be expected to find and finance their own accommodation. This may not present a problem if there is plenty available, but in university towns especially there is a high demand from students for low-cost rented accommodation. You may find that you have to pay a premium on the rent — up to a year in advance — or you could be presented with a formidable looking legal document to sign.

Finding help
One way to overcome such obstacles is to confront your employers with the problem and find out if they can help. They may be able to offer the landlord certain guarantees or negotiate a better deal. If you can persuade them to sign the contract and deduct the rent from your salary, so much the better. Organisations tend to have more clout than individuals. If you are a student teacher (assistant) in a university town you may be able to use the accommodation bureau of the university. Newspapers and private accommodation bureaux are other sources of accommodation addresses. However, some of the best value accommodation is found by word of mouth, so it pays to ask around.

YOUR FIRST PROFESSIONAL CONTACTS

One of the first things you will need to do is establish contact with your workplace. First meetings can be crucial and your aim must be to make a favourable impression on everybody. So it is sensible to dress smartly for the occasion, unless advised otherwise.

Women have to be particularly scrupulous about dress. In Muslim countries, in particular, long dresses and covered shoulders are *de rigueur* — and trousers could cause offence in places. In educational establishments it is best to dress decorously — which can mean drably, I'm afraid — so you will have to save your natty outfits for social occasions.

If you are not certain what to wear, ask for advice. You may find, to your relief, that Savile Row elegance is not expected of you. Informal attire is more likely to be accepted in expatriate-run language schools than in more formal educational establishments.

Ideally the first encounter should be limited to meeting people and having a quick look round. If there are any pressing problems, such as accommodation, by all means bring them up, but it is wise to leave the nitty gritty till later.

Not every first encounter is necessarily an ideal one, unfortunately. Term may have started, and you could find yourself being pushed into a classroom within minutes of your arrival! You may find your colleagues so rushed off their feet that a lengthy briefing is just out of the question.

Even if you arrive in advance of the start of term, you cannot assume that you will be put fully into the picture. Not all heads of departments or principals are particularly good at briefing people. They just take it for granted that everybody knows the intricacies of their establishment. Be prepared for this by compiling in advance a list of questions you will need to ask.

Suggested questions

In general, you will need to know:

- Who is who in the establishment and to whom am I responsible?
- What precisely are my duties?
- Will I have extra duties apart from teaching?
- What are the working hours?

More specifically:

- What is the syllabus?
- How much discretion do I have in teaching methods and materials?
- Am I expected to produce detailed lesson plans for inspection?
- Is there a register in which I have to record attendance and/or the content of my lessons?
- What teaching facilities does the school/college have, apart from blackboards and classrooms, and how do I book them?

About your students:

- What is the background of my students?
- How motivated are they?
- What disciplinary problems arise and how are they dealt with?
- How are students assessed?
- Which marking schemes are used and how should marks be recorded?

Concerning your financial position:

- When are salaries paid?
- What, if any, deductions are made?
- Is it possible to get an advance if I need one?

If there are **expatriate staff** in the establishment they will probably be able to tell you what you need to know without too much prodding. Beware, however, of taking every remark at its face value. Some 'old hands' may have a tendency to mix opinion with facts, and it is the facts that you are after at this stage, not other people's prejudices.

On the other hand you may be the only expatriate on the staff, and may find you have to probe for answers. Don't bombard your colleagues with too many questions as they may find this intimidating. Try instead to extract information from them by degrees. Some of this can be learned by example. See if you can sit in on lessons to find how other teachers handle their classes.

SORTING OUT PROBLEMS

Not every landing proves to be a happy one. The institution and the job may fall far short of your expectations. There may be some kind of confusion as to your role. Perhaps your accommodation is not up to standard, or certain conditions relating to your contract are not being fulfilled. You may even find that you are superfluous to staffing requirements or that no-one knows what to do with you.

There are three options open to you:

● You can walk out.
● You can complain.
● You can shrug your shoulders and decide to make the best of a bad job.

Walking out can prove costly. Not that you will necessarily be sued for breach of contract, but you may have to pay your fare home and find yourself out of work for a while. However, if after careful consideration you feel that you have been placed in an impossible situation which is unlikely to improve, retreat may be the best solution.

Complaining can be more fruitful, if you find the right person. The obvious people to turn to are the organisation that recruited you. This should present no problem if they happen to have a local representative. Even if they don't, I think it is important to put the onus on them to solve any misunderstanding rather than wade into the fray yourself. Only do this when all other approaches fail.

The third alternative, to **grin and bear it**, may be the wisest move in the long run. If your employers recognise that you have been lured to their establishment under false pretences, they may be prepared to go some way to meeting your demands. This will not happen, however, if you go round making mountains out of molehills or asking for things which are not specified in the contract.

Bear in mind that during this initial period you are, in effect, establishing a bridgehead. Once you have a secure and comfortable base you will be able to concentrate on the important task of establishing a good relationship with your colleagues, superiors, and ultimately, your students.

GETTING DOWN TO WORK

The first days or weeks in a new environment often have something of the character of a holiday. It is a stimulating period much enjoyed by people who revel in novel experiences, and something of a shock for people who acclimatise more slowly.

This period does not last. The novelty begins to wear off, and you settle into a routine. Teachers in the first category may discover that the place where they have landed is not as attractive as they thought at first, while the slow adapters gradually come to terms with it, and may even come to like it. But it is only now that you discover whether you have made the right decision or not.

This section points out potential problems. Not that you will necessarily encounter more than a few. However, it is just as well to be aware of what could happen in order to avoid trouble.

BUILDING RELATIONSHIPS

With colleagues

You could find yourself in a tightly-knit expatriate community where everyone lives virtually on top of each other, perhaps on the same campus. On the other hand you might be the only foreigner on the staff and find yourself practically ignored.

In the first situation you will certainly not lack for professional advice. In fact, you could get smothered by it. In the latter case you may not get any advice at all, so it is important to establish at least a professional relationship. Try to pin someone down, preferably your head of department if you have one, and ask for direction. It is a mistake to concentrate solely on doing your own thing.

Unless it happens to be part of your brief, don't cast yourself as a new broom that has come to sweep clean, otherwise you could cause resentment. After all, your colleagues have a headstart on you as they are already familiar with the teaching situation. Admittedly not all will be as well qualified as you may be, and as a result may nurse an inferiority complex. This could manifest itself in downright opposition to any proposals you make designed to improve teaching. You need to recognise that change can only come about gradually and with the approval of all concerned.

With students

Your relationship with your students will vary according to their age and cultural background. Many of the younger ones in the state system will be used to quite formal teaching methods, and may act disruptively if you adopt a more relaxed approach in the classroom. In parts of the Third World rote learning is still very much entrenched. Ask if you can observe a few lessons to see how other teachers handle their classes.

Generally speaking, students like teachers they can respect, not someone who panders to them. It is a wise policy not to cultivate familiarity — in the early stages, at least — unless you are dealing with mature students.

With other expatriates

There is no need to go completely native. Cultivate the friendship of other expatriates, by all means. A lot of them will be more comfortably off than you are, particularly if they are in business or the diplomatic service. Nevertheless you probably have a lot to offer them. If you are in an international school, for example, you could be teaching their children.

Aim for a lifestyle that is congenial rather than extravagant, and avoid becoming a member of an inward-looking clique who do nothing but bemoan the customs of the natives — even if the natives do happen to be fellow-Europeans!

With local people

'When in Rome do as the Romans do'. This is a useful adage, but should not be taken to extremes, particularly if you find yourself living in an obscure village in a remote Third World country. Indeed, the locals could find it offensive if you try to ape them in every way.

Most nationals have a concept of how a British person behaves. It may be an old-fashioned concept fashioned by P.G. Wodehouse novels, but it is on the whole positive. If you deviate too much from the conceived norm, people will be puzzled and even outraged. There is no need to cultivate the image of the stiff upper lip, but you will need to exercise discretion in your behaviour and your relationships. In a sense you are an ambassador for your own country, and you set the standard by which your fellow-countrymen will be judged!

UNDERSTANDING LOCAL ATTITUDES AND CUSTOMS

Your relationships with local people will be much enhanced if you take pains to understand and respect their local customs. Even in societies which you believe to be similar to your own there can be surprisingly different attitudes. Here are a few matters where circumspection may be necessary.

Politics

Avoid political discussions except with people that you have come to know very well. While people may feel free to criticise their own government quite mercilessly, they may resent a foreigner doing so. In less secure countries criticism of the government by a foreigner could land you in jail.

Religion

Religious practices in certain countries may seem bizarre but religion is a sensitive issue, and you must learn to live with it. Be careful about discussing your own religious beliefs in case you are suspected of proselytising. (If you are a teacher in a missionary school this advice may not apply!)`

Girl meets boy

Many societies adopt very protective attitudes towards their women, and arranged marriages are often the norm. For a foreign male even to invite a girl out to dinner unchaperoned could provoke a scandal in some countries. Women teachers have to be particularly circumspect in male dominated societies, as friendly interest can easily be misinterpreted. Make sure you are aware of local attitudes before you enter into any close relationship with someone of the opposite sex.

The law

Foreigners are not above the law, and have no special rights and privileges. Therefore, it is important not to flout the law of the land, even if you feel that certain aspects of it are nonsensical (for example, a ban on the consumption of alcohol). In some countries sentences can be severe — drug trafficking offences may incur the death penalty, working illegally without a work permit could well lead to instant deportation. Ignorance of the local laws is no defence in the courts.

PROFESSIONAL PROBLEMS

Textbooks

You may well find that the textbooks issued to students are inappropriate, biased or just plain hopeless. However, if you try to change them right at the outset you could cause an uproar. In schools, particularly, you may find that books are prescribed by the Ministry of Education and cannot be changed. Or there may be a problem in getting new supplies. Try to make the best of a bad job — for the time being, at least. Inspired teaching, however, can compensate for a great deal, even an inadequate textbook.

A more serious problem arises when there are no textbooks at all. This is a common occurrence in Third World countries which are short of foreign exchange, and it can also happen in the most exclusive schools and colleges in the most developed of countries where orders have gone astray.

Facilities

If you have worked in a well-equipped establishment with videos, photocopiers, overhead projectors, visual aids and so on, you could be in for a shock. Chalk and a blackboard in every room may be the sum total of facilities in your educational establishment. The notion of specially prepared worksheets done on duplicators or photocopiers may have to be given a miss.

A situation like this can be particularly frustrating for a teacher of science or practical subjects. Students may have no opportunity to learn by doing, but instead have to rely exclusively on textbooks.

On the other hand you may be in an establishment where equipment is locked away and never used, or just doesn't work. In cases like this, make a few discreet enquiries and offer to show your colleagues how these items can be used. If you demonstrate tremendous zeal, you may even end up in charge of all the teaching aids.

Syllabus

In many countries the syllabus for schools, and sometimes even for universities, is laid down by the government. Education inspectors will come round occasionally to check not on the quality of the teaching but on whether teachers are adhering to the syllabus.

The syllabus may be unbelievably bad, but you will have to cope with it as best you can. In the long-term, however, you may be able to influence future policy. Schools or professional bodies sometimes have the right to make recommendations to the Ministry regarding possible changes.

Standards

Educational standards vary from country to country and often within countries. You may be pleasantly surprised; on the other hand you could be appalled — especially at the tertiary level, when you compare the amount of knowledge you had to acquire to gain your own first degree with the abysmal standards your students have to attain.

There is no easy solution to this problem. If you try to raise standards, students complain that the exams are too difficult. If you don't, you are really deluding people into thinking they are more competent than they probably are. The moment of truth comes when they apply to do a post-graduate course at a foreign university.

Irregularities

In some countries a diploma is worth its weight in gold, and people will stop at nothing in order to gain one. One matter that you may have to come to terms with is cheating — or 'co-operation' — in examinations and written assignments.

You could also find that some of your poorly-paid colleagues are accepting inducements to pass students, or that pressure is put on you to upgrade the marks of students that you consider hopeless, particularly if they come from influential families.

Red tape

Most educational systems, particularly highly centralised ones, have their share of red tape. Permission may have to be applied for to leave the country for a short holiday; minutes of staff meetings have to be read and signed; you may be confronted with a plethora of forms; and towards the end of the academic year when marks have to be totted up and examinations held, things can get even worse.

In most cases there is little you can do, since these procedures are laid down by law. So don't make a fuss, but try to understand them and comply with them. Your colleagues probably detest the administrative details every bit as much as you.

HEALTH

You will not be able to cope with all the rigours of your professional duties unless you are in the peak of condition, so maintenance of good health is a top priority. This doesn't mean you should become a hypochondriac. You just need to take sensible precautions and act swiftly if your condition deteriorates.

Physical health

The aims must be prevention, and in tropical areas this means avoiding tap water and uncooked vegetables, taking prescribed prophylactics, as well as deterring disease carrying insects. (The Ross Institute Health booklet gives some very useful tips — see p.65).

Exercise ought to form part of your daily routine, whether it be sport or a less strenuous activity such as walking.

If you fall ill, don't put off a visit to a physician. He is much more familiar with local diseases and ailments than you are, and will normally be able to prescribe a speedy cure.

Mental health

In a strange environment there is always a minority who find that they are unable to cope. All of us feel depressed at one time or another, and the problem can be accentuated if you find yourself in strange surroundings.

Depression may spring from homesickness, a feeling of isolation, overwork, an inability to come to terms with your surroundings, social pressures, and so on. It can be associated with abuse of alcohol and may lead to a breakdown of some kind.

There are various ways to avoid drifting into a state of acute depression:

● Keep your brain active. Read, study, learn the local language, write your memoirs!
● Keep in touch with home through letters, magazines and newspapers, short wave radio broadcasts and satellite TV.
● Get away for weekends and short holidays as often as possible.
● Meet people. If you are not far from a large expatriate community, join a club, go to the local church.
● If everything else fails, consult a doctor.
● Don't hit the bottle! Excessive alcohol consumption could make you even worse.

PREMATURE TERMINATION OF CONTRACT

In principle, contracts are meant to be kept rather than broken, and you should endeavour to complete yours unless you have good reasons not to do so. This is important not only from the point of view of your employer but also for your future. When you apply for posts in the future, a prospective employer may have second thoughts about taking you on if he sees that you have walked out on a job.

You therefore need to weigh up the pros and cons very carefully to make sure you have good reasons to quit. Otherwise, try to see your contract out.

The following are justifiable reasons for leaving the post prematurely:

● Ill-health
● Family problems
● Fundamental disagreement with your employer
● Failure by the employer to honour the terms of your contract

● Problems with the job that will never be resolved (this may be a tricky one).

Wherever possible ensure that the contract is terminated by mutual agreement, and that you and your employers and/or superiors part on good terms. After all, you may need to approach them for a reference in the future.

9
Taking the Next Step

When you read this chapter you may have a sense of *déjà vu*. It may remind you of where you came in at the first chapter. The last six months of your contract are a time for making decisions. Indeed, you may find yourself pressed by your employers to make up your mind even sooner as to whether you intend to renew your contract.

Decisions, decisions! If you are back home, you do not have to go through this exercise so frequently. However, since virtually all teaching positions abroad tend to be fixed contract posts, every one, two or three years the teacher has to consider his future. Even if you enjoy the rare privilege of security of tenure, it is wise to **review your options** periodically.

YOUR CAREER OPTIONS

Renewing your contract

The end of your contract need not necessarily betoken upheaval. In many instances contracts can be renewed. Indeed, if you have acquitted yourself well at your place of work, superiors and colleagues will no doubt encourage you to stay on.

But, given the uncertain nature of an overseas teaching career, is this the best option? If you are content with your work and your circumstances, you may well feel that it is. After all, at home teachers and lecturers stay in the same job for years — even right up to retirement. Not everyone considers it beneficial to chop and change.

On the other hand, staying on might be regarded as an easy way out. You are postponing your decision until the next time your contract comes up for renewal, and the longer you stay in the place the more difficult it is to uproot yourself and move elsewhere.

The financial factor should not be disregarded. Generally speaking, if you agree to renew, you should be offered a carrot in the shape of **increased remuneration**. On the other hand, you could find yourself worse off if your hitherto tax-free salary becomes liable to income tax, as is the case, for example, in Sweden when the initial two years are up.

Finding another job in the same country

If you feel very much at home in your adoptive country, and really don't want to leave, you could consider taking up another job. If there is a **prestigious opportunity** going, by all means apply, even if it stipulates higher qualifications than you possess.

Remember that by dint of your experience you will be a strong contender for the post, particularly against an outsider however well qualified.

Don't change for the sake of change however, since it may cause resentment among your current colleagues and employers.

Finding another job abroad

Should you opt to move on, it is wise to get cracking at an early stage — certainly six months or so before the termination date of your contract.

The first people to inform and consult are those at the agency that recruited you. If they are happy with you and you are with them, ask them to keep you in mind for another post and state your preferences.

If you have home leave it makes sense to visit a number of different recruitment agencies to let them see your face, and to find out the lie of the jobs market. Ask to be added to the candidate database of those which operate one.

Some organisations issue vacancy bulletins, notably **Christians Abroad** and **International House**. Ask to be put on the mailing lists of those that do. Otherwise spend time browsing through the job advertisement columns of the appropriate newspapers. Most British Council libraries, for instance, take the *Times Educational Supplements.*

If you have colleagues in other countries in the same line of business, contact them to see if they know of any openings.

In the early stages of your quest make up your mind that you want to move forward. Try for a job with more responsibility than the one you have at present. Alternatively, consider moving sideways into a field that is connected with your present work but not exactly the same — **teacher training**, for example.

Finding another job at home

This may be trickier. For one thing you are less accessible when it comes to interviews, and most home institutions are not prepared to consider you unless they have had a chance to see you face to face. Moreover, you may have to pay your own travel expenses to and from the interview.

In addition to keeping your eyes glued to recruitment advertisements, send **speculative letters** to local authorities, schools and colleges in both the state and the public sector to find out if they know of any vacancies. Contact recruitment agencies which recruit for UK schools as well as overseas ones, such as Gabbitas Educational Services. It might be sensible to contact your union as well.

If you have not managed to fix up a job before you return to Britain, there is no need to despair. You can resort to stop-gap measures.

- **A temporary job.** This is particularly easy in the summer when language schools all over Britain require staff in the form of teachers, social organisers and course leaders. Don't overlook opportunities in tourism and related industries.

- **Supply teaching.** Either register with the education authority in the area in which you normally live and offer your services, or try one of the big metropolitan education authorities which are constantly on the lookout for supply staff. You might also consider putting your name on the books of a private agency.

Opportunities for EFL teachers in the UK

One problem facing returnees is that the number of all the year round posts in TEFL is limited. If you wish to continue in your chosen profession you should investigate

- **Private language schools**. There are language schools dotted all over Britain offering courses for foreigners, most of them private, and many of them open all through the year. Business tends to be slack for most of them during the autumn and winter, so you may only be offered a short-term contract at first. The more reputable ones are members of the Association of Recognised English Language Services (ARELS) which publishes a newsletter for its members. For a modest charge they will circulate your details.

- **Public sector colleges and universities**. Many institutions in the public sector offer English language courses to foreign students as well as courses which prepare teachers for the RSA/Cambridge and Trinity College TEFL/TESOL examinations. Several university education departments also run TEFL/TESOL teacher training courses. Opportunities tend to be restricted and competition for jobs is keen. For a list of public institutions in this field you should contact the British Association of State Colleges in English Language Teaching (BASCELT).

- **Local education authorities**. LEAs with a substantial immigrant community often have special units within schools to improve the language of non-natives. Many of these jobs are full-time and offer the same terms and conditions as those enjoyed by other teachers employed by the authority.

- **Department for Education and Employment**. Among the Government's training schemes is one designed to upgrade the language skills of immigrant workers. More details are available in the booklet *Action for Jobs* or alternatively from Job Centres or Training and Enterprise Councils.

If you plan to settle in the British Isles, it may be necessary to consider a change of career direction. Here are a few suggestions:

- **Modern language teaching**. Good language teachers are currently in short supply.
- **Publishing**. Publishers involved in the lucrative EFL textbook market are often on the lookout for editors and writers.
- **Working with foreign firms or missions**. Opportunities arise in UK based diplomatic and commercial missions, foreign banks and companies. Your knowledge of a particular country could compensate for your lack of experience in this area.

ENROLLING FOR A COURSE

Absence from home for a considerable number of years may mean that you are out of touch with the latest developments in your field, in which case a period of study might be appropriate. The Department for Education and Employment arranges a number of short **refresher courses** under the direction of HM inspectors lasting between three and fourteen days. Longer courses, both full-time and part-time, are dealt with in the DFEE handbook *Long Courses for Teachers*. The Teachers' Branch of the DFEE can provide further information.

Assessing deterrents
There are certain factors which may act as a deterrent to taking a course.

Lack of finance?
While some teachers arrive home with their finances in a very healthy state, this is not true of everybody, and you may think twice about spending all your assets on a course of study. Moreover, you are proba-

bly not eligible for a local authority grant, even a discretionary one, having just returned from abroad. Don't be deterred from trying though, and also investigate other sources of finance (see *The Grants Register* published by Macmillan).

The (DFID) operates the **Educational Development Scheme** which offers a small number of awards to anyone wishing to continue working in the Third World.

Investigate training grants at the local Job Centre. These are for approved vocationally-orientated courses in technology, management, computers, etc, of up to one year. Even if you want to embark on a course of study which is not approved, the Training Agency may approve it if you put up a good enough case.

Too late to register?
While you often have to register for an undergraduate course up to nine months in advance, this is not the case with all postgraduate or training courses. Decide which course you would like to do and contact a number of the establishments which offer it, explaining your position.

Too old to learn?
This is a nonsense. We live in the age of the mature student. Middle-aged people are returning to study in increasing numbers these days. They have to, in order to keep abreast of modern developments. You'll need to brush up your study skills, of course, and the first month may be traumatic getting back in the old routine. But the stimulus should prove well worthwhile.

Unwilling to commit yourself to full-time study?
The number of opportunities for part-time study is increasing. Many tertiary institutions offer part-time study courses, notably Birkbeck College of London University. You can also study by correspondence with the Open University, the Open College, and several other institutions for all manner of degrees and certificates including external degrees of London University.

CHANGING DIRECTION AND GETTING ADVICE

It may be that you want to strike out into new territory or are uncertain which direction your career should follow. One way of resolving the dilemma is to talk things over with your superiors or colleagues and listen to their views. VSO and SCE are two organisations that offer advice and assistance to their returnees. Most others don't. In such a situation you could turn to one of the following organisations for advice:

- Christians Abroad
- The Department of Employment (Job Centre)
- the careers counselling unit of your old university or college. Some local colleges offer a similar service, as do some LEA careers offices
- independent careers counsellors.

Many of the larger independents such as Connaught, Chusid Lander, and the Vocational Guidance Association (now a private company), advertise nationally. Smaller, more localised outfits can be found in the *Yellow Pages*.

The cost of private counselling can range from £250 to a few thousand pounds. The different fees charged indicate the level of service offered. A basic service will usually consist of an aptitude and personality test followed by a counselling session and/or written report. An intermediate service will offer the basic service plus counselling sessions, help with interview techniques, CV preparation, and so on, until you land a new job. A full service will be the intermediate service plus an extensive marketing campaign, mounted by the organisation, and temporary assignments.

The following organisations offer basic guidance to individuals at fees starting at around £300 or less:

- Career Analysts
- Career Counselling Services
- Independent Assessment & Research Centre
- Mid-Career Development Centre
- Vocational Guidance Association
- Career Development Centre for Women.

Teaching abroad long term

Is it possible to spend one's whole career abroad? That very much depends on the nature and location of your job. Very few posts apart from those in the missionary field are to be seen as long-term engagements.

In some developed countries security of **tenure** is possible in an educational institution, particularly at the tertiary level. This is not generally the case, though, in the Third World, where governments hope eventually to replace expensive expatriate teachers and lecturers by their own nationals. Another possibility, if you are prepared to take on more of an **administrative role**, is to find a permanent post with an educational organisation with outlets in foreign countries, such as the British Council or a language school group.

The majority of teaching posts abroad, however, tend to be **contract based**, and however permanent your prospects look, remember that unforeseen events such as war, an economic downturn or revolution could put an end to your dreams of permanence. You therefore cannot afford to rest on your laurels. You need to keep up with the latest developments in your field and treat yourself to the occasional refresher course in order to remain a marketable proposition. Otherwise you may find yourself at a disadvantage when you are obliged to move on to another post, and returning to work in your chosen field in the British Isles could prove very difficult.

A BRIGHT FUTURE AHEAD

Throughout this book I have tended to focus on the perils of venturing abroad as a teacher or lecturer and understate the advantages. My motive has not been to discourage you from taking such a step but rather to prepare you for the type of eventuality you might have to face.

But let me end on a positive note.

To start with, the chances are that you will need to face up to only a fraction of the problems detailed in this book. Indeed, many teachers and lecturers enjoy trouble-free contracts during which they encounter fewer hassles than they would at home. Secondly, teaching abroad can be immensely stimulating if you approach it in the right frame of mind. An overseas posting can open up marvellous opportunities to travel and get to know people. It is an experience that few regret and many cherish. Thirdly, provided you are suitably qualified, there will continue to be a ready market for your skills. Education is an expanding business, and there are opportunities galore for people of all ages who are prepared to look for them.

Education is also an international business, and there is now a much freer flow of teachers between countries.

For teachers wanting to return to the UK the prospects look better than they have for a decade. Demographic trends mean that Britain is facing a shortage of trained people, particularly at the younger end of the scale. After a downturn in teaching posts, teachers are now in short supply, particularly in such subjects as languages, commercial subjects, science and mathematics. Another consideration is that the jobs market in Britain is more fluid these days, so changing direction has become much easier.

Finally your cosmopolitan outlook and experience of other countries and cultures could prove a considerable asset to a firm or organisation that is having to think internationally — perhaps for the first time.

In short, prospects have never looked brighter for teachers and lecturers wishing either to work abroad or to return to Britain. Develop awareness of your abilities and potential and of the many opportunities available, and you can look to the future with optimism.

10
The Teaching Scene
Worldwide

AFRICA

The problems with many countries in Africa is that they are short of teachers and short of cash, South Africa being the main exception. Although most aspire to the goal of universal education, it is often something of an achievement if 50% of children in a particular country receive a primary education. Secondary education is the privilege of a much smaller percentage.

In many African schools classes are large, with a ratio in excess of 50 pupils per teacher in many cases. The best educational provision tends to be in the towns and cities. Facilities in the rural areas are poor, and illiteracy rates are correspondingly high. Civil war, famine, low commodity prices or mismanagement compound the problems in certain countries.

Yet it is not all gloom and doom. Resource-rich countries with small populations, such as **Botswana**, have been able to invest in schools and colleges. In parts of French-speaking Africa there are innovative schemes designed to improve education in rural areas and attempts to tailor the school curriculum more precisely to the needs of the country. International agencies such as the World Bank and UNDP are particularly active in this field, and so are a number of voluntary agencies.

Africa is by no means a homogeneous continent. Its destiny over the past century has been shaped by the colonial powers that have imposed their own languages, methods and educational systems on the people under their control. As a consequence, education tends to be conducted in English, Portuguese or French rather than in indigenous languages, particularly at the secondary level.

Missionary societies played a key role in developing the educational system of many of the Commonwealth countries of Africa, and their involvement continues. In most cases their schools have been incorporated into the state system of education. Secondary education was highly selective, geared to producing administrators rather than people with practical skills. Such a tradition dies hard.

There is still considerable British involvement in Commonwealth Africa. The voluntary agencies and missionary societies recruit for Africa, and there are also a significant number of contract teachers in schools and universities subsidised by the Department for International Development.

In many of the former French territories the colonial power assumed complete responsibility for education. There is still considerable French involvement in the educational systems of these countries, with French teachers making up a significant proportion of secondary school staffs. French is the medium of instruction, though there is also a keen interest in learning English.

Two of the largest states on the continent — **Angola** and **Mozambique** — are former Portuguese possessions. Their governments are faced with the uphill task of building up their educational system from a low level after fighting a civil war. The peace settlement in Southern Africa has improved matters considerably for both of them. In former **Zaire** Belgian influence is still very noticeable.

Virtually every country in Africa has achieved nationhood during the last 20 or 30 years. Yet few of these countries are natural unities. Their boundaries enclose a diversity of tribes, races, languages and religions, and it is a monumental task to reconcile these differences without resorting to force. To be fair, some countries have made remarkable strides forward considering the difficulties they have had to contend with. Others have degenerated into chaos or seem to have lost their way. Many Africans are sensitive to criticism from Westerners, and put much of the blame for their current plight on colonialism.

Africa is very much the Third World. Many countries suffer from poor communications and shortages of equipment and food. If you are posted to the provinces you will need to display resilience and ingenuity. Yet expatriates who manage to make the transition effectively fall in love with Africa and its people, and are reluctant to leave when the time comes.

There is considerable variation. The quality of education seems directly proportional to the wealth of the country, and in this respect **South Africa** comes out top. Currently it is implementing ambitious plans to iron out inequalities of education provision and train up its workforce.

For the expatriate there can be considerable variations in the cost of living both within and between countries, and it is wise to get up-to-date information. A course of vaccinations will be necessary against such diseases as cholera and yellow fever, and scrupulous care needs to be given to health matters.

One should not overlook the network of private and international schools in Africa which recruit regularly from the UK and elsewhere.

Useful addresses:
● Association of International Schools in Africa, c/o International School of Kenya, PO Box 14103, Nairobi, Kenya. Tel: 00 254 2 582578. Fax: 00 254 2 580596.

● Independent Schools Council of South Africa, PO Box 87430, Houghton 2041, South Africa. Tel: 00 27 11 648 7208. Fax: 00 27 11 648 1467. E-mail: zaibmeym@ibmmail.com

ASIA

The countries of Asia are remarkably diverse, and most can boast a long and distinguished cultural heritage. While many are regarded as Third World countries, others — such as **Singapore, Taiwan, South Korea** and, above all, **Japan** — are developed and prosperous. Most have well-established educational systems which have been influenced by Western models.

This is one of those areas of the world where teachers are held in very high regard by their pupils, although the high regard is not usually reflected in their salaries. There are few discipline problems in schools and colleges, but on the other hand students tend to be somewhat passive and unwilling to think for themselves. The teacher is regarded as the fount of all wisdom.

Generally speaking, people of this area are polite — certainly to foreigners — and they expect this politeness to be returned. People have to be handled with tact and understanding in order not to cause loss of face. In South East Asia particularly, frankness is equated with rudeness.

SE and E Asians tend to appear reserved and distrustful of shows of affection or temperament. Everyone expects to be treated with respect, no matter what his station in life. This can be very frustrating for the kind of person who likes to let off steam. Many can quote instances of Asians who are so anxious to please that they give the answer you want rather than the correct one!

An appreciation of the religion(s) of the country (Islam, Hinduism or Buddhism), is important, as religion often exerts a strong influence on the lives of the people. Mainstream religious beliefs are often tinged with animism — a belief in the spirit world. There is a tendency to be fatalistic and superstitious, to believe in luck and astrology.

In several countries goods are cheap and plentiful (though this is not the case with **Burma**); labour is cheap, too, and expatriate teachers can often afford a servant or two (but not in **Japan** or **Singapore**). In the urban areas, at least, women seem to be reasonably liberated, and indeed a number of education systems seem to be dominated by women teachers.

The Indian subcontinent is self-sufficient in teachers, so opportunities for expatriates are few and far between though there are increasing opportunities in the voluntary sector. South East Asia is more promising, particularly **Indonesia, Brunei, Malaysia, Singapore** and **Thailand. Cambodia, Laos** and **Vietnam** are making use of foreign teachers now especially in the TEFL field.

Eastern Asia is dominated by the most populous country in the world (**China**) and the most successful (**Japan**).

To understand the Chinese it is important to understand the country's turbulent history. The country, once the most advanced in the world, rested on its laurels for centuries, and when the West arrived with its more advanced ideas and technologies in the last century the country had a rude awakening. This century has been particularly turbulent with the establishment of a republic, civil war and the establishment of a Communist regime by Mao Tse Tung in the late 1940s. Because of the purges of the Cultural Revolution the older Chinese used to be wary of each other and of foreigners, but now there has been a general relaxation of attitudes and contact with foreigners is no longer frowned on.

Family life means a lot to the Chinese. Many families are Confucian in outlook and ancestor worship is part of their tradition. They are generally very hospitable, but one must take care not to offend their sensibilities.

China has developed independently of the West, and by its very size it might seem to be a nation of endless opportunity for the expatriate teacher. In fact, China is a poor country with one of the lowest GNPs per capita in the region. Demand for foreign teachers, usually in the TEFL field, has soared in recent years but the majority are volunteer type posts.

Japan, on the other hand, has been exposed to a good deal of Western influence, and since the Second World War this influence has been predominantly American. Yet beneath the surface Japanese society differs markedly from Western society. It is highly competitive with a great deal of pressure put on students to achieve. It is also a strongly conformist and disciplined country, where there is little scope for individualism. It is also very much a man's world. The typical businessman spends his leisure time with his colleagues in bars rather than at home with his wife. Wives of executives tend not to go out to work, but spend much of their time at home worrying about the academic progress of their children.

In Japan there are some well paid jobs, the salaries taking account of the high cost of living, particularly in the large cities.

South Korea and **Taiwan** also have booming economies, and there are certainly opportunities there. But of all the countries of the region **Hong Kong** is probably the one which offers the most openings for British teachers and lecturers. The education system is very much in the British mould. It is also the place where expatriates feel most at home. Hong Kong has a large foreign community, and first class amenities. Its main drawbacks are that it is very cramped, and there is some uncertainty as to what incorporation into mainland China will mean for the man and woman in the street. Over the long term there could be a reduction in demand for expatriate teachers.

AUSTRALASIA, NORTH AMERICA AND THE PACIFIC

Australia and **New Zealand** will seem like a home from home for many teachers. Although there is no longer any drive to attract immigrants on the same scale as in the past, there are opportunities in school teaching for the foreigner, especially in New Zealand. Universities in this area are also keen to recruit foreign staff.

Most of the opportunities in **Canada** and the **USA** are on an exchange basis, but opportunities do exist for well-qualified people who are prepared to seek them out, especially in higher education.

The Pacific consists for the most part of small island states a long way from anywhere. Most have airlinks, but travel is expensive, and you are likely to find yourself existing in a small community with a very restricted cultural life. But for anyone who enjoys sunshine and glistening beaches these islands can be paradise.

Some of the larger ones, such as **Fiji** can offer much more. Fiji accommodates the campus of the University of the South Pacific. **Papua New Guinea** is a more substantial territory than the others and offers plenty of interesting terrain. It is also perhaps one of the most fruitful places to find a job.

THE CARIBBEAN

Belize, Surinam, Guiana and **Guyana** fall outside the Spanish/Portuguese cultural community of Latin America and have much more in common with the English speaking countries of the Caribbean. This area is culturally very diverse, and the countries reflect their colonial heritage — French, British, Spanish, Dutch.

The Commonwealth countries are strongly influenced by British ideas and the British system of education, and universal education is very much the norm. Often the education system is a partnership between church schools and the state. The countries have pooled their resources to finance a regional university, the University of the West Indies, which has branches on many of the islands.

Some — like **Jamaica, Trinidad and Tobago**, and **Dominica** — are independent, but many of the smaller ones, like **Bermuda**, are dependencies with a measure of internal self-government. Levels of prosperity differ widely.

Guiana and the French-speaking islands are dependent territories administered by France. Their tertiary centre is the Université Antilles Guyane at Cayenne (Guiana). Independent **Haiti** is also French speaking, but this turbulent backward country has few attractions.

There is a small Dutch presence in the area, in **Surinam** (now independent) and the **Netherlands Antilles**. The Dutch-speaking university is situated in Suriname.

The Dominican Republic, once a Spanish colony, has much more in common with South America than its neighbours. Spanish-speaking **Cuba** is somewhat different. The only avowedly Communist country in the Western hemisphere, it is somewhat like Eastern Europe transplanted to the Caribbean. Its brand of education is unique in the area, and has had some major successes — notably in the reduction of illiteracy.

American influence is also strong in the area. The Caribbean is a playground for American tourists, and the island of **Puerto Rico** is in association with the US, although not a state of the union as such.

On the whole, teachers enjoy living in the Caribbean. Most places are readily accessible and the climate good. But it is wrong to look on the islands as a tropical paradise. There is poverty and squalor in the towns and cities and genuine hardship on some of the smaller less prosperous islands.

EUROPE

Europe is perhaps the most accessible place for any teacher from Great Britain. It is easy to travel to, and in the countries of the European Union there are few, if any, impediments to taking up a job if you are a national of another EU country. In other words, it is quite possible to turn up on spec and look around for a suitable position.

On the whole it is more satisfactory to arrange a job in advance, especially since there are a number of well established organisations recruiting for educational institutions in Europe. If you intend to teach in a country outside the European Union (eg Switzerland, Eastern Europe) pre-arranged employment is vital in order to obtain the necessary work permit.

Most European countries are self-sufficient in teachers. While there are opportunities to teach in state secondary schools and universities under exchange schemes administered by the Central Bureau (usually as English assistants), long-term employment with security of tenure has been much less common. The main problem is that until recently foreign teaching qualifications were not recognised in certain countries.

In the European Union that should be changing. According to European Union law any EU citizen qualified to teach in the school system of his or her own country may not be excluded from working in schools in member states. There has been some resistance to this directive by some ministries of education and the European Commission has seen fit to intervene. In some cases you may be required to take a short conversion course to achieve qualified teacher status.

Elsewhere there are fewer problems. **Turkey**, for instance, is currently suffering from a shortage of English, maths and science teachers to staff the bi-lingual (Turkish and English medium) schools both in the state and private sectors. This problem should be solved eventually when the country has trained enough teachers of its own.

The private sector, where it exists, is more promising territory for expatriates (particularly TEFL specialists). In some cases a teacher's qualifications have to be approved by the state educational authorities. There are, however, opportunities for teachers of most subjects and at all levels in English-medium international schools, of which there is at least one (and often half a dozen or more) in virtually every European capital, including Eastern Europe. The European Union schools (although not strictly speaking private) are a particularly attractive proposition.

The main demand is for TEFL teachers, at the adult level — at British Council Language Institutes, for example — and increasingly for primary and secondary age children. While there are some jobs at public institutions, like the adult evening colleges in **Sweden**, the bulk of the jobs are in the private sector. It is unusual to find a city in Western Europe which does not have at least one private language school specialising in English teaching. Some of these language schools are linked to British institutions like International House; others may be part of a national chain, as is the case with the British Schools in **Italy**; while others may be completely independent. Most insist on a TEFL qualification; a few are prepared to accept virtually anyone, though such institutions are apt to prove unsatisfactory both professionally and salary-wise.

There are also opportunities in higher education, particularly in TEFL and related fields. Many European universities handle their own recruitment, sometimes advertising vacancies, but more often relying on personal contact. The British Council has usually handled recruitment for tertiary institutions in Eastern Europe but now more organisations are coming forward to recruit for this region.

In countries where companies are encouraged to provide training for their staff, expatriate teachers may be included on the payroll. The demand is in the main for English tuition, but could also embrace other fields such as management, computers, banking, and so on. This is particularly true of **Germany**.

EASTERN EUROPE AND THE FORMER SOVIET UNION

Since the end of the Cold War teaching opportunities have increased considerably in this particular region. Many of the capital cities now have a very cosmopolitan workforce with the result that international schools have been set up or expanded. There has also been a demand for training in modern management techniques.

However, of greater importance has been an upsurge of interest in English (TEFL), demand for which continues to outstrip supply. The less prosperous areas have come up against the problem of a lack of ready cash to employ expatriate teachers, though there have been a number of initiatives (eg the British government's Know-How Fund) to overcome the difficulty.

The British Council continues to recruit lecturers and advisers in TEFL and English Studies, and a number of private language training institutions (eg Bell, Inlingua, International House, Linguarama) have set up language schools. One of the most interesting initiatives has come from VSO which has set up a subsidiary, Eastern European Partnership, to recruit teachers for Eastern Europe and the Soviet Union. The Central Bureau now sends teachers to selected countries and there are also short-term opportunities for non-qualified teachers with organisations such as Teaching Abroad in various locations, including **Siberia**.

While some countries of the region, notably **Hungary**, **Slovenia** and the **Czech Republic** are rapidly becoming as prosperous and developed as Western Europe, in others the standard of living is relatively low and many of the people have a struggle making ends meet. Expatriates planning to work in these countries have to accept that they will encounter shortages and frustrations – not least with a bureaucracy which may seem little changed from Communist times.

A number of countries around the Caspian Sea which were once part of the Soviet Union are included in this handbook for the first time. Most are starting to recruit teachers from abroad, and this process is likely to accelerate as Western oil firms move in to develop oil reserves. Training and teaching opportunities are likely to follow, notably in TEFL and practical skills, and international schools are starting to appear in the capital cities to cater for the children of the expatriates who are moving in.

LATIN AMERICA

There are more similarities between Latin American countries than differences. One half of the region speaks Spanish; the other half (Brazil) speaks Portuguese. All have undergone colonialisation, but most have been independent entities for as long as many European countries. Christianity is the predominant religion, with Roman Catholicism particularly well entrenched.

While people of European stock may predominate in **Argentina, Costa Rica, Chile** and **Uruguay**, in other countries other racial groups form the majority — the South American Indians in the Andean countries. In the north east people are more similar to those in the Caribbean — of mixed African and European stock.

South American society has a strong *machismo* element, which feminists might find trying. Political instability is a problem in certain countries, but actual dictatorships are few and far between. Several have experienced economic problems, rampant inflation and massive international debts, but this should cause few headaches to expatriates who are remunerated in hard currency.

While many of the cities, particularly on the Atlantic seaboard, are sophisticated and advanced, there are often extremes of wealth and poverty existing side by side. Some countries are poor and backward, and virtually all have their underdeveloped regions where people live on the breadline. This can be disconcerting to Europeans with a strong social conscience. Yet most people who have lived in Latin America — particularly the cities — find it an exhilarating place. There is ethnic variety, breathtaking scenery, and plenty of *joie de vivre*.

In several of the main cities there are sizeable British communities established for several generations, and in places like these you will often find a private British-style English medium secondary school. In view of the number of US citizens resident in Latin America, American-style international schools are also common.

At the tertiary level there are a number of opportunities for people who can speak the local language, though some of the more technical and scientific subjects may be taught in English. There are posts in the

TEFL field, both permanent and short term, usually recruited through the British Council.

In some countries the British Council runs its own English language teaching operations. A more usual pattern is for language institutes to be run by an independent cultural foundation linked to the Council, such as the Sociedade Brasileira de Cultura Inglâsa. The majority of the students tend to be in their teens, and the courses generally lead to Cambridge Lower Certificate and Cambridge Proficiency.

Latin America as a whole lacks teaching personnel at all levels. Various bi-lateral and multi-lateral technical co-operation programmes are endeavouring to make up some of the shortfall. There is also a selective immigration programme administered by the Intergovernmental Organisation for Migration (IOM) designed to attract well-qualified Europeans who will provide a stimulus to priority areas of the economy where there is insufficient indigenous talent.

Health warning: Mexico City and a number of cities on the Western side of South America are at high altitudes, and may prove trying for all but the exceptionally fit. There is a risk of malaria in jungle areas, notably in **Brazil, Paraguay** and eastern **Bolivia**.

Useful addresses

● Intergovernmental Organization for Migration (IOM), Geneva Office for Latin America, 17 route des Morillons, PO Box 100, 1211 Geneva 19, Switzerland can help anyone wishing to work in Latin America and publishes a bulletin of job listings which includes teaching posts. Usually these are bachelor status appointments, and knowledge of Spanish or Portuguese is required.

● Hispano and Luso Brazilian Council, Canning House, 2 Belgrave Square, London SW1X 8PJ. Tel: 071-235 2303. Library and Resource Centre for South America and Iberian Peninsula.

● Latin American Bureau, 1 Amwell Street, London EC1R 1UL. Tel: 071-278 2829. Library and resource centre.

THE MIDDLE EAST AND NORTH AFRICA

This area encompasses the Arab World from **Morocco** in the West to **Oman** in the East plus **Iran** and **Israel**.

The binding force in the Arab world is Islam, though within this framework there are considerable differences between the countries that make up this area with regard to wealth, political orientation and cultural attitude. Very few can claim to be democratic in the Western sense of the word.

Working in the Arab World calls for a large measure of adaptability. One has to be extremely careful to avoid giving offence. Political discussion is to be avoided, particularly in countries like **Libya**, where strong anti-Western attitudes prevail. Above all, be careful to avoid offending people's religious sensibilities.

A study of Islam and its traditions is a prerequisite for anyone visiting the Arab world for the first time. It will enable you to understand the people better, and perhaps appreciate the positive aspects of their religious beliefs which are bound to affect you in some way. This is especially so where attitudes are extremely strict and traditional. In **Saudi Arabia**, for instance, alcohol is forbidden; women are not allowed to drive cars; shops and offices have to close at prayer time; religious police patrol the streets. Not all Europeans, particularly women, can stand the social restrictions. Even in the most liberal countries, the Ramadan fast is often scrupulously observed, and tempers can get frayed in the heat of the day.

The school system tends to follow the primary-intermediate-secondary pattern. Co-education is rare, and in some countries this can extend to university level. The Koranic system of learning by rote is still quite deeply entrenched in many areas.

The best teaching opportunities in terms of salary occur in the eastern states —**Bahrain, Kuwait, Oman, Qatar, Saudi Arabia** and the **United Arab Emirates** which now boast fine modern cities. Although the salaries and conditions offered are generally more than adequate, some of these posts are on bachelor-status terms. In recent years opportunities have declined slightly, partly due to the fall in the oil price, but also because these countries are now starting to develop expertise among their own nationals.

Expatriate Arabs are much in evidence in the schools of the oil-producing countries, but there is a considerable number of British and other European nationals in the field of EFL, in bilingual and international schools, working as instructors with oil and aerospace companies, and at the tertiary level. The British Council has several language institutes dotted around this area, and there are a number of private language schools in operation as well.

In North Africa the French influence is still noticeable in **Morocco, Algeria** and **Tunisia**. These countries are virtually self-sufficient in teaching personnel, though there are a number of openings for TEFL specialists. In **Libya,** despite the government's hostility to Britain, there is still a sizeable contingent of teachers from Britain, and this is also true of **Egypt**.

There are opportunities in the other countries of the Arab world, notably in international schools and at the tertiary level. The situation in **Lebanon**, the cultural centre of the region, now looks very promising but prospects in **Iraq** have worsened.

Iran stands apart culturally from the Arab world. In the days of the Shah there was a significant expatriate presence in education, but this has disappeared. Nowadays expatriates are definitely not welcome, but this could change.

Useful addresses:
- Near East/South Asia Council of Overseas Schools, c/o American College of Greece, PO Box 60018, 153 10 Aghia Paraskevi, Attikis, Greece.

Country
Information
A-Z

This section offers a survey of job opportunities in education in over 180 countries. Each entry lists addresses (typically ministries of education, diplomatic and cultural missions) from which you should be able to obtain further information. At the end of most entries is a selection of organisations that are involved in recruitment. If no address is supplied, you should turn to the section on teacher recruitment organisations for further details. In some cases the names have been abbreviated.

Local British Council offices are included in most cases, since their staff are normally aware of the current educational situation in their locality. Some of these offices publish lists of schools in their locality which employ expatriates. The British Council's information centre in Manchester can provide the telephone and fax numbers or e-mail addresses of individual offices. (Tel: 0161 957 7755. Fax: 0161 957 7762.)

Other sources of information are the British Embassy/High Commission, the United States Information Service, or the Australian, Canadian or New Zealand cultural attaché in the country concerned. Most American international or community schools (AIS) can be contacted through the US Embassy of the country in which they are situated.

A-Z DIRECTORY

Afghanistan
Pop: 20.5 m   *Area*: 652,225 sq km
Afghanistan Embassy: 31 Prince's Gate, London SW7 1QQ Tel: 0171 589 8891
Ministry of Education: Char Raki Malek Ashgar, Kabul.

The political future of Afghanistan is somewhat unclear. The educational system is relatively undeveloped except in the main towns and adult literacy is around 20%. The situation is not helped by the denial of education to women and girls, though there are signs that the fundamentalist Taliban leaders are relaxing this policy. There are universities at Kabul and Nangarhar and state secondary schools in provincial capitals.

Further information: The charity SAFE is supporting educational initiatives in Afghanistan though it is not actively recruiting foreign staff in 1998. Address: Denver Cottage, Venham Dean, Andover, Hants SP11 0JY.

Albania
Pop: 3.42 m   *Area*: 27,398 sq km
Albanian Embassy: 4th Floor, 38 Grosvenor Gardens, London SW1W. Tel: 0171 730 5709.
Ministria e Arsimit: Tirana.
Office of British Chargé d'Affaires: Rruga Vaso Pasha 7/1, Tirana. (For British Council see Yugoslavia)

After years of isolation Europe's poorest country has finally come in from the cold. The British Council now has a TEFL adviser there and EEP has a programme for people with learning difficulties. There is an international school in Tirana.
Recruitment: BC, EEP.

Algeria
Pop: 28.6 m   *Area*: 2.4 m sq km
Algerian Embassy: 54 Holland Pk, London W11 3RS. Tel: 0171 221 7800.
Ministry of Education: 8 ave de Pékin, Mouradia, Algiers.
British Council: 7 chemin des Glycines, BP 43, Alger-Gare, Algiers.

The education follows the traditional French pattern modified to suit local circumstances. All the schools are state run. There is an American School in Algiers and the British Council has a language institute here. There are sometimes opportunities in TEFL in the universities situated In Algiers, Boumerdes, Constantine, Annaba, Oran, Sétif. However, in 1998 the political situation was unstable.
Recruitment: BC, ECIS.

Angola
Pop: 11.5 m   *Area*: 1.25 m sq km
Angolan Embassy: 98 Park Lane, London W1. Tel: 0171 495 1752.
Ministry of Education: Avda Comte Jika, Luanda.
British Embassy: Rua Diogo, Cao, CP 1244, Luanda.

The civil war in this former Portuguese possession seems to be over and the country is rebuilding its infrastructure. Teaching opportunities now exist, notably at the British Council's language institute in Luanda. Other opportunities may exist at the Universidade Agostinho Neto in Luanda and with foreign oil companies operating in the country.
Recruitment: AIM, AEF, BC, Concern.

Anguilla
Pop: 11,000   *Area*: 155 sq km
Education Department: The Secretariat, The Valley.
This British dependency in the Caribbean boats six primary schools and one secondary school.
Recruitment: VSO.

Antigua and Barbuda
Pop: 81,500   *Area*: 442 sq km
High Commission of Antigua and Barbuda: 15 Thayer St, London W1M 5DL. Tel: 0171 486 7073.
Ministry of Education, Culture and Youth Affairs: Church Street, St John's.
British High Commission: Price Waterhouse Centre, 11 Old Parham Road, PO Box 483, St Johns.
Opportunities sometimes arise in secondary schools, of which there are sixteen. The State Island College provides technical and teacher training, and there is an extramural department of the University of the West Indies.
Recruitment: VSO.

Argentina
Pop: 36 m   *Area*: 2.77 m sq km
Argentine Embassy: 65 Brook Street, London W1Y 1YE. Tel: 0171 318 1300.
Ministry of Education: Pizzurno 935, 1020 Buenos Aires.
British Council: Marcelo T de Alvear 590, 1058 Buenos Aires.
Argentina has one of the highest standards of education in South America. It also has a sizeable British colony which has lived in the country for several generations. As a result the country has some well established British-type English medium schools — Northlands, St Catherine's, St George's, St Andrew's and St Hilda's — all in Buenos Aires. Other international schools include Barker College, Belgrano Day School and the American Community School (Asociacion Escuelas Lincoln). In Cordoba there is the Reydon School for Girls.
There are Anglo-Argentinian Cultural Institutes in all the major cities offering English language tuition. The country has over 29 state and 23 private universities — notably in Buenos Aires, Cordoba, Catamarca, Coyo, Entre Rios, Jujuy, La Pampa, Patagonia, La Plata, Litora, Tandil.
Recruitment: BC, Gabbitas, ECIS, IH, SA, Saxoncourt.

Armenia
Pop: 3.7 m   *Area*: 29,800 sq km

Armenian Embassy: 25A Cheniston Gardens, London W8 6TE. Tel: 0171 938 5345/5415.
Ministry of Education and Science: Movses Khorenatsi Street 13, Yerevan 375010.
British Embassy: Charents Street 58, Yerevan 375010.

Formerly part of the Soviet Union Armenia boasts two universities (one an American foundation), an engineering university and ten other HE institutions. There is an international school at Yerevan. The British Council has been asked to set up a language centre in Yerevan.

Australia

Pop: 18.3 m   *Area*: 7.7 m sq km
High Commission: Australia House, Strand, London WC2B 4LA. Tel: 0171 379 4334.
British Council: Edgecliff Centre, 401/203 New South Head Road, PO Box 88, Edgecliff, Sydney, NSW 2027.

The country boasts some 7,500 Government Schools; 2,454 Non-government Schools; 36 universities; 47 colleges and institutes of Advanced Education (vocationally oriented education); 271 technical and FE Colleges. However, Australia is virtually self-sufficient in teachers.

Primary and secondary education is in the hands of the different states. For information on posts in secondary schools it is advisable to contact the various ministries of education direct.
Federal State Departments of Education:
New South Wales: GPO Box 33, Sydney, NSW 2001.
Western Australia: 151 Royal Street, East Perth, WA 6000.
Victoria: 2 Treasury Place, Melbourne, VIC 3002.
Queensland: Old Treasury Building, Queen Street, Brisbane, QLD 400.
South Australia: 9th Floor, 31 Flinders Street, Adelaide, SA 5000.
Northern Territories: T & G Building, 69 Smith Street, Darwin NT 5794.
Tasmania: 116 Bathurst Street, Hobart, TAS 7001.
Australian Capital Territory: PO Box 826, Woden, ACT 2606.

Some London offices of the different state governments are able to offer advice. The Government of South Australia is particularly keen to attract well qualified immigrants and has an active immigration programme. Opportunities occur in the tertiary sector — usually on a contact basis — and advertisements for these positions appear frequently in the *THES*.
Reference: How to Emigrate; *How to Get a Job in Australia*; *Australian News* (Outbound); *Australian Outlook* (Consyl).
Recruitment: ACU; IH, LECT.

Austria

Pop: 8 m   *Area*: 84,000 sq km

Austrian Embassy: 18 Belgrave Mews West, London SW1X 5HU. Tel: 0171 235 3731.

The Austrian Institute: 28 Rutland Gate, London SW7 1PQ.

Ministry of Education: Minoritenplatz 5, A-1014 Vienna.

British Council: Schenkenstrasse 4, A1010 Wien.

Teachers in the state system normally have to be Austrian nationals, but this practice may no longer be tenable under EU regulations. Teacher exchanges continue, and there are opportunities in private schools, adult institutes, private language institutes and Austria's twelve universities for English teachers. Vienna has two international schools: the American International School (Salmanndörferstrasse 47) and the Vienna International School (Strasse der Menschenrechte 1). Innsbruck has an international high school and Salzburg an international preparatory school.

Since the last edition of this book Austria has become a member of the European Union, and for EU citizens EU immigration procedures now apply.

Recruitment: CB, ECIS, Inlingua, IH, Linguarama, SA.

Azerbaijan

Pop: 7.5 m   *Area*: 86,600 sq km

Azerbaijani Embassy: 4 Kensington Court, London W8 5DL. Tel: 0171 938 3412.

Ministry of Education: 1 Azadlyg Square, Baku 370016.

British Embassy: 2 Izmir Street, Baku 370016.

Azerbaijan's economic future looks promising thanks to extensive oil reserves. The Azerbaijan International Operation Co (AIOC) is a consortium of major oil companies, and this may open opportunities for skills trainers. There is a state university at Baku and two international schools. A number of language institutes have opened including a British Council operation at the Baku Institute of Social Management and Politology which also undertakes teacher training at local HE institutes.

Recruitment: BC, ECIS, Language Solutions.

Bahamas

Pop: 280,000   *Area*: 14,000 sq km

Bahamas High Commission: 10 Chesterfield Street, London W1X 8AH. Tel: 0171 408 4488.

Ministry of Education: Shirley Street, PO Box N3913, Nassau.

British High Commission: Bitco Building, East Street, PO Box N7516, Nassau.

There are state and private secondary schools — all English medium — including Freeport High School and St Paul's Methodist College in Freeport; Kingsway Academy, Lyford Cay School, St Andrew's School, St Anne's Parish School and St John's College in Nassau. Also the College of the Bahamas — a junior community college affiliated to the University of the West Indies and some American universities which offer associate degree programmes to some 3,000 students.

Recruitment: LECT, ECIS.

Bahrain

Pop: 586,000   *Area*: 706 sq km

Bahrain Embassy: 98 Gloucester Road, London SW7 4AU. Tel: 0171 370 5132.

Ministry of Education: PO Box 43, Isa Town.

British Council: AMA Centre, 146 Sheikh Salman Highway, PO Box 452, Manama 356.

Bahrain is perhaps the most cosmopolitan of the Gulf states, and has a well established educational system. There are opportunities in most subjects in private international schools, such as Bahrain School (PO Box 934), Bahrain Bayan School (PO Box 32411), Naseem School (PO Box 28502) and St Christopher's School (PO Box 32052).

A number of expatriates are employed by the tertiary institutions: the Arabian Gulf University, the University College of Arts, Science and Education, the Gulf Polytechnic and the College of Health Sciences.

The British Council has a language centre here and there are are a number of private language schools, such as Polyglot, the Gulf Academy and Gulf Language Services. The Government and companies such as Gulf Air and the Bahrain Petroleum Co provide in-service training for their employees.

Recruitment: BC, ECIS, SA.

Bangladesh

Pop. 120.5 m   *Area*: 148,400 sq km

Bangladeshi High Commission: 28 Queen's Gate, London SW7 5JA. Tel: 0171 584 0081.

Ministry of Education: Bangladesh Secretariat, Bhaban 7, 2nd 9-Storey Building, 6th Floor, Dhaka.

British Council: PO Box 161, 5 Fuller Road, Ramna, Dhaka 1000.

There is some expatriate involvement in the state sector and the British Council has a language centre here. There may be opportunities in English medium schools such as the American International School and St Francis Xavier's Greenherald International School. The British Council has a teaching centre in Dhaka. There are universities at Dhaka, Rajshahi, Chittagong, Jahnagirnagar, an Engineering University at Dhaka and an Agricultural University at Mymensingh staffed almost exclusively by Bangladeshis.

Recruitment: BC, Concern, LECT, Methodist, SIM, VSO, WCM.

Barbados

Pop: 264,000   *Area*: 430 sq km

Barbados High Commission: 1 Great Russell Street, London WC1B 3NH 0171 631 4975.

Ministry of Education and Culture: Jemmot's Lane, St Michael

British High Commission: Lower Collymore Rock, PO Box 676, Bridgetown.

One of the most prosperous islands of the Caribbean, Barbados has a well developed schools system. There are twenty-one government secondary schools and fifteen private ones, a polytechnic, a teacher training college, a technical institute and the Cave Hill Campus of the University of the West Indies.

Belarus

Pop: 10.3 m   *Area*: 207,600 sq km

Belarus Embassy: 6 Kensington Court, London W8 5DL. Tel: 0171 938 3223/3288.

Ministry of Education: Ulitsa Savetskaya 9, Minsk 220010.

British Embassy: Ulitsa Karl Marx 37, Minsk 220030.

British Council: Minsk State Linguistic University, Ulitsa Zakharova 21, Minsk 220662.

Belarus boasts four universities plus other specialist institutes. The British Council has a teaching resource centre and a TEFL consultant and is supporting teacher training, British Studies courses and a public service language centre for civil servants. A few private language schools are now operating. There is an AIS in Minsk.

Recruitment: BC, IH.

Belgium

Pop: 10 m   *Area*: 30,500 sq km

Belgian Embassy: 103 Eaton Square, London SW1 9AB. Tel: 0171 470 3700.

Ministry of Education (Flemish Sector): Centre Arts Lux, 4th and 5th Floors, 58 avenue des Arts, B P 5, 1040 Brussels

Ministry of Education (French Sector), 68a rue du Commerce, 1040 Brussels.

British Council: rue de la Charité, 1210 Brussels.

The Embassy publishes useful notes on living conditions and administrative procedures. Apart from having Flemish medium schools and French medium ones, there are two separate educational systems; the écoles officielles (state-owned) and the écoles libres (privately owned but subsidised by the state). Until recently there were no opportunities in state schools, except under teacher exchange schemes. There are schools for service children, for the children of European Community employees, as well as private international schools catering for expatriate children. They include:

British School of Brussels, 19 Steenweg op Leuven, 1980 Tervuren.

Le Verseau International School (French/English medium) 60 Rue de Wavre, 1301 Bierges.

British Primary School, 6 Stationstraat, Vossem (Tervuren).

International School of Brussels, 19 Kattenberg, Brussels 1170.

International School of Liege, 64 Rue Pierre Henvard, 4920 Embourg.

Antwerp International School, 180 Veltwijkelan, 2070 Erkeren.

St John's International School, 146 Dreve Richelle, 1410 Waterloo.

EEC International School, 103 Boulevard Louis Schmidt, 1040 Brussels.

Brussels English Primary School, 23 Avenue Franklin Roosevelt, 1050 Brussels.

SHAPE International School, Mons.

There are opportunities in language schools and universities, particularly Vesalius College, a new English language medium college linked to the Flemish Free University of Brussels. Address: 2 Pleinlaan, 1050 Brussels.

The Bulletin, 1036 Chaussée de Waterloo, 1180 Brussels, and English language newspapers sometimes advertises teacher vacancies.

Notes: No work permit or visa is required for EU nationals, but within eight days of arrival you should report your intended place of residence to the local town hall to obtain a certificate of registration (CIRE) valid for one year or a three-month provisional certificate.

Recruitment: CB; DFEE, ECIS, Inlingua, SCE, SA.

Belize

Pop: 210,000   *Area*: 23,000 sq km

Belize High Commission: 200 Sutherland Avenue, London W9 1RX. Tel: 0171 499 9738.

Ministry of Education: Belmopan, Belize.

British High Commission: PO Box 91, Belmopan.

Situated on the east coast of Central America Belize has 225 primary schools and 23 secondary schools. Post-secondary institutions include the University College of Belize, a teachers' college, a school of nursing and a technical college. A work permit is necessary and is applied for by the employer on behalf of the employee.
Recruitment: APSO, VSO.

Benin
Pop: 4.3 m   *Area*: 113,000 sq km
Benin Embassy: 87 av Victor Hugo, 75116 Paris.
Honorary Consulate: Dolphin House, 16 The Broadway, Stanmore, Middlesex HA7 4DW. Tel: 0181 954 8800.
Ministry of National Education: BP 348, Cotonou.
British Consulate: BP 147, Cotonou.

Formerly Dahomey. The educational system follows the French system and the adult literacy rate stands at 25%. The International Development Association and OPEC Development Fund are assisting in educational improvements, including teacher training. There are opportunities in TEFL at the University of Benin, Porto Novo. There is a British School at Cotonou.
Recruitment: BC.

Bermuda
Pop: 60,000   *Area*: 53 sq km
Ministry of Education: Old Hospital Building, 7 Point Finger Road, Paget.

This prosperous group of 150 islands is still a colony with its own representative government. There are nine private and government secondary schools, including Bermuda High School (in Pembroke), Mount St Agnes Academy and Saltus Grammar School (both in Hamilton). Bermuda College offers post-secondary education.
Recruitment: ECIS

Bhutan
Pop: 1.3 m   *Area*: 45,000 sq km
Ministry of Health and Education: Tashichhodzong, Thimpu.

Only 20% of children attend school in this remote Himalayan kingdom. There are eight high schools, one junior college, six technical schools and one higher education institute. There are no private schools. English is the medium of instruction and a British type syllabus is followed. The country has a large number of expatriate teachers, largely Indian.
Recruitment: VSO.

Bolivia

Pop: 8 m   *Area*: 1.1 m sq km
Bolivian Embassy: 106 Eaton Square, London SW1 9AD. Tel: 0171 235 4255.
Ministry of Education: Avda Arce, La Paz.
British Embassy: Avda Arce 2732-2754, Casilla 696, La Paz.

Opportunities exist in private schools, particularly for science and maths teachers. These include Cochamba Co-operative School, La Paz American Co-operative School, Orura Anglo-American School and Santa Cruz Co-operative School. The Ministry of Education in La Paz can provide further information. La Paz University is the most important tertiary sector institution. The oldest is St Francis Xavier University founded in 1624.
Recruitment: Crosslinks, SA, SIM.

Bosnia-Herzegovina

Pop: 4.5m   *Area*: 51,000 sq km
Embassy of Bosnia-Herzegovina: Morley House, 314-320 Regent Street, London W1R 5AB. Tel: 0171 255 3758.
Ministry of Education: Zmaja od Bosne 3A, Sarajevo 71000.
British Council: Obala Kulina Bana 4, 2nd Floor, Sarajevo.

For much of the 90s conflict has raged in this part of the Balkans. Now an uneasy peace is allowing the Bosnians to reconstruct their education system. Sarajevo has an AIS. The British Council is assisting the government with teacher training seminars and workshops and is considering the possibility of client funded TEFL facilities.
Recruitment: BC

Botswana

Pop: 1.4 m   *Area*: 582,000 sq km
Botswana High Commission: 6 Stratford Place, London W1N 9AE. Tel: 0171 499 0031.
Ministry of Education: Private Bag 005, Gaborone.
British Council: c/o British High Commission, Queens Road, The Mall, PO Box 439, Gaborone.

This large country with a small population is making great strides forward with its education system. The current pattern of seven years primary — two years intemediate — three years senior secondary is now changing to a six-three-three system. There is virtually universal education at the primary level and the government aims to provide universal education at intermediate level by the 1990s. Northside School and Westwood International School in Gaborone are the main international

establishments. At the higher education level there is the University of Botswana and Molepole College of Education. Most educational institutions have expatriate teachers on their staffs.
Recruitment: AEF, BC, DFID, Skillshare.

Brazil

Pop: 156 m   *Area*: 8.5 m sq km
Brazilian Embassy: 32 Green Street, London W1Y 3FD. Tel: 0171 499 0877; Consulate: 6 St Albans Street, London SW1Y 4SG.
Ministry of Education: Esplanada dos Ministeris, Bloco L, 70.444 Brasilia
British Council: Edificio Morro Vermilho, Quadra 1, Bloco 21, SCS, 70399-900 Brasilia DF.

Portuguese-speaking Brazil is the giant of the South American continent. It has some of the largest cities including Rio de Janeiro and São Paolo with highly developed educational systems. In rural areas educational provision is not as good. The NE region, for example, still has 55% adult illiteracy. There are a number of international schools in Belem, Belo Horizonte, Campina, Curitiba, Porto Alegre, Recife and Salvador. There are two in Rio de Janeiro (the American School and the British School) and four in São Paulo (including St Paul's School, 166 Jardim Paulistino). Many large Anglo-Brazilian cultural centres (Sociedade Brasileira de Cultura Inglesa) flourish in the major cities. The society in Rio, for instance, has no fewer than eighteen branches in the city plus two in Brasilia. There are also a number of Brasil-American foundations involved in English language teaching.

There are no fewer than 114 universities in the country, of which 53 are privately owned. For information on teaching at university level contact CAPES, Recrutamento de Recursos Humanos no Exterior SAS, Quadra 6, Lote 4, Bloco L, 4° andar Brasilia – 70.000.DF.
Information on work permits and diploma recognition:
Secretaria de Assuntos Internacionais, Ministério de Educacão, Esplanada do Ministérios, Bloco L, 8° andar 70.074 – Brasilia DF.
Recruitment: BC, Callan, CB, ECIS, EWW, Gabbitas, IH, Saxoncourt, TA.

Brunei Darussalem

Pop: 280,000   *Area*: 5,765 sq km
Brunei High Commission: 19-20 Belgrave Square, London SW1X 8PG. Tel: 0171 581 0521.
Ministry of Education: Old Airport, Berakas, Bandar Seri Begawan 1170.

British Council: 45 Simpang 100, Jalan Tunku Link, Gadong, Bandar Sri Begawan 3192.

This small, oil-rich sultanate has both state and private schools which may be Malay medium, English medium, Arabic medium or Chinese medium. There are also vocational and technical schools, as well as a brand new university. CBT has a large programme here both at the secondary and the pre-university levels. The Brunei Shell Petroleum Co operates a primary school for expatriates at Seria and there is an international school at Berakas. The British Council has a language centre here.
Recruitment: BC, CFBT, Timeplan.

Bulgaria
Pop: 8.5 m   *Area*: 111,000 sq km
Bulgarian Embassy: 186 Queen's Gate, London SW7 5HL. Tel: 0171 584 9400.
Ministry of National Education: Blvd Knjaz Donkukov 2A, 1000 Sofia.
British Council: 7 Tulova Street, 1504 Sofia.

There is a growing interest in learning English in schools and the three universities at Sofia, Veliko Turnovo and Plovdiv. There are two international schools – the Anglo American School of Sofia and the American College of Sofia. The British Council has a language institute in Sofia and is heavily involved in in-service teacher training.
Recruitment: BC, CB, ECIS, EEP, SA.

Burkina Faso
Pop: 10 m   *Area*: 274,000 sq km
Burkina Faso Embassy: 16 Place Guy d'Arezzo, 1060 Brussels. Tel: 00 32 3 345 9911.
Honorary Consulate: 5 Cinnamon Row, Plantation Wharf, London SW11 3TW. Tel: 0171 738 1800.
Ministry of Primary Education: BP 1179, Ouagadougou
Ministry of Secondary and Higher Education: BP 7130, Ouagadougou
British Consulate: BP 1918, Ouagadougou.

Formerly Upper Volta. With World Bank help the country has redically reformed its education system in rural areas with the establishment of 750 centres which combine elementary schooling with agricultural training. This should help to reduce the high adult illiteracy rate of 81%. There is an International School at Ouagadougou (BP 35) as well as the University of Ouagadougou where there may be TEFL opportunities. The Ministry of Education has a British Council recruited adviser.
Recruitment: APSO, BC.

Burma (Myanmar)
Pop: 45 m   *Area*: 676,000 sq km
Burmese Embassy: 19a Charles Street, London W1X 8ER. Tel: 0171 629 6966.
Ministry of Education: Ministers' Office, Rangoon (Yangon).
British Embassy: 80 Strand Road, PO Box 638, Rangoon (Yangon).

Burma is a country where time seems to have stood still, and this applies very much to the educational system. English is not widely used as a medium of instruction and there is little expatriate involvement in either education or business life, except at the International School of Rangoon. There are two universities, at Rangoon and Mandalay. The British Council has a language centre in Rangoon (Yangon).
Recruitment: BC.

Burundi
Pop: 5 m   *Area*: 29,000 sq km
Burundi Embassy: 46 Place Marie Louise, 1040 Brussels.
Ministry of Education: Bujumbura

A country shattered by conflict in the 90s is slowly starting to reconstruct.
Recruitment: BC, MAM.

Cambodia
Pop: 10 m   *Area*: 181,000 sq km
Ministry of Education: 80 Boulevard Norodom, Phnom Penh
British Embassy: 29 rue 75, Phnom Penh.

After two decades of strife Cambodia is returning to normality and a number of mainly voluntary organisations are working there, particularly in the TEFL field. There is a university and a fine arts university in Phnom Penh as well as an international school.
Recruitment: APSO, Concern, SA, VSO.

Cameroon
Pop: 13 m   *Area*: 475,000 sq km
Cameroon Embassy: 84 Holland Park, London W11 3SB. Tel: 0171 727 0771.
Ministry of National Education: Yaounde
Ministry of Higher Education: Yaounde
British Council: Immeuble Christo, rue Charles de Gaulle, BP 818, Yaounde.

There are two distinct patterns of education which date from the colonial era. The western part follows the British system; the rest of the country follows the French system; but the two systems are being harmonised. Two-thirds of the children receive primary education — quite a high proportion for Africa — and some 38% of the schools are under mission or private ownership. There is an International School at Douala (BP 1909), an American School aand Rain Forest International School at Yaounde. At the tertiary level there is the University of Yaounde and the École Nationale Superieure Polytechnique.

Recruitment: BC, CA, ECIS, SA, VSO.

Canada

Pop: 30 m   *Area*: 10 m sq km

Canadian High Commission: Canada House, Trafalgar Square, Macdonald House, 1 Grosvenor Square, London W1X 0AB. Tel: 0171 258 6600. *Immigration Department*: 38 Grosvenor Street, London W1X 0AA. Tel: 0171 409 2071.

British High Commission: 80 Elgin Street, Ottawa, ON K1P 5KT.

Canada is well supplied with teachers, and consequently teaching positions for foreigners are hard to come by — except in the case of exchange teachers. It is usually only possible for a work permit to be issued if the local Canada Employment Centre is convinced that there is no suitably qualified Canadian national available to fill a post for which a foreign teacher has been accepted. The most fruitful areas for vacancies are in the North West Territories and the remoter parts of Saskatchewan and Alberta. There are international schools in Ottawa, Toronto, Vancouver and Windsor, Nova Scotia. The Leicester Pearson United World College of the Pacific is at Victoria, BC.

Sources of information: The Canadian High Commission keeps a list of current vacancies in its reception area, but these do not usually include teaching posts. Alternatively contact the British Columbia Government Office (1 Regent St, London SW1Y 4NS) or the Quebec Government Office (59 Pall Mall, London SW1 5JH). Canadian Education Association, Suite 8-200, 252 Bloor St West, Toronto, Ontario M5S 1V5 issues a leaflet *Information for teachers thinking of coming to Canada*. Canadian Teachers' Federation, 110 Argyle Street, Ottowa, Ontario K2P 1B4, issues a booklet *Teaching in Canada*. Canadian Association of Independent Schools, c/o Appleby College, Oakville, Ontario L6K 3P1. Canadian Association of University Teachers, Suite 1001, 75 Albert Street, Ottawa, Ontario K1P 5E7, advertises vacancies in the CAUT Bulletin. Association of Universities and Colleges of Canada, 151 Slater Street, Ottawa, Canada K1P 5N1, publishes vacancies in *University Affairs*.

Reference: Canada News (Outbound); *How to Emigrate* (How To); *Finding a Job in Canada* (How To); *Canada Employment Weekly*, 15

Madison Avenue, Toronto M5R 2S2. Tel: 001 416 964 6069. Fax: 001 416 964 3202. www.mediacorp2.com
Recruitment: ACU; CB (for Quebec); LECT.

Cayman Islands

Pop: 20,000   *Area*: 256 sq km
Cayman Islands Government Office: Trevor House, 100 Brompton Road, London SW3 1WX. Tel: 0171 581 9418.
Department of Education: George Town, Grand Cayman

Around 200 expatriate teachers are currently employed by the Cayman Islands Government, private schools and the International College of the Cayman Islands, Newlands, Grand Cayman. There is also a community college. The three islands are a British dependency, and no visas are required for British and Commonwealth passport holders. Teachers working in the private sector will need to obtain work permits and register with the Department of Education.
Recruitment: Crown Agents.

Central African Republic

Pop: 3 m   *Area*: 623,000 sq km
Central African Republic Embassy: 30 rue des Perchamps, 75016 Paris. Tel: 00 33 1 4224 4256.
Ministry of National Education: BP 791, Bangui

The educational system is based on the French model. There may be opportunities for English-speaking expatriates at the University of Bangui, BP 1450, Bangui.
Recruitment: AIM.

Chad

Pop: 6.3 m   *Area*: 1.3 m sq km
Chad Embassy: Blvd Lambermont 52, 1030 Brussels. Tel: 00 32 215 1975.
Ministry of National Education: N'Djamena

This is a desperately poor country which exists largely on aid. French influence is strong, but there is an American International School at N'Djamena. There may be opportunities for non-Francophone teachers at the University of Chad, BP 1117, N'Djamena.
Recruitment: AIM.

Chile

Pop: 14.7 m   *Area*: 757,000 sq km
Chilean Embassy: 12 Devonshire Street, London W1N 2DS. Tel: 0171 580 6392.

Ministry of Education: Avda Liberator B o'Higgins 1371, Santiago.
British Council: Eliodoro Yañez 832, Casilla 15T, Tajamar, Santiago.

There are several international schools here: the Colegio Ingles St John's, Concepcion; the American School, Puerto Montt; MacKay School and St Margaret's School for Girls in Viña del Mar; Grange School, International School, Lincoln International Academy and Redland School in Santiago. The Chileno-Britanico Cultural Association flourishes in many towns, and there is a British-type school in Santiago known as the Grange School. There are a number of flourishing universities, notably in Santiago (University of Chile, Catholic University of Chile), Atacama, Antofagasta, Bibo, Concepcion, La Serena, Talca, Valdivia and Valparaiso.
Recruitment: BC, CB, ECIS, SA, SAMS, SIM.

China (People's Republic)

Pop: 1,200 m   *Area*: 9.5 m sq km
Chinese Embassy: 49-51 Portland Place, London W1N 3AH. Tel: 0171 636 5726. Consular Section: 31 Portland PLace, London W1N 3AG.
Education Commission: 37 Damuchang Hutong, Xicheng District, Beijing.
British Embassy: Cultural and Education Section, 4th Floor, Landmark Building, 8 North Songsanhuan Road, Chaoyang District, Beijing 100026.(Also in Shanghai and Guangdong.)

The most populous country of the world, China is nevertheless a Third World country with few natural resources. The country is now keen to have expatriate teachers, notably in the TEFL field, but most opportunities are on a volunteer basis. A number of agencies recruit for Chinese state educational institutions. There are three international schools in Beijing (Beijing Biss, International, Western Academy), two in Guandong (AIS, Clifford), two in Shanghai (American, Yew Chang) and one in Tianjin.
Recruitment: Bell, BC, CB, CIEE, EF, ELT, EWW, Church of Scotland, Gabbitas, SA, Saxoncourt, Skola, TA, WCM, VSO.

China (Republic) See Taiwan

Colombia

Pop: 33 m   *Area*: 1.1 m sq km
Colombian Embassy: 3 Hans Crescent, London SW1X 0LR. Tel: 0171 589 9177. Consulate: 140 Park Lane, London W1Y 3DF Tel: 0171 493 4233.
Ministry of Education: Centro Administrativo Nacional, 501 Avda El Dorado, Bogota.

British Council: Calle 87 No 12-79, Apartado Aereo 089231, Santafe de Bogota.

There are international schools in Baranquilla (British American School, Colegio Karl C Parrish), Bogota (Anglo Colombian School, English School), Cali (Colegio Colombo Britanico). Cartagena (George Washington School), Medellin (Columbus School). The British Council has language institutes in Bogota and Medellin. Colombia has over 200 HE institutions, many of them with US backing.
Recruitment: BC, CB, ECIS, EWW, IH, SA, Timeplan.

Comores Islands
Pop: 500,000   *Area*: 2,171 sq km
Ministry of National Education: B P 446, Moroni
British Consulate: PO Box 986 Moroni.
This former French territory situated in the Indian Ocean between Madagascar and the African mainland is self-sufficient in primary school teachers but employs French-speaking teachers at the secondary level. The island of Mayotte which forms part of the archipelago has opted to remain a French overseas territory.
Recruitment: AIM.

Congo
Pop: 3 m   *Area*: 342,000 sq km
Honorary Consulate: Alliance House, 12 Caxton House, London SW1H 9DH. Tel: 0171 222 7575.
Congolese Embassy: 37 bis rue Paul Valéry, 75116 Paris. Tel: 00 33 1 4500 6057.
Ministry of Education: B P 169, Brazzaville
Honorary British Consulate: Pointe Noire.

There is no private education sector in this former French possession which boasts one of the highest literacy rates in Africa — 63%. The Marien Ngouabi University in the capital is the main HE institution.
Recruitment: BC, MAM.

Congo, Democratic Government of
Pop: 45 m   *Area*: 2.3 m sq km
Embassy: 26 Chesham Place, London SW1X 8HH. Tel: 0171 235 6137.
Ministry of Education: Avenue des Ambassadeurs, BP 32 Kinshasa/Gombe.

Formerly the Belgian Congo, then Congo Kinshasa and most recently known as Zaire, Belgian influence remains strong here, and French is the official language. School teachers are expected to have a good work-

ing knowledge of French, except in the two international schools — the American School (BP 4702) and the Zaire British Association school (BP 940) both in Kinshasa. There is expatriate TEFL involvement at the English Language Centre, Kinshasa and the Institut National de Science et de l'Education. The country has four universities: Kinshasa, Kinshasa/Limete, Kisangi and Lumumbashi. The country is starting to regain normality after the turmoil of recent years.
Recruitment: AIM, BC, SA.

Costa Rica

Pop: 3.4 m   *Area*: 51,000 sq km
Costa Rican Embassy: 14 Lancaster Gate, London W2 3LH. Tel: 0171 796 8844.
Ministry of Education: Apdo 10,087, San José.
British Embassy: Apartado 815, Edificio Centro Colon, 1007 San José.

Costa Rica is one of the most stable and developed countries in Central America and perhaps the most European in character. There are several international schools in San José including the Anglo-American School (PO Box 3188), Costa Rica Academy (PO Box 4941), Lincoln School (PO Box 1919). At the HE level there is: University of Central America, University of Costa Rica (both in San José), the University of Herdeia, the Open University and a number of private universities. Documentation required for residence and work permits: letter of application, contract, references, birth certificate, marriage certificate, police record or good conduct declaration signed by three witnesses, chest X-ray and blood test reports, photocopies of used pages in passport, six front and six profile photographs.
Recruitment: CB, ECIS, SA.

Cote D'Ivoire.

See **Ivory Coast**.

Croatia

Pop: 5 m   *Area*: 56,610 sq km
Croatian Embassy: 21 Conway Street, London W1P 5HL. Tel: 0171 387 1144.
Ministry of Education: Ave Vukovar 78, 10000 Zagreb.
British Council: PO Box 55, 12/1 Ilica, 10000 Zagreb.

Formerly part of Yugoslavia, Croatia seems to have put the conflicts of the early 90s behind it and is now able to turn its attention to rebuilding its infrastructure. There are four universities: Zagreb, Rijeka, Osijek and Split.
Recruitment: BC.

Cuba

Pop: 10 m   *Area*: 111,000 sq km
Cuban Embassy: 167 High Holborn, London WC1 6PA. Tel: 0171 240 2488.
Ministry of Education: Obispo No 160, Havana
British Embassy: Calle 34 No 708, Miramar, Havana.

Since its revolution Cuba has virtually eradicated illiteracy and increased educational provision. Over 85% of Cubans now receive a secondary education, higher than in most Latin American countries. Education is based on Marxist-Leninist principles and combines study with manual work, particularly at HE level. More than 250,000 students are said to be receiving higher education. The international school in Havana (c/o British Embassy) serves the expatriate community. There are universities at Havana, Santiago de Cuba, Santa Clara and Camagey as well as 26 other HE institutions.
Recruitment: I to I.

Cyprus

Pop: 665,000   *Area*: 9,250 sq km
Cyprus High Commission: 93 Park Street, London W1Y 4ET. Tel: 0171 499 8272.
Ministry of Education: Greg Axentiou Street, 1434 Nicosia .
British Council: 3 Museum Street, 1097 Nicosia.
Turkish Rep of N. Cyprus Office: 28 Cockspur St, London SW1 Tel: 0171 837 4577.
TRNC Ministry of Education: Lefkosa, Mersin 1, Turkey.

Cyprus is a divided country politically. There is the Turkish Republic of Cyprus in the north of the island, and the Republic of Cyprus in the south. Attempts have been made to reunite both parts of the country in the past, and currently there is a glimmer of hope that they will be successful. International and English medium schools can be found in Larnaca (American Academy, PO Box 112); Limassol (Limassol Grammar School, Homer St), Logos School of English Education (PO Box 1075); Nicosia (American Academy, Falcon School, Grammar School); Paphos (Anglo-American International School). There are several private language schools teaching English plus the British Council's own institute. Most other educational institutions are state run except for the English School which used to have links with the British Council and is now run by a foundation. There is also a school attached to the British base. At the tertiary level there is the University College of Arts and Science in Limassol and the Pedagogical Academy. There are also

government run adult evening institutes. A university opened in the Turkish part of the island in 1986.
Recruitment: BC, SA, SCE.

Czech Republic
Pop: 10.3 m   *Area*: 78,664 sq km
Czech Embassy: 26-30 Kensington Palace Gardens, London W8 4QY. Tel: 0171 727 3966/7.
Ministry of Education: Karmelitska, 8, 118.12 Prague.
British Council: Narodni 10, 125.01 Prague.

There is a particular demand for people with TEFL expertise in schools and in the country's various universities in Prague (Charles U), Brno (Purkyne U), Olomouc (Palacky U). There are government and privately run language institutes in the principal towns and the British Council has its own language centre and resource centres. Prague has several international schools (AIS, British International School, English College, English International School).
Recruitment: BC, CB, ECIS, EEP, EWW, IH, Linguarama, Nord Anglia, SA, Saxoncourt.

Denmark
Pop: 5.3 m   *Area*: 43,000 sq km
Royal Danish Embassy: 55 Sloane Street, London SW1X 9SR. Tel: 0171 333 0200.
Ministry of Education: Frederiksholms Kanal 21-25, DK-1220 Copenhagen K.
British Council: Gammel Mont 12.3, DK-1117 Copenhagen K.

The International Relations Division of the Ministry publishes a booklet on the Danish educational system and regulations governing the employment of foreign teachers. Generally speaking, a foreign teacher can only be employed in state schools in a temporary capacity until he or she takes a supplementary qualifying examination. The provision of primary and lower secondary education in the Folkeskoler is the responsibility of the local authorities (Kommunalbestyrelse). The upper secondary schools (Gymnasia) are administered by the counties (Amtsrad), and applications should be made to the appropriate authority. There are also a number of private institutions which are not subject to the same regulations. Information about employment in the private sector is obtainable from Frie Grundskolers Faellesrad, Nygade 6, DK-4200 Slagelse. There are a number of international schools: Aarhus (Interskolen); Copenhagen (International School, Rygaards International School); Esbjerg (International School); Svendborg (International School). Denmark has five universities at Copenhagen, Aarhus, Aalborg, Odense and Roskilde. It also has a well developed system of adult education centres independent of the state known as Folk High Schools. Details are available from Efterskolernes Sekretariat, Farvergade 27, DK-1463 Copenhagen-K. Finally there are several private language schools.

EC citizens are allowed to work (or look for work) in Denmark for three months. If you intend to continue, at least two weeks before the end of this period you should apply to the Department of Aliens for a residence and work permit. Address: Direktoratet for Udlaendinge, Absolonsgade 9, 1658 København V.

Reading: The ICU, Bremerholm 6, 4th Floor, 1069 Copenhagen K publish a useful booklet entitled *Guide for young visitors to Denmark*. It would also be useful for the not-so-young.

Recruitment: CB, ECIS, Inlingua, SLS.

Djibouti

Pop: 405,000   *Area*: 22,000 sq km
Djibouti Embassy: 26 rue Emile Ménier, 75116 Paris. Tel: 00 33 1 4727 4922.
Ministry of Education: B P 2101, Djibouti
British Consulate: PO Box 81, 9-11 rue de Genve, Djibouti.

Two ethnic groups live in this territory: the Issa (of Somali origin) and the Afar (of Ethiopian origin). There are nineteen secondary schools, many of them private, and a teacher training college. Official languages are Arabic and French, and French influence is strong.

Dominica

Pop: 75,000   *Area*: 751 sq km
Dominican High Commission: 1 Collingham Gardens, London SW5 0HW. Tel: 0171 370 5194.
Ministry of Education: Government Headquarters, Kennedy Avenue, Roseau.
British Consulate: PO Box 6, Roseau.

There are both government and church schools on the island, together with a teacher training college, a technical college and a branch of the University of the West Indies.

Recruitment: VSO

Dominican Republic

Pop: 7.8 m   Area: 48,000 sq km
Dominican Honorary Consulate: 6 Queens Mansions, Brook Green, London W6 7EB. Tel: 0171 602 1885.
Ministry of Education: Avda Máximo Gomez, Santo Domingo, DN.
British Embassy: Avenida 27 de Febrero 233, Santa Domingo, DN.

Sharing an island with Haiti this country was first a Spanish colony and then a French colony. There are international schools at Jarabacoa (Escuela Caribe); La Romana (Abraham Lincoln School); Santo Domingo (Carol Morgan Schools). The Republic has twelve universities including the University of Santo Domingo founded in 1538.
Recruitment: SA.

Ecuador

Pop: 11.7 m   *Area*: 284,000 sq km
Ecuador Embassy: 3 Hans Crescent, London SW1X 0LN Tel: 0171 534 1367
Ministry of Education: Méjia 348, Quito.
British Council: Av Amazonas 1646, Casilla 17 07 8829, Quito.

Ecuador has a mix of state and private schools, and it is in the private sector that opportunities exist — mainly for English teachers. There are language schools (including British Council centres in Quito and Guyaquil) and international schools exist at Guyaquil (American School, Inter-American Academy); Quito (American International School, Alliance Academy). There are 30 state HE institutions and two private ones.
Recruitment: BC, CB, SA.

Egypt

Pop: 60 m   *Area*: 1 m sq km
Egyptian Embassy: 2 Lowndes Street, London SW1X. Tel: 0171 235 9719. Egyptian Education Bureau, 4 Chesterfield Gardens, London W1Y 8BR
Ministry of Education: 6 Amin Samy Street, El-Sayed El-Zeinab, Cairo.
British Council: 192 Sharia el Nil, Agouza, Cairo. Also in Alexandria.

Egypt is a major exporter of teachers to other countries in the Arab world. There are, however, opportunities for TEFL teachers in private schools, language schools, including British Council operations in Cairo, Heliopolis and Alexandria, and teacher training colleges. International education is provided by the Schutz American School in Alexandria (PO Box 1000), and by the British International School (PO Box 137), Cairo American College (PO Box 39) and the Heliopolis International School – all in Cairo. There are thirteen universities at

Alexandria, Assiut, Cairo, Mansoura, Menia, Ismailia, Tanta, Zagazig and elsewhere. The American University of Cairo enjoys a particularly high reputation.
Recruitment: AP, BC, Church of Scotland, ECIS, EWW, Gabbitas, IH, SA.

El Salvador
Pop: 5.5 m   *Area*: 21,000 sq km
Embassy: 159 Great Portland Street, London W1N 5FD. Tel: 0171 436 8282.
Ministry of Education: Calle Delgado y 8a Avde Norte, San Salvador.
British Embassy: Edificio Inter-Inversiones, Paseo General Escalaon 4828, PO Box 1591, San Salvador.

The best opportunities here exist in the private sector at such schools as the Academia Britanica Cuscatleca (PO Box 121, Santa Tecla) and the Escuela Americana (PO Box 01-35, San Salvador). There are three state universities including the University of El Salvador plus 35 private ones. Normally your employer should obtain a work permit for you in El Salvador before you can obtain a temporary residence visa through a Salavadorean consulate. In certain cases it is possible to enter the country with a tourist visa and obtain temporary residence once you arrive. This is, however, at the discretion of the Ministry of the Interior.
Recruitment: APSO, BC, ECIS.

Eritrea
Pop: 3.5 m   *Area*: 93,679 sq km
Eritrean Embassy: 15-17 avenue Wolvendael, Brussels. Tel: 00 32 2 374 4434.
Ministry of Education: PO Box 5610. Asmara.
British Council: Lorenzo Ta'zaz Street No 23, PO Box 997, Asmara.

Since becoming independent from Ethiopia Eritrea has been rebuilding its shattered educational system. There is a university at Asmara.
Recruitment: BC, VSO.

Estonia
Pop: 1.6 m   *Area*: 45,215 sq km
Estonian Embassy: 16 Hyde Park Gate, London SW7 5DG. Tel: 0171 589 3428
Ministry of Education: Tönismägi 11, Takkinn 0106
British Embassy: Kentmanni 20, Tallinn 0100.
British Council: Resource Centre, Vani Posti 1, Tallinn 0001.

Together with the other Baltic States Estonia is keen to develop TEFL. The British Council is involved in in-service teacher training and

there are expatriate lecturers at Tartu University and some of the other eight HE education institutions.
Recruitment: EEP, IH.

Ethiopia
Pop: 55 m   *Area*: 1,128,000 sq km
Ethiopian Embassy: 17 Princes Gate, London SW7 1PZ. Tel: 0171 589 7212.
Ministry of Education: PO Box 1176, Addis Ababa
British Council: Artistic Building, Adwa Avenue, PO Box 1043, Addis Ababa.

Drought and civil war are just two of the problems that the government has to cope with, and educational plans have therefore been set back. There are a number of expatriates, including Indians and British, teaching in schools, often on volunteer terms. International education is provided at the International Community School, PO Box 70282, Addis Ababa and Sandford English Community School, PO Box 30056, Addis Ababa. Ethiopia has two universities: Addis Ababa (POB 1176) and Dire Dawa.
Recruitment: BC, ECIS, SIM, Concern, SA, VSO.

Falkland Islands
Pop: 2,600   *Area*: 12,172 sq km
Falkland Islands Government Office: Falkland House, 14 Broadway, London SW1H 0BH. Tel: 0171 222 2542.

Teaching opportunities arise from time to time at the primary school and community school at Port Stanley.

Fiji
Pop: 804,000   *Area*: 18,300 sq km
Fiji High Commission: 34 Hyde Park Gate, London SW7 5BN. Tel: 0171 584 3661.
Ministry of Education: Marela House, Suva.
British High Commission: Victoria House, 478 Gladstone Road, Suva.

Fiji, with its 300 islands and population mainly of Indian and Polynesian stock, has virtually achieved universal education. The most important educational institution here is the University of the South Pacific in Suva which serves 11 countries in the region. There are also colleges of agriculture, technology and medicine. International schools exist at Pacific Harbour (PO Box 50) and Suva (PO Box 2393).
Recruitment: ACU, VSO.

Finland

Pop: 5 m   *Area*: 338,000 sq km
Finnish Embassy: 38 Chesham Place, London SW1X 8HW. Tel: 0171 235 9531.
Ministry of Education: Rauhankatu 4, 00170 Helsinki 17.
British Council: Hakaniemenkatu 2, 00530 Helsinki.

There are large number of foreign teachers in Finland in state schools, private schools, language schools, universities and Finnish-British Societies whose headquarters is at Puistikatu 1bA, 00140 Helsinki. The principal need is for TEFL teachers. Helsinki has an International School and an English School. There are universities in Helsinki, Jyväskylä, Oulu, Tampere, Joensuu, Kuopio, Lapland, Vaasa and Turku plus three technological universities, three business schools and four art universities.
Recruitment: ECIS, IH, Inlingua, Linguarama, SA.

France

Pop: 58 m   *Area*: 544,000 sq km
French Embassy: 58 Knightsbridge, London SW1X 7JT. Tel: 0171 201 1000.
French Institute: 14 Cromwell Place, London SW7 2JR. Tel: 0171 581 2701.
Ministry of Education: 110 rue de Grenelle, 75007 Paris
British Council: 9 rue de Constantine, 75007 Paris. Also in Bordeaux.

The country is divided into 27 educational districts called académies reponsible for the administration of education in that particular region. For expatriate teachers without a French pedagogical qualification opportunities in state schools used to be available only on an exchange basis, but the situation is changing. Fifteen per cent of French children attend private schools, and there are also employment opportunities in this sector, particularly in TEFL. For more information consult: Enseignement privé catholique, 277 rue St Jacques, 75005 Paris; Fédération de l'Enseignement Laïque, 5 rue de la Santé, 75013 Paris. International schools exist in Cannes (Anglo American School, Mougins; Centre International de Valbonne); Chambon-sur-Lignon (Collège Cevenol); Nice (American International School); and Paris where there are several, including the British School, the American School and the International School. There are 72 state, five Catholic and seven private universities as well as the highly selective grandes écoles. Several of these employ TEFL staff. Private language institutes abound.
Recruitment: BC, Callan, CB, Crosslinks, ECIS, ELT, EWW, IH, Inlingua, Crosslinks, SA.

French Overseas Departments and Territories

Ministry of Overseas Departments and Territories: 27 rue Oudinot, 75007 Paris.

Opportunities in TEFL may exist in Guadeloupe, Guiana, Martinique — at the Université Antilles Guyane, for instance. The Université de la Runion, 24 Avenue de la Victoire, St Denis, Réunion might also be worth trying.

Recruitment: AIM (for Réunion).

Gabon

Pop: 1 m   Area: 268,000 sq km

Gabon Embassy: 27 Elvaston Place, London SW7 5NL. Tel: 0171 823 9986.

Ministry of Educations: Libreville.

British Embassy: See Democratic Republic of Congo

One of the more prosperous countries in Africa south of the Sahara thanks to abundant mineral resources and a small population, it is also one of the most advanced educationally. Seventy per cent of all children attend primary and secondary school. Half the teachers here are expatriates, mostly French nationals. There are two universities: Université Omar Bongo, BP 13, Libreville and the Université des Sciences et Techniques at Masuka. Libreville has an AIS.

Recruitment: AEF.

Gambia

Pop: 1 m   *Area*: 11,000 sq km

Gambian High Commission: 52 Kensington Court, London W8 5DG. Tel: 0171 937 6316

Ministry of Education: Bedford Place Building, Banjul.

British High Commission: PO Box 507, 48 Atlantic Road, Fajara,

There are sixteen secondary technical, eight secondary high and nine post-secondary schools in this former British enclave surrounded by Senegal. Among the institutions employing expatriates is Gambia College, which provides teacher training, agricultural courses and health training. There is an American Embassy School and Marina International Primary School in Banjul.

Recruitment: BC, LECT, VSO.

Georgia

Pop: 5.5 m   *Area*: 69,700 sq km

Georgian Embassy: 3 Hornton Place, Kensington, London W8. Tel: 0171 937 8233 (or 45 Avonmore Rd, London W14 8RT).

Ministry of Education: Uznadze 52, 38002, Tbilisi.
British Council: 13 Chavcharaze Avenue, 2nd Floor, Tbilisi 380079.
This small Black Sea state, once part of the Soviet Union, has had a chequered history of late. It boasts one university and a technical university. The British Council has a resource centre at the university and its professional staff includes an English language development officer. A few private language institutes operate here.
Recruitment: IH.

Germany

Pop: 82 m   *Area*: 357,000 sq km
German Embassy: 34 Belgrave Square, London SW1X 8PZ. Tel: 0171 235 5033.
Goethe Institut: 50 Princes Gate, London SW7 2PH. Tel: 0171 581 3344.
British Council: Hahnerstrasse 5, D-50667 Köln 1; Herdenbergstrasse 20, D-10623 Berlin 12. Also Hamburg, Leipzig and Munich.

Education is the responsibility of the federal states which make up Germany, and the state ministries of education can provide information on opportunities in state schools. Baden Württemburg: Neues Schloss, D-70173 Stuttgart. Bayern (Bavaria): Salvatorplatz 2, D-80333 München. Berlin: Storkopwer Strasse 104-106, D-10407 Berlin. Brandenburg: Heinrich-Mann-Alle 107, D-14467 Potsdam. Bremen: Rembertiring 8-12, D-28195 Bremen. Hamburg: Hamburger Strasse 31, D-22083 Hamburg. Hessen: Luisenplatz 10, D-65185 Wiesbaden. Mecklenburg-Vorpommern: Werderstrasse 124, D-19055 Schwerin. Niedersachsen (Lower Saxony): Schiffgraben 12, D-30159 Hanover. Nordrhein-Westfalen: Völklinger Strasse 49, D-40221 Düsseldorf. Rheinland Pfalz: Mittlere Bleiche 61, D-55116 Mainz. Saarland: Hohenzollernstrasse 60, D-66119 Saarbrücken. Sachsen (Saxony): Carolaplatz 1, Westflügel, D-01097 Dresden. Sachsen-Anhalt: Turmschanzerstrasse 32, D-39114 Magdeburg. Schleswig Holstein: Brunswiker Strasse 16-22, D-24105 Kiel. Thüringen: Werner-Seelenbinder-Strasse 1, D-99099 Erfurt. For a list of private schools contact the Bundesverband Deutscher Privatschulen, Darmstädter Landstrasse 85a, D-60598 Frankfurt/Main.

In addition there are opportunities in private language schools (such as the Benedictschulen), adult institutes (Volkshochschulen), companies, universities (including the new International University which teaches through the medium of English (PO Box 1550, D-76605 Bruchsal). For information on vacancies in the British service schools in Northern Germany contact HQ SCE, Building 5, Wegberg Military

Complex, BFPO 40. There are international schools in several major cities including Berlin (John F Kennedy School, British School), Bonn (British, American), Dresden, Düsseldorf, Frankfurt, Hamburg, Leipzig, Munich, Stuttgart and the Black Forest.

The Zentralstelle für Arbeitsvermittlung, Feuerbachstr 42, D-60325 Frankfurt/Main 1 recruits teachers for both the public and the private sector.

Recruitment: BC, CB, CFBT, DFEE, ECIS, ELT, EWW, Inlingua, IH, Linguarama, OPU, SCE, SLS, SAS.

Ghana
Pop: 16.5 m   *Area*: 239,000 sq km
Ghana High Commission: 104 Highgate Hill, London N6 5HE. Tel: 0171 8686.
Secretariat for Education: PO Box M45, Accra.
British Council: Liberia Road, PO Box 771, Accra. (Branch in Kumasi)

Ghana has five universities including University of Cape Coast; University of Ghana (Accra); University of Science and Technology (Kumasai). There are two international schools in Accra.

Recruitment: AP, BC, LECT, TA, VSO; Universities of Ghana Office, 321 City Road, London EC1V 1LJ.

Gibraltar
Pop: 29,000   *Area*: 5 sq km
Gibraltar Government Office: Arundel Great Court, 179 Strand, London WC2R 1EH. Tel: 0171 836 0777.

The educational system amounts to twelve primary and two secondary schools. There are two primary schools for the children of ser vice personnel and a College of FE.

Greece
Pop: 10.5 m   *Area*: 132,000 sq km
Greek Embassy: 1a Holland Park, London W11 3TP. Tel: 0171 229 3850.
Ministry of Education: 15 Mitropoleos Street, Athens.
British Council: 17 Plateia Philikis Etairias, Kolonaki Square, PO Box 34388, Athens 10210. Branch in Thessalonika.

Many private language schools, private primary and secondary schools employ expatriate teachers and advertise regularly in the *TES*. There are also opportunities in TEFL at the British Council centres in Athens and Thessalonika and in the country's sixteen universities. Among the international schools are the American Community Schools,

Athens College, Campion School (Athens) and St Catherine's British Embassy School.
Recruitment: BC, ECIS, CB, EWW, IH, SA, Skola.

Grenada
Pop: 96,000   *Area*: 344 sq km
Grenada High Commission: 1 Collingham Gardens, London SW5 0HW. Tel: 0171 373 7808.
Ministry of Education: St George's.
British High Commission: 14 Church Street, St George's.
Expatriate teachers are involved in secondary education and special education here. The main tertiary institutions are St George's University School of Medicine, a technical college, a teacher training college, School of Agriculture (Mirabeau), School of Fishing (Victoria) and a branch of the University of the West Indies.
Recruitment: VSO

Guatemala
Pop: 10.7 m   *Area*: 109,000 sq km
Guatemalan Embassy: 13 Fawcett Street, London SW10 9HN. Tel: 0171 351 3042.
Ministry of Education: Palacio Nacional, Guatemala City
British Embassy: 7a Avenida 5-10, Zona 4, Guatemala City.
    The country has five universities but its adult illiteracy rate is the second highest in the Western hemisphere. The Colegio Maya, Colegio Valle Verde and American School provide international education.
Recruitment: SA, Saxoncourt.

Guinea
Pop: 6.5 m   *Area*: 246,000 sq km
Guinea Embassy: 51 rue de la Faisanderie, 75061 Paris. Tel: 00 33 1 4704 8148.
Ministry of National Education: BP 2201, Conakry.
British Consulate: BP 834 Conakry.
    This former French possession has good mineral and agricultural potential and could become quite prosperous, but the centralised economy of the socialist minded government has proved inefficient. Liberalisation is now in the air, and one consequence is that private schools have been legalised. There is an American international school at Conakry. Educational institutions include the brand new University of Conakry and the Polytechnique Gamal Abdul Nasser. There are also colleges of health, administration and vocational skills. Most of these

tertiary courses have a strong practical element akin to the sandwich course system practised in the UK.
Recruitment: BC.

Guinea-Bissau
Pop: 1 m   *Area*: 36,125 sq km
Guinea-Bissau Embassy: Ave Franklin D Roosevelt 70, 1050 Brussels. Tel: 00 32 2 647 0890.
Ministry of Education: Bissau.
British Embassy: See Senegal.
  This former Portuguese possession is currently setting up a university.
Recruitment: VSO.

Guyana
Pop: 950,000   *Area*: 215,000 sq km
Guyanan High Commission: 3 Palace Court, Bayswater Road, London W2 4LP. Tel: 0171 229 7684.
Ministry of Education: 21 Brickdam, Georgetown.
British High Commission: 44 Main Street, PO Box 10849, Georgetown.
  The Guyanan High Commission acts as a point of contact for teachers wishing to work in Guyana. There are foreign teachers at the secondary and tertiary level paticularly in maths, science and technical subjects. All education is in the hands of the state, including the University of Guyana, PO Box 1110, Georgetown.
Recruitment: LECT, VSO.

Haiti
Pop: 6.8 m   *Area*: 28,000 sq km
Ministry of Education: Rue Audain, Port au Prince
  There are two international schools in this turbulent, poor and least developed of all the Caribbean countries: Ecole Flamboyant and the Union School, both at Port au Prince. The address of the University of Haiti is Box 2279, Port au Prince.
Recruitment: SA.

Honduras
Pop: 5.3 m   *Area*: 112 sq km
Embassy: 115 Gloucester Place, London W1H 3PJ. Tel: 0171 486 4880.
Ministry of Education: Comayaguela, DC.
British Embassy: Edificio Palmira, 3er Piso, Colonia Palmira, PO Box 290, Tegucipulca.
  Basic education is compulsory in this Central American republic.

Everyone who completes this stage of their education is required to teach two illiterate adults to read and write. Opportunities may arise at international schools in La Ceiba (Mazapan School), San Pedro Sula (Escuela Internacional Sampedrana) and Tegucigalpa (American School). Honduras has six universities (state and private) including the Universidad Nacional Autonoma at Tegucigalpa.

Recruitment: APSO.

Hong Kong

Pop: 5.8 m   *Area*: 1,000 sq km

Hong Kong Government Office: 6 Grafton Street, London W1X 3LB. Tel: 0171 499 9821.

Directorate of Education: Lee Gardens 5f, 33-37 Hysan Avenue, Causeway Bay, HK.

British Council: 3 Supreme Court Road, Admiralty, Hong Kong.

Now a special adminstrative region of China, Hong Kong has free and compulsory education up to the age of 15. There are three types of school: government schools, schools run by voluntary bodies (usually the churches) which receive government assistance, and private independent schools. In addition there is a small group of English schools for English speaking children, notably the twelve schools operated by the English Schools Foundation. In the past the British Council has recruited a sizeable number of EFL teachers for the state sector. The authorities have plans to make many English medium schools change their language of instruction to Chinese (Cantonese), but protests from parents and teachers have led to a scaling down of this policy.

The Vocational Training Council operates eight technical institutes, and there are four teacher training colleges: Grantham, Northcote, Sir Robert Black, and the HK Technical Teachers' College. There are currently seven HE institutions: University of Hong Kong, the Chinese University of Hong Kong, the Hong Kong Polytechnic University, the City University, the Hong Kong Baptist University, Lingnan College and the Hong Kong University of Science and Technology. The Government Office publishes a useful fact sheet on living conditions in HK.

Useful addresses: English Schools Foundation, GPO Box 11284, HK. HK International School, South Bay Close, Repulse Bay, HK (American style). Chinese International School, 7 Eastern Hospital Road, Causeway Bay, HK. Kellet School, 2 Wak Lok Path, Wah Fu Estate, HK. Sir Ellis Kadoorie School, 9 Eastern Hospital Rd, Sookunpo, H K (govt school).

Recruitment: ACU, Baptist, BC, ECIS, OMS, OPU, SA, WES.

Hungary

Pop: 10.6 m   *Area*: 93,000 sq km

Hungarian Embassy: 35 Eaton Place, London SW1X 8BY. Tel: 0171 235 2664.

Ministry of Education: Szalayu U 10/14, 1055 Budapest.

British Council: Benczur Utca 26, 1068 Budapest.

Hungary offers opportunities in government schools, private schools, universities and language schools teaching EFL, science, maths and technical subjects. The government has set up two bi-lingual Hungarian/English schools. There is an American School in Budapest. There are six universities at Budapest, Pécs, Szeged, Debrecen, Miskolc and Veszprén and 85 other HE institutes. International education is provided at the Magyar British International School and the International Christian School.

Recruitment: Bell, BC, CB, EEP, IH, Linguarama, Nord Anglia, SA.

Iceland

Pop: 270,000   *Area*: 103,000

Icelandic Embassy: 1 Eaton Terrace, London SW1W 8EY. Tel: 0171 730 5131/2.

Ministry of Education: Hverfisgata 4-6, 150 Reykyavik.

British Embassy: Laufásvegar 49, Reykjavik 101.

The two universities in Iceland employ a few expatriates and the American Embassy has a school there.

India

Pop: 890 m   *Area*: 3.3 m sq km

Indian High Commission: India House, Aldwych, London WC2B 4NA. Tel: 0171 836 8484.

British Council: British High Commission, 17 Kasturba Gandhi Marg, New Delhi 1100-01. Also Bombay, Calcutta, Madras.

Public education is the responsibility of the state governments, and education departments are usually based in the state capitals (given in brackets): Andhra Pradesh (Hyderabad); Arunchal Pradesh (Itangar); Assam (Dispure); Bihar (Patna); Goa (Panaji); Gujarat (Gandhingar); Haryana (Chandigarh); Himachal Pradesh (Shimla); Jammu and Kashmir (Srinagar/Jammu); Karnataka (Bangalore); Kerala (Trivandrum); Mahdya Pradesh (Bhopal); Maharashtra (Bombay); Manipur (Imphal); Meghalaya (Shillong); Mizoram (Aizawl); Nagaland (Kohima); Orissa (Bhubaneswar); Punjab (Chandigarh); Rajasthan (Jaipur); Sikkim (Gangtok); Tamil Nadu (Madras); Tripura (Agartala); Uttar Pradesh (Lucknow); West Bengal (Calcutta). Private education, including church schools, exists alongside the state sector and there seem to be increasing opportunities for foreign teachers in the voluntary sector. There are also international schools, notably in Bangalore (ADITI, International), Bombay (American, International), Calcutta, Hyderabad, Mussoorie (International, Woodstock), New Delhi (American Embassy School, British School), Ootacamund (Hebron School) and Tamil Nadu (Kodaikanal International). India has some thirteen central universities and about 151 state universities in addition to a number of specialist HE institutions.

Recruitment: BC, I to I, LECT, Interserve, SA, TA, SPW, VSO, WCM.

Indonesia

Pop: 192 m   *Area*: 1.9 m sq km

Indonesian Embassy: 38 Grosvenor Square, London W1X 9AD. Tel: 0171 499 7661.

Ministry of Education: Jalan Jenderal Sudirman, Senayan, Jakarta Pusat.

British Council: S Widjojo Centre, 71 Jalan Jenderal Sudirman, Jakarta 12190.

There have been plentiful opportunities in the past for teachers and lecturers, but the sudden downturn in the economy at the end of 1997 is bound to reduce the number of teaching jobs — at least for a time. There are international schools at Balikpapan, Bandung (two), Bogor, Bontang, Jakarta (two), Malang, Medan (two), Salatiga, Semarang, Sentani, Serukam, Sumatra, Surabaya and Tembagapura. The British Council has language centres in Jakarta and Surabaya, and there are a large number of private language schools. Indonesia has 31 state and 66 private universities, and there are also opportunities in teacher training and with oil companies.

Recruitment: Bell, BC, ECIS, EF, ELT, Inlingua, SA, Saxoncourt, Skola, VSO, WES.

Iran

Pop: 63 m   *Area*: 1.65 m sq km

Iranian Embassy: 27 Prince's Gate, London SW7 1PX. Tel: 0171 584 8101.

Ministry of Education: Teheran.

British Embassy: 143 Ferdowsi Avenue, PO Box 11365-4474, Teheran 11344.

After a period of isolation Iran's attitudes to the West appear to be softening, and there may be opportunities here in the future notably in the 30 universities, 30 medical universities and the thirteen specialist HE institutes.

Iraq

Pop: 19 m   *Area*: 435,000 sq km
Iraqi Interests Section: Royal Jordanian Embassy, 21 Queen's Gate, London SW7 5JG. Tel: 0171 584 7141.
Ministry of Education: PO Box 258, Baghdad
British Interests Section: Russian Embassy, House 12, Street 218, Al Khelood, Baghdad.

In the current political climate there are few, if any, opportunities for foreign teachers here. Iraq has eight universities (notably in Baghdad, Mosul and Basra) and nineteen technical universities. There is an international school in Baghdad. Currently Britain and several other countries have suspended diplomatic relations with Baghdad.

Israel

Pop: 5.7 m   *Area*: 21,000 sq km
Israeli Embassy: 2 Palace Green, London W8 4QB. Tel: 0171 957 9300.
Ministry of Education: Hakirya, 14 Klausner St, Tel Aviv.
British Council: 140 Hayarkon Street, PO Box 3302, Tel Aviv 61032.

Generally speaking, Israel is self-sufficient in teachers. Even the staff at the British Council's language institutes in Tel Aviv, Nazareth and Jerusalem tend to be locally recruited. There may, however, be opportunities at the three international schools: The Anglican School, PO Box 191, Jerusalem. England Israel High School, Kfar Hanoar Hadatoi, Kfar Hasidim 20494. Walworth Barbour American International School, Rehov Hazorea, Kfar Shmaryahu, Tel Aviv. There are very few private language schools since the district authorities usually fulfil this need. At the HE level there is the Israel Institute of Technology (Haifa), Hebrew University of Jerusalem, Bar-Ilan University, Tel Aviv University, Haifa University, Ben-Gurion University of the Negev.
Reference: Mark Taylor: *Education in the service of the State of Israel* (Anglo Israel Association, 9 Bentinck Street, London W1M 5RP).
Recruitment: ECIS, Church of Scotland.
(For Palestine-administered territories see **West Bank and Gaza**).

Italy

Pop: 57 m   *Area*: 301,000 sq km
Italian Embassy: 14 Three Kings Yard, London W1Y 2EH. Tel: 0171 629 8200. Consulates: 38 Eaton Place, London W1; 111 Piccadilly, Manchester 2; 7-9 Greyfriars, Bedford MK40 1HJ.
Italian Institute: 39 Belgrave Square, London SW1X 8NX.
Ministry of Education: Viale Trastevere 76A, 00100 Rome.

British Council: Via Quatro Fontane 20, 00184 Rome. Also in Bologna, Milan, Naples.

Until recently there have been no opportunities in state schools for foreigners except under an exchange scheme, though opportunities certainly exist in the private sector. There are international schools in Florence, Genoa, Imperia (Liceo Internazionale), Milan (American, International, Sir James Henderson), Naples, Rome (Ambrit, American Overseas, Castelli, Greenwood Garden, International Academy, Kendale Primary, Marymount, New, Notre Dame International, Southlands, St George's, St Stephen's, Summerfield), Trieste (International, UWC), Turin, Varese (EC School) and Venice. Language schools abound, some affiliated to an international group, others to an Italian organisation, such as the British School Group which alone has 74 branches (Vilae Liegei 14, 00198, Roma) and the British College (Via Luigi Rizzo 18, 95131 Catania). The British Council has institutes in Italy, too, and there are opportunities particularly for EFL lecturers in Italy's many universities, but on contract terms only. The Italian Embassy issues a booklet on employment in Italy

Recruitment: BC, Callan, CB, DFEE, ECIS, ELT, EWW, IH, Inlingua, Linguarama, Nord Anglia, SA, Saxoncourt, Skola, Timeplan.

Ivory Coast (Côte D'Ivoire)

Pop: 14 m   *Area*: 322,000 sq km
Embassy of the Côte d'Ivoire: 2 Upper Belgrave Street, London SW1X 8BJ. Tel: 0171 235 6991.
Ministry of National Education: BP V120, Abidjan
Ministry of Higher Education: BP V151, Abidjan.

This used to be one of the most prosperous countries in the whole of Africa, but the collapse of world prices for timber, cocoa and coffee (the Ivory Coast's main resources) reduced the per capita GNP by almost half. Nevertheless, the proportion of children in primary school remains relatively high, and the Government has invested in five new technical training institutes. The National University of the Ivory Coast is at Abidjan and there is a campus at Yamoussoukro. There are international schools at Abidjan, Kingston (Priory School), and Mandeville (Belair School).
Recruitment: BC, ECIS, SIM, OMOCI (Office de la Main d'Oeuvre en Côte d'Ivoire, BP 108, Abidjan).

Jamaica

Pop: 2.5 m   *Area*: 11,425 sq km
Jamaican High Commission: 1-2 Prince Consort Road, London SW7 2BZ. Tel: 0171 823 9911.

Ministry of Education: 2 National Heroes Circle, Kingston 4.
British Council: PCMB Building, 64 Knutsford Blvd, PO Box 575, Kingston 5. This office handles the whole of the Caribbean.

Opportunities might arise at the tertiary level institutions: College of Arts, Science and Technology, School of Agriculture, University of the West Indies (Mona Campus). The AIS and Priory School offer international education.
Recruitment: CA, LECT, WCM.

Japan

Pop: 125.5 m   *Area*: 378,000 sq km
Japanese Embassy: 101-104 Piccadilly, London W1V 9FN. Tel: 0171 465 6500.
Ministry of Education: 3-2 Kasumigaseki, Chiyoda-ku, Tokyo.
British Council: 2 Kaguruzaka 1-Chome, Shinjuku-ku, Tokyo 162. Branches in Fukuoka, Kyoto, Nagoya, Osaka and Sapporo.

The Japanese authorities are keen to promote international contacts, and the Ministry of Education administers a scheme known as the Japan Exchange and Teaching Programme (JET). This is open to the nationals of most English-speaking countries and the agents of the scheme in the UK are CIEE. The scheme is limited to under-35s, and would suit an unattached graduate. Teaching qualifications, though desirable are not obligatory. What is required is an interest in TEFL and Japan. Most teachers are based in schools, but some may be assigned to the local education inspectorate. Japan has become a Mecca for foreign businessmen these days and as a consequence there are a good many international schools. Salaries tend to be high, but so is the cost of living. There are international schools in Fukuoka, Hiroshima, Kobe (three), Kyoto, Nagoya, Okinawa (two), Sapporo, Tokyo (nine), Yokohama (three).

Most of the 400 or so private language schools are Japanese owned and many have an American link. However Japan's economy has been faltering since the mid-nineties and this has led to the closure of several schools. The British Council has language schools in Kyoto, Osaka and Fukuoka, while in Tokyo they have gone into partnership with a Japanese whisky firm to run the Cambridge School of English. Opportunities exist, especially for TEFL teachers, in both the state and private universities. At one time many such posts offered security of tenure, but now universities only offer short term contracts, and there are now fewer opportunities for foreigners than previously.
Reference: *Directory of English Studies in Japan* (British Council, Tokyo).

Recruitment: BC, CA, CIEE, ECIS, ELT, EWW, Hilderstone, Linguarama, Methodist, Nord Anglia, SA, Saxoncourt, Skola.

Jordan

Pop: 4.1 m   *Area:* 98,000 sq km
Jordanian Embassy: 6 Upper Phillimore Gardens, London W8 7HB. Tel: 0171 937 3685.
Ministry of Education: PO Box 1646, Amman.
British Council: Rainbow Street, Jabal Amman, PO Box 434, Amman.

There are several English medium international schools in Amman including the American Community School, the Ammam Baccalaureate School, the International Community School, Mashrek International School and the New English School. English is the medium of instruction in the upper classes of some private secondary schools. Jordan has six state universities, including the Universities of Jordan (Amman), Yarmouk and Mo'ata, and there are a further eleven private universities. TEFL is the subject most in demand and the British Council has a language centre in Amman.
Recruitment: BC, ECIS, SA.

Kazakhstan

Pop: 16.5 m   *Area*: 2.7 sq km
Kazakhstan Embassy: 33 Thurloe Square, London SW7 2SD. Tel: 0171 581 4646.
Ministry of Education: Jambula 25, Almaty.
British Council: Ulitsa Panfilova 158/17, Almaty 480046.

This vast country, formerly part of the Soviet Union, boasts 68 HE sector institutions. The British Council organises TEFL seminars and workshops and is developing a new English textbook for schools. It runs teacher training courses and is planning to set up an English language teaching centre in the near future. There is a small AIS in Amaty.
Recruitment: BC, EEP.

Kenya

Pop: 30.5 m   *Area*: 583,000 sq km
Kenyan High Commission: 45 Portland Place, London W1N 4AS. Tel: 0171 636 2371/5.
Ministry of Education: PO Box 30040, Nairobi
British Council: ICEA Building, Kenyatta Avenue, PO Box 40751, Nairobi. Also in Kisumu and Mombasa.

The educational system comprises both government and government assisted schools. There are a number of international schools, including the International School and St Mary's School (both in Nairobi) which prepare pupils for the International Baccalaureate. Apart from the Universities of Nairobi, Moi, Kenyatta and Egerton there are three Polytechnics (Mombasa, Kenya and Eldoret), as well as the Jomo Kenyatta University of Agriculture and Technology. The British Council has a language centre in Nairobi and libraries in Kisumu and Mombasa. *Recruitment*: AIM, APSO, BC, DFID, ECIS, Church of Scotland, SA, VSO.

Kiribati

Pop: 80,000   *Area*: 861 sq km
Honorary Consulate: 7 Tufton Street, London SW1P 3QN. Tel: 0171 222 6952.
Ministry of Education: PO Box 263, Bikenibeu, Tarawa.
British High Commission: Tarawa.

Kiribat's 33 atolls are scattered over 5m sq km of sea, yet every inhabited atoll has at least one primary school. There is a Marine Training School at Tarawa, a Technical Institute at Betio and an extra-mural centre of the University of the South Pacific on South Tarawa.
Recruitment: British Council, VSO, WCM.

Korea, Democratic People's Republic (North Korea)

Pop: 23 m   *Area*: 121,000 sq km
Ministry of Education: Pyongyang.

Until recently N Korea was strongly isolationist. Now the country is trying to develop relations with the outside world, so there has been some relaxation. Whether that means there will be opportunities for expatriate teachers remains to be seen. English is a compulsory second language from the age of 14 onwards. If opportunities occur they are likely to be in the TEFL field, notably Pyongyang University.

Korea, Republic of (South Korea)

Pop: 44 m   *Area*: 99,000 sq km
Korean Embassy: 60 Buckingham Gate, London SW1E. Tel: 0171 227 5500.
Ministry of Education: 77-6 Sejong-no, Chongno-ku, Seoul.
British Council: Room 401, Anglican Church Annex, 3-7 Chung Dong, Choong-ku, Seoul.

The country's economy, which has made rapid strides in recent years, is now experiencing a downturn, and it is difficult to predict what impact this will have on teaching opportunities and when the situation will improve. Educational standards are high and in the past there has been a demand for foreign teachers, particularly in TEFL. There are three inter-

national schools in Seoul (British, Foreign, International) and one in
Taejon (Korea Christian Academy). Opportunities exist for TEFL
teachers at the Sogang University Language Institute, Korea Herald
Language Training Centre, Sisa Young-Ho-Sa, and numerous other lan-
guage institutes. The country boasts some 131 universities.
Recruitment: BC, SA, Saxoncourt.

Kuwait
Pop: 2 m   *Area*: 18,000 sq km
Kuwaiti Embassy: 2 Alberts Gate, London SW1X. Tel: 0171 590 3400.
Ministry of Education: PO Box 7, Safat, Hilali St.
British Council: 2 al Arabi Street, Mansouriyah, PO Box 345, 13001, Safat.

This oil state which for four decades has spent much of its wealth on
creating efficient social services and a good educational system seems to
have recovered from the trauma of the Gulf War. In view of the large
expatriate presence there are international schools at Fahaheel (The
English School), Jabriya, (New English School, Al-Bayan School — the
latter a bilingual English/Arabic school), Khaldiya (Universal American
School), Safat (Sunshine School), Salmiya (Kuwait English School),
Salwa (American School, Gulf English School), Surra (The English
School), Yarmuk (Modern School). Expatriates are also employed in
language schools, such as the Pitman School, and in tertiary institutions:
University of Kuwait; Teacher Training Institute, Commercial Institute,
Institute of Applied Technology, Clinical Institute. The social system is
highly conservative, and expatriates must take care not to offend local
sensibilities. The consumption of alcohol is forbidden by law.
Recruitment: BC; ELT, PACES, SA, WES.

Kyrgyzstan
Pop: 4.5 m   *Area*: 200,000 sq km
Ministry of Education: Tynystanova 257, 720040 Bishkek.
British Council: see Kazakhstan.

This former Soviet republic situated between Russia and China has
33 HE institutions, notably the Kyrgyz State University and the Kyrgyz
Russian University. The British Council is planning to extend its operations here in the near future. There is a small AIS in Bishkek.

Laos
Pop: 4.6 m   *Area:* 237,000 sq km
Lao Embassy: 74 ave Raymond Poincare, 75116 Paris.
Tel: 00 33 1 4553 0298.
Ministry of Education: Vientiane

Laos is beginning to open up again and there are foreign teachers again in this former French colony which has undergone so many upheavals during the past three decades. It has a university of medical science in Vientiane and ten other HE institutions. There is a small international school in Vientiane (PO Box 3180).
Recruitment: Concern, VSO.

Latvia
Pop: 2.5 m   *Area*: 65,000 sq km
Latvian Embassy: 45 Nottingham Place, London W1M 3FE. Tel: 0171 312 0040
Ministry of Education: Valnu Iela 2, Riga 1098.
British Council: Blaumana Iela 5a, Riga 1011.

Like Lithuania and Estonia the country is keen to improve EFL teaching. The British Council is involved in in-service teacher training and is managing a project to help teachers of other subjects to requalify as English teachers. There are British lecturers at the Liepaja Pedagogical University. Riga has a small international school.
Recruitment: BC, EEP.

Lebanon
Pop: 3 m   *Area*: 10,400 sq km
Lebanese Embassy: 21 Kensington Palace Gardens, London W8 4QM. Tel: 0171 229 7265.
Ministry of Education: Campus de l'Unesco, Beirut
British Embassy: Azar Building, Sidani Street, Ras Beirut, Beirut.

Formerly regarded as the cultural centre of the Arab world with the highest literacy rate, Lebanon is returning to normal after years of conflict. The British Council has a language centre in Beirut. There are eight universities, including the highly regarded American University of Beirut. The American Community School and the International School of Choueifat provide international education.
Recruitment: BC, SA.

Lesotho
Pop: 2.1 m   *Area*: 30,000 sq km
Lesotho High Commission: 7 Chesham Place, London SW1X 8HN. Tel: 0171 235 5686
Ministry of Education: PO Box 47, Maseru 100
British Council: Hobson's Square, PO Box 429, Maseru 100.

This landlocked country is surrounded by South Africa and enjoys

a mild climate. It has a high level of literacy, with much of the edu-
cation being provided by mission schools (Evangelical, Roman
Catholic and Anglican). There are international schools at Mafeteng
(Kingsgate High School), Maseru (Machabeng High School and
Maseru English Medium Preparatory School). The National
University of Lesotho at Roma (which once formed part of the
University of Botswana) has an international primary school taking
children till the age of 13.
Recruitment: AIM, APSO, BC, DFID, ECIS, SA, Skillshare.

Liberia
Pop: 2.8 m   *Area*: 111,000 sq km
Liberian Embassy: 2 Pembridge Place, London W2 4XB. Tel: 0171 221
1036.
Ministry of Education: PO Box 1545, Monrovia.
British Embassy: Mamba Point, PO Box 120, Monrovia (currently closed).

Liberia has been in turmoil for the past few years and this has had a
devastating effect on the educational system which used to be extensive.
When normality resumes there should be opportunities in the private
sector and at the international schools — the American Co-operative
School in Monrovia and the British Preparatory School. Science, maths
and technical subject specialists are most in demand, particularly at the
tertiary level which includes a College of Technology, a computer science institute, Cuttington Episcopalean University College and the
University of Monrovia.
Recruitment: VSO (but not currently).

Libya
Pop: 5.6 m   *Area*: 1.76 m sq km
Libyan Interests Section: Saudi Arabian Embassy, 119 Harley Street,
London W1. Tel: 0171 937 0925.
Secretariat of the General People's Committee for Education: Tripoli.
British Interests Section: Italian Embassy, PO Box 912, Sharia Uahran
1, Tripoli.

There are a large number of expatriates working in Libya — including British — as instructors with oil companies, sometimes out in the
field, and as teachers in the secondary and tertiary sector. The oil companies run two international schools for the children of their expatriate
staff: the English Community School at Marsa El Brega (Sirte Oil Co)
and the Oil Companies School, PO Box 860 Tripoli. Libya now boasts
six universities at Tripoli, Benghazi (two), Marsa Brega, Sebha and
Ajdabia.

Recruitment: Umm Al-Jawaby Oil Service Co Ltd, 15 Lodge Road, London NW8 8NX. Tel: 0171 266 4545.

Lithuania

Pop: 3.7 m   *Area*: 65,000 sq km
Lithuanian Embassy: 84 Gloucester Place, London W1H.
Tel: 0171 486 6401.
Ministry of Education: A Volano 2/7, Vilnius 2691.
British Council: Teachers Resource centre, Vilnaius 39/6, Vilnius 2001.
See also **Latvia**.

The country has five universities and there are expatriate TEFL lecturers at the Vilnius Pedagogical University. Vilnius has a small AIS. The British Council is supporting in-service teacher training and there are a number of flourishing private language schools.
Recruitment: EEP, EF, IH, Saxoncourt.

Luxembourg

Pop: 413,000   *Area*: 2,600 sq km
Luxembourg Embassy: 27 Wilton Crescent, London SW1X 8SD.
Tel: 0171 235 6961.
Ministry of Education: 6 boulevard Royal. L-2449 Luxembourg.

The education system of the Grand Duchy is a unique amalgamation of French and German curricula, since students go on to study at Belgian, French, German and Swiss universities. The Centre Universitaire with its multinational staff offers only a preliminary year of university studies (162a avenue de la Faiencerie). There is also an Institut Supérieur de Technologie, and Institut Supérieur d'Etudes Pédagogiques, and the European Institute for Information Management. There are two international schools: Ecole Européenne, Plateau de Kirchberg — for the children of EC bureaucrats; and the American School, 188 ave de la Faiencerie. There are also a number of private language schools, such as the International Language Centre and the English Language Centre.
Recruitment: DFEE, CB, ECIS, SA

Macedonia

Pop: 2 m   *Area*: 25,700 sq m
Macedonian Embassy: Suite 10, Harcourt House, 19A Cavendish Square, London W1M 9AD. Tel: 0171 499 5152.
Ministry of Education: 9 Ulica Veljko Vlahovic, 91000 Skopje.
British Council: British Information Centre, Bulevar Goce Delcev 6, PO Box 562, 91000 Skopje. See also **Yugoslavia**.

Once part of Yugoslavia, Macedonia seems to have avoided any conflict so far despite having minorities living within its borders. It has two universities – at Skopje and Bitola. Skopje has an AIS.
Recruitment: BC, EEP, IH.

Madagascar
Pop: 13 m   *Area*: 587,000 sq km
Madagascar Honorary Consulate: 16 Lanark Mansions, Pennard Road, London W12 8DT. Tel: 0181 746 0133.
Madagascar Embassy: 4 Avenue Raphael, 75016 Paris.
Ministry of Secondary and Basic Education: Anuso, Antananarivo.
Ministry of Higher Education: Tsimbazaza, Antananarivo.
British Embassy: First Floor, Immeuble Ny Havana, Cité de 67 Ha, BP 167, Antananarivo. (British Council: see **Mauritius**)
   The fourth largest island in the world received its independence from France in 1960. The educational system is basically French but the Malagasy language is being promoted these days. There are American schools at Antananarivo and Antsirabe. There is also a university with six regional centres.
Recruitment: AIM, AEF, WCM.

Malawi
Pop: 11 m   *Area*: 118,500 sq km
Malawi High Commission: 33 Grosvenor Street, London W1X 0DE. Tel: 0171 491 4172.
Ministry of Education: Private Bag 328, Capital City, Lilonge 3
British Council: Plot No 13/20, City Centre, PO Box 30222, Lilongwe 3. Also in Blantyre.
   A considerable number of foreign teachers work at schools in the public sector, including the prestigious Kamazu Academy for high-fliers, the 'Eton of Africa'. There is a particular demand for teachers of maths, science and technical subjects. The Embassy handles recruitment for technical schools. On arrival in the country the Ministry of Education arranges a six-week induction course for new teachers. Up to two-thirds of net earnings can be remitted out of the country. There are international schools at Blantyre (St Andrew's), Lilongwe (Bishop Mackenzie), Libe (Hillview Primary), Zomba (Sir Harry Johnston Primary). Among the tertiary level institutions are the University of Malawi, Chacellor College, Malawi Polytechnic, Bunda College and the Kamazu School of Nursing.
Recruitment: APSO, AEF, BC, Christians Abroad, Church of Scotland, Gabbitas, SA, VSO.

Malaysia

Pop: 21.3 m   *Area*: 330,000 sq km
High Commission: 45-46 Belgrave Square, London SW1X 8QT. Tel:
0171 491 4172.
Ministry of Education: Block J, Pusat Level 9, Bandar Damansara,
50604 Kuala Lumpur.
British Council: Jalan Bukit Aman, PO Box 10539, 50916 Kuala
Lumpur. Also in Kota Kinabalu, Kuching and Penang.

Malaysia — consisting of mainland Malaysia, Sarawak and Sabah is
a comparatively prosperous country. It is racially a very mixed country
with Malays in the majority and substantial Chinese, Indian and Dayek
communities. CFBT recruits TEFL teachers mainly for the secondary
sector. The British Council has its own language institutes in Kuala
Lumpur and Penang. There are international schools in the Cameroon
Highlands (Chefoo School), Kota Kinabalu (International), Kuala
Lumpur (Garden International, International) and Penang (Dalat, St
Christopher's, Uplands). The country boasts seven universities, four
polytechnics, 21 teacher training colleges. In addition there is a region-
al centre for science and mathematics teaching (RECSAM) in Penang.
Recruitment: BC, CFBT, ELT, SA.

Maldives

Pop: 225,000   *Area*: 298 sq km
Maldives High Commission: 22 Nottingham Place, London W1M 3FB.
Tel: 0171 224 2135.
Ministry of Education: Ghaazee Building, Ameer Ahmed Magu, Malé.
British Embassy: See **Sri Lanka**.

This Indian Ocean republic of 1,200 coral islands, most of them unin
habited, boasts a high literacy rate. It has three types of formal education: the traditional Koranic schools; Dhivehi medium primary schools;
and English medium primary and secondary schools. In addition, it has
a vocational training centre, a teacher training institute, a science education centre, an Islamic education centre, and institute of hotel and catering services and a centre for management and admininistration. The
Maldives Institute of Technical Education opened recently.
Recruitment: VSO.

Mali

Pop: 9.2 m   *Area*: 1.24 m sq km
Mali Embassy: Av Molière 487, 1060 Brussels. Tel: 00 32 2 345 7432
Ministry of National Education: BP 71, Bamako.

An extremely poor country with only 25% of its people receiving a

basic education. With assistance from agencies such as the World Bank and UNDP there is a drive to make education more vocationally oriented. Emphasis is being put on agricultural training and functional literacy programmes. There are five tertiary level institutions and an institute of higher studies where French is the teaching medium. There is an American International School in Bamako.
Recruitment: BC, SA.

Malta
Pop: 376,000   *Area*: 316 sq km
Malta High Commission: 36-38 Piccadilly, London W1V. Tel: 0171 292 4800.
Ministry of Education: Floriana CMR 02.
British Council: 7 St Anne Street, Floriana, VLT 15.

The country's substantial private education sector includes 80 Roman Catholic schools. International schools are St Edward's College and Verdala School, both in Cottonera. The main demand is for science, technical and commercial subject teachers. Malta also has a university and several English language schools catering for Continental Europeans.
Recruitment: SA.

Mauritania
Pop: 2.3 m   *Area*: 1 m sq km
Mauritanian Embassy: 5 rue de Montevideo, 75016 Paris. Tel: 00 33 1 4504 8854.
Ministry of Education: BP 183, Nouakchott.

With one of the lowest literacy rates in Africa and a largely nomadic population, Mauritania is struggling to improve its educational standards. There is an American international School at Nouakchott, and at the tertiary level there is the University of Nouakchott, the Ecole Nationale des Sciences, and the Ecole Nationale d'Administration.

Mauritius
Pop 1.1 m   *Area*: 2,000 sq km
Mauritius High Commission: 32 Elvaston Place, London SW7 5NW. Tel: 0171 581 0294.
Ministry of Education: New Government Centre, Port Louis.
British Council: Fondoon Building, Royal Road, PO Box 111, Rose Hill.

This prosperous Indian Ocean island with high educational standards appears to be largely self-sufficient in teachers. There is an international school — Alexandra House — in Vacoas and Le Bocage International

School at Moka. At the HE level there is the University of Mauritius, Mauritius Institute of Education and the Mahatma Gandhi Institute. *Recruitment*: AEF.

Mexico

Pop: 81 m   *Area*: 1.97 m sq km

Mexican Embassy: 43 Hertford Street, London W1Y 7TF. Tel: 0171 459 8568. Consulate: Halkin Street, London SW1X 7DW.

Ministry of Education: República de Argentina y Gonzales Obrégon 28, 06029 Mexico, DF.

British Council: Maestro Antonio Caso 127, Col San Rafael, Apdo Postal 30-588, Mexico 06470 DF. Also in Guadalajara.

Mexico has universal education at the primary level, as well as a high enrolment in secondary schools. There are American international schools in Durango, Guadalajara, Mexico City, Monterrey (two), Pachuca, Puebla, Queretaro and Torreon. Also in Mexico City are El Colegio Britanico and Greengates School. Among the language schools operating are those of the Anglo-Mexican Cultural Institute. There are 38 state universities which follow the American academic pattern, the most important being the Universidad Autónoma de México in Mexico City. In addition, there are 48 private universities.

Recruitment: BC, CB, EF, Saxoncourt, TA.

Moldova (Moldavia)

Pop: 4.4 m   *Area*: 33,700 sq km

Ministry of Education: Piata Marii Adunari Nationale 1, 2033 Chisinau.

British Council: See **Russia**.

This relatively poor country in the extreme south west corner of the former Soviet Union has substantial Russian and Ukrainian minorities. Teaching Abroad used to send teaching assistants here, but that programme has been discontinued. The British Council organises summer schools for English teachers.

Mongolia

Pop: 2.3 m   *Area*: 1.6 m sq km

Mongolian Embassy: 7 Kensington Court, London W8 5DL. Tel: 0171 937 5238.

Ministry of Education: Ulan Bator.

British Embassy: 30 Enkh Taivny Gudamzh, PO Box 703, Ulan Bator 13.

This central Asian republic has a developed educational system which includes one university and seven other higher education institutions.

Recruitment: BC, VSO, SA.

Morocco
Pop: 26 m   *Area*: 447,000 sq km
Moroccan Embassy: 49 Queen's Gate Gardens, London SW7 5NE. Tel: 0171 581 5001.
Ministry of Education: Quartier des Ministères, Rabat.
British Council: 36 rue de Tanger, BP 427, Rabat.

Education follows the French model and the teachers are nowadays largely Moroccan. However, there are still opportunities in the state system for foreigners. American International Schools flourish at Casablanca, Rabat and Tangier. The British Council has a language institute in Rabat, and there are a few commercial private schools of English, such as the International Language Centre, Rabat; the Tutor Centre, Agadir; and the English Institute, Casablanca. There are universities at Rabat, Fez, Casablance (two), Kenitra, Marrakesh, Oujda, Meknes, Tetnan and El Jadida and an English medium university at Ifrane.
Recruitment: BC, CB, Crosslinks, IH, SA.

Mozambique
Pop: 16 m *Area*: 801,590 sq km
Mozambique Embassy: 21 Fitzroy Square, London W1P 5HJ. Tel: 0171 383 3800.
Ministry of Education: Avda 24 de Julho 167, Maputo.
British Council: Rua John Issa, PO Box 4178, Maputo.

This former Portuguese colony is getting back on its feet after the disastrous civil war, and education is a top priority. Higher education is provided by the Eduardo Mondlane University, Maputo.
Recruitment: AEF, AIM, Church of Scotland, Concern, Skillshare.

Myanmar
See **Burma**

Namibia
Pop: 1.5 m   *Area*: 824,292 sq km
Namibian High Commission: 6 Chandos Street, London W1M 0LQ. Tel: 0171 636 6244.
Ministry of Education: Private Bag 13186, Windhoek.
British Council: 74 Bulow Strasse, PO Box 24224, Windhoek 9000.

Namibia, once a German colony and then administered by South Africa, is fully independent and taking important steps in adult literacy and primary education. It has four teacher training colleges and a university.
Recruitment: AIM, AEF, APSO, Skillshare, SPW, VSO.

Nepal

Pop: 20 m   *Area*: 141,000 sq km
Nepalese Embassy: 12a Kensington Gardens, London W8 4PQ. Tel: 0171 229 6231.
Ministry of Education: Kathmandu.
British Council: PO Box 640, Kathmandu.

There are a number of opportunities for foreign teachers in this Himalayan kingdom. The British government is supporting the Budhanilkantha School and there are also foreign lecturers at Tribhuvan University and the Campus of International Languages. VSO is involved with a UNICEF women's education project. Expatriate education is provided by the British Primary School and the Lincoln School in Kathmandu.
Recruitment: BC, ECIS, Church of Scotland, ECIS, Interserve, Methodist, SPW, VSO.

Netherlands

Pop: 15.4 m   *Area*: 41,000 sq km
Netherlands Embassy: 38 Hyde Park Gate, London SW7 5DP. Tel: 0171 590 3200.
Ministry of Education: Post Bus 25000, 2700 LZ Zoetermeer.
British Council: MD Keizersgracht 343, 1016 Amsterdam.

Foreign teachers not in possession of a Dutch qualification may have permission to teach as an unqualified teacher at the secondary level, but the employing school has to apply to the Inspector of Education for approval. The Foreign Countries and Minorities Branch (Information Division), Ministry of Education, Post Bus 25000, 2700 LZ Zoetermeer can provide further information. Vacancies are often advertised in *Het Weekblad voor Leraren bij het VWO en HAVO,* the weekly journal for secondary school teachers c/o Intermedia BV, Postbus 371, 2400 AJ Alphen aan de Rijn. The Netherlands has a large number of international schools including the EC School at Bergen, British Schools in Amsterdam and The Hague, and others in Amsterdam, Arnhem, Brunssum, Eindhoven, Groningen, Hilversum, Leiden, Maastricht, Ommen, Rotterdam, Vilsteren and Werkhoven. There are universities at Leiden, Utrecht, Groningen, Limburg, Rotterdam (Erasmus), Amsterdam (University of Amsterdam and Free University of Amsterdam), Nijmegen (Catholic University).

EU nationals should contact the local police for a residence permit within a week of their arrival if they intend to work for more than three months.
Recruitment: BC, CB, DFEE, ECIS, SCE, Linguarama, SA, Timeplan.

New Zealand

Pop: 3.7 m   *Area*: 269,000 sq km

New Zealand High Commission: New Zealand House, Haymarket, London SW1Y 4TQ. Tel: 0171 930 8422.

Department of Education: Private Bag, Wellington. Website: www.teachnz.govt.nz

British Council: c/o British High Commission, 44 Hill Street, PO Box 1812, Wellington 1.

New Zealand is currently experiencing a teacher shortage especially at the secondary school level, and immigration restrictions have been waived for well-qualified teachers who meet requirements. Teachers of maths, science, technology, computing and graphics are in particularly high demand. Timeplan acts as an agent in the UK for the New Zealand Ministry of Education. The academic year starts at the end of January. A teacher exchange scheme continues to operate. For information on opportunities in the private sector contact: Association of Heads of Independent Secondary Schools of NZ, PO Box 5028, Greenmeadows, Hawkes Bay. There are six universities (Auckland, Hamilton, Palmerston North, Wellington, Christchurch (two) and Dunedin); 22 technical institutes or community colleges, and six teachers colleges. Advertisements for vacancies appear regularly in the *THES*.

Reference: *Destination New Zealand* (Outbound); *New Zealand Outlook* (Consyl); *Newz New Zealand*, PO Box 247, Taurangi, NZ (vacancy pages from NZ newspapers); *How to Emigrate*; *Finding a Job in New Zealand* (How to Books).

Recruitment: ACU, LECT, Timeplan.

Nicaragua

Pop: 4.4 m   *Area*: 130,000

Nicaraguan Embassy: 36 Upper Brook Street, London W1Y 1PE. Tel: 0171 409 2536.

Ministry of Education: Apdo 108, Managua, JR.

British Embassy: Reparto Los Robles, Primera Etapa, Entrada Principal de la Carretera à Mano Derecho, Managua.

There are opportunities for volunteer teachers in this beautiful Central American state. In Managua there is an American-Nicaraguan School and the country boasts five universities. In order to get a visa the employing organisation must apply to the Ministry of External Co-operation for a technical visa to be issued by the Nicaraguan Embassy.

Recruitment: APSO.

Niger

Pop: 9.5 m   *Area*: 1.3 m sq km
Niger Embassy: 154 rue de Longchamp, 75116 Paris. Tel: 00 33 1 4504
8060.
Ministry of Education: Niamey.

The World Bank is involved in a number of educational projects in
Niger and the British Council provides an adviser to the Ministry of
Education. There is an American School in Niamey. Opportunities could
exist at the University of Niamey.
Recruitment: AP, BC, SIM.

Nigeria

Pop: 97 m   *Area*: 924,000 sq km
Nigerian High Commission: Nigeria House, 9 Northumberland Avenue,
London WC2 5BX. Tel: 0171 839 1244; Education Division, 180
Tottenham Court Road, London W1P 9LE.
Ministry of Education: 3 Moloney Street, Lagos.
British Council: 11 Kingsway Road, PO Box 3702, Ikoyi, Lagos. Also
in Enugu, Ibadan, Kaduna, Kano, Port Harcourt.

Nigeria has an extensive educational system, but because of expansion in the tertiary sector is by no means self-sufficient in teachers.
There are international schools in Ibadan, Jos, Kaduna and Lagos
(three). Nigeria has 50 HE insitutions and their recruitment is handled in
the UK by the Nigerian Universities Office in the Education Division of
the High Commission.
Recruitment: AP, BC, ECIS, Gabbitas, SIM, VSO.

Norway

Pop: 4.4 m   *Area*: 324,000 sq km
Norwegian Embassy: 25 Belgrave Square, London SW1X 8QD. Tel:
0171 235 7151.
Ministry of Education: PO Box 8119, 0032 Oslo
British Council: Fridtof Nansens Plass 5, 0160 Oslo 1.

It is not easy for a foreign teacher to find a full-time post in the
schools system, since knowledge of Norwegian is required. Moreover,
the country appears to be more than self-sufficient in teachers. Teaching
appointments are made by the local school board (skolestyre) in the case
of schools dealing with the 7-16 age group. The regional school board
(fylkesskolestyre) appoints teachers at the upper secondary level.
Tertiary institutions handle their own recruitment. There are international schools in Bergen, Oslo (American School, British School),
Stavanger (American School, British School) and Trondheim (Birralee).

TEFL teachers can find employment with language schools and two voluntary adult educational organisations: Studenteramfundets Friundervisning, Nedre Vollgt 20, Oslo 1; Arbeidernes Opplysningsforbund, Storgt. 23d, Oslo 1. Vacancies in Norwegian schools and colleges are advertised in Norsk Lysingsblat (Akersgt. 34, Oslo 1). Norway has four universities: Bergen, Oslo, Tromso, Trondheim.

Recruitment: BC, Inlingua, ECIS, SA.

Oman

Pop: 2.2 m   *Area*: 213,000 sq km
Embassy of the Sultanate of Oman: 167 Queen's Gate, London SW7 5HE. Tel: 0171 225 0001.
Ministry of Education: PO Box 3, Muscat 113.
British Council: Road One, Medinat Qaboos West, PO Box 73, PC 115, Muscat. Also in Soharand and Salalah.

Since the early seventies vast sums have been invested in the modernisation of the country, including education. There is a strong British influence here. A large number of instructors and TEFL teachers work with the armed forces, and there are several private language institutes in the main cities. Most of the positions are bachelor status ones. Education for expatriates is provided by the Muscat English Speaking School at Ruwi, while the Sultan's School at Seeb provides a bilingual education largely for Arab pupils. At the tertiary level there is a teacher training institute and a university has opened recently.

Recruitment: BC, CFBT, ECIS, EWW, IH, SA, Omani Embassy.

Pakistan

Pop: 130 m   *Area*: 796,000 sq km
Pakistan High Commission: 35 Lowndes Square, London SW1X 9JN. Tel: 0171 235 2044.
Ministry of Education: Block D, Pakistan Secretariat, Islamabad.
British Council: Block 14, Civic Centre G6, , PO Box 1135, Islamabad. Also in Karachi, Lahore and Peshawar.

Pakistan is more or less self-sufficient in teachers, but opportunities for expatriates exist in private schools run along British public school lines. There are international schools for the full age range at Islamabad, Karachi (American Society School), Lahore (American Society School), Murree (Christian School) and a British Primary School in Karachi. The British Council has a language centre in Karachi and there are universities in all the major cities including the private Lahore University of Management Sciences which employs expatriates.

Recruitment: BC, Church of Scotland, Gabbitas, Interserve, LECT, SIM, SA, VSO.

Panama
Pop: 2.3 m   *Area*: 77,000 sq km
Panamanian Embassy: 48 Park Street, London W1Y. Tel: 0171 493 4646.
Ministry of Education: Apdo 2440, Panama 3.
British Embassy: Torre Swiss Bank, Urb Marbella, Calle 53, Piso 4 & 5, PO Box 889, Panama City 1.

This small Central American state enjoys good educational standards. There are international schools in Balboa, Colon and Puerta Armuelles (Escuela Las Palmas).The state has three universities.
Recruitment: ECIS.

Papua New Guinea
Pop: 4 m   *Area*: 462,000 sq km
Papua New Guinea High Commission: 14 Waterloo Place, London SW1R 4AR. Tel: 0171 930 0922.
Ministry of Education: PSA Haus, Independence Drive, Waigani.
British High Commission: Kiroki Street, Waigani, PO Box 4778, Boroko, Port Moresby.

There is still a strong Australian influence in PNG, and Australia still contributes a generous amount of aid. The educational system is well developed in the main centre, less so in the remote rural areas. The International Education Agency of PNG operates 22 independent English medium international schools from pre-school upwards, including two secondary schools at Port Moresby and Lae. At the tertiary level there is the University of Papua New Guinea and the Papua New Guinea University of Technology.
Recruitment: ACU, ECIS, SA, VMM, VSO, Essential Development (PO Box 331, Crows Nest, NSW 2065, Australia).

Paraguay
Pop: 5 m   *Area*: 406,000 sq km
Paraguayan Embassy: Braemar Lodge, 51 Cornwall Gardens, London SW7 4AQ. Tel: 0171 937 1253.
Ministry of Education: Chilé, Humanita y Piribebuy, Asunción.
British Embassy: Calle Presidente Franco 706, PO Box 404, Asunción.

There are international schools in Asunción (American School, Christian Academy). Paraguay has two universities: the National University and the Catholic University, both in Asunción.
Recruitment: British Council, Central Bureau, SAMS, SA.

Peru

Pop: 24 m   *Area*: 1.3 m sq km
Peruvian Embassy: 52 Sloane Street, London SW1X 9SP. Tel: 0171 235 6867.
Ministry of Education: Parque Universitario s/n, Lima.
British Council: Calle Alberto Lynch 110, San Isidro, Lima 14.

Among the international schools are the Colegio Anglo-American Prescott, Arequipa; the Southern Peru Staff Schools, Ilo; the American School and the Sanata Margarita School, Markham College, Lima. The British Peruvian Cultural Institute tends to recruit its TEFL teachers locally. American Bi-national Centres teach English in nine cities and and there are a number of private language institutes. Peru has 28 state universities and 23 private universities. Despite stringent labour laws governing expatriates, there have been several instances of globe-trotters landing temporary teaching jobs. Salaries tend to be low.
Recruitment: British Council, Central Bureau, Crosslinks, SA, SIM.

Philippines

Pop: 70 m   *Area*: 300,000
Philippines Embassy: 9a Palace Green, London W8 4QR. Tel: 0171 937 1600; Consulate: 1 Cumberland House, Kensington High Street, London W8.
Ministry of Education: Palacio del Gobernador, General Luna Street, cnr Aduanda Street, Intramuros, Manila.
British Council: 7 3rd Street, New Manila, PO Box AC 168, Cubao, Quezon City, Metro Manila.

There is a strong American influence on the educational systems, with instruction in English and Pilipino right from the primary stage. International schools exist in Baguio City, Cebu City, Makati (Faith College), and Manila (British School, Casa Montessori Internationale, International School). English is widely spoken in the Philippines and as a consequence there are virtually no private language schools. Opportunities may exist in the University of the Philippines or the other 20 state and 49 private universities.
Recruitment: ECIS, VSO, SIM, SA, VSO.

Poland

Pop: 38.5 m   *Area*: 313,000 sq km
Polish Embassy: 47 Portland Place, London W1N 3AG. Tel: 0171 580 4324.
Cultural Institute: 34 Portland Place, London W1N 4HQ. Tel: 0171 636 6032.

Ministry of Education: 00-918 Warsaw, Al I Armii WP 25.

British Council: Al Jerozolimskie 59, 00-697 Warsaw.

There is a strong demand for TEFL in Poland and a number of private language schools have appeared in recent years. There are also TEFL opportunities in the state system, notably in the country's 12 universities and 30 polytechnics. Warsaw boasts a number of international schools including: American, American International, British, St Paul's British.

Recruitment: BC, Callan, CB, ECIS, EEP, EF, ELT, EWW, IH, Inlingua, Linguarama, Nord Anglia, SA, Saxoncourt.

Portugal

Pop: 10 m   *Area*: 92,000 sq km

Portuguese Embassy: 11 Belgrave Square, London SW1X 8PP. Tel: 0171 235-5331; Consulate: 62 Brompton Road, London SW3 1BJ. Tel: 0171 581 8722.

Ministry of Education: Av 5 de Outubro 107, 1000 Lisbon.

British Council: Rua de Sao Marcal 174, 1294 Lisbon Codex. Also in Cascais, Coimbra, Oporto, Parede.

Portugal has a number of international schools on the Algarve (International School, Colegio Internacional de Vilamoura); in Lisbon (AIS, St Anthony's, St Dominic's, St George's School, St Julian's School); in Loulé (Prince Henry); in Oporto (British). There are also a few schools with only a primary section. The main TEFL opportunities would appear to be in the language school sector. The British Council has its own teaching operations in Lisbon and Coimbra and the British Institute in Oporto has a British Council connection. Among the private languages institutes are the Cambridge School and the Central School of Languages. Among the HE institutions are the Universities of Coimbra (established 1290), Porto, Aveiro, Minho, Evora, Azores and five universities in Lisbon (Technical, Catholic, New University, Free University, University of Lisbon).

Recruitment: BC, Crosslinks, ECIS, ELT, IH, SA.

The Portuguese possession of **Macao** (pop: 425,000), which reverts to China in 1999, is home to the international University of East Asia. For further details contact: Macao Govt Information Service, Rua de S Domingos 1, CP 706, Macao.

Qatar

Pop: 540,000   *Area*: 11,000 sq km

Qatar Embassy: 30 Collingham Gardens, 27 Chesham Place, London SW1X 8HG. Tel: 0171 370 6871.

Ministry of Education: Doha.
British Council: 93 Al Sadd Street, PO Box 2992, Doha.

There are plenty of opportunities principally for TEFL teachers in this small oil state, where only one-fifth of the population is actually Qatari. Expatriates (both Arab and European) teach at the secondary level, at the Language Teaching Institute, the Higher Teacher Training College and the University of Qatar. The Doha College for English Speaking Students (PO Box 7506) is an international secondary school. There are two primary schools for expatriates — the English Speaking School and the Independent School, both in Doha.
Recruitment: BC, PACES, SA.

Romania

Pop: 23 m   *Area*: 237,500 sq km
Romanian Embassy: 4 Palace Green, London W8 4QD. Tel: 0171 937 9666.
Ministry of Education: Str. Gen Berthelot 28-30, 70663 Bucharest.
British Council: Calea Dorobalintor 14, Bucharest.

Poverty-stricken Romania is anxious to make progress in TEFL and there are a number of voluntary organisations attempting to cope with demand. The country boasts nineteen universities at Iasi, Bucharest, Cluj, Timisora, Craiova, Brasov and elsewhere and sixteen specialist HE institutions. There is an American school in Bucharest.
Recruitment: BC, CB, EEP, IH, Linguarama.

Russia

Pop: 150 m   *Area*: 17,075,000 sq km
Russian Embassy: 18 Kensington Palace Gardens, London W8 4QX. Tel: 0171 229 6412.
Ministry of Education: Christoprudny Bul 6, Moscow.
British Council: Biblioteka Inostrannoi Literaturi, Ulitsa Nikolo-Yamskaya 1, Moscow 109189.

Politically and educationally this is a time of tremendous change. A number of private educational organisations are involved in TEFL and business training, some of it funded by the British government's Knowhow Fund. There are international schools operating in Moscow (Anglo-American, British International, Moscow International), St Petersburg (Anglo-American) and Vladivostok (International).
Recruitment: BC, CB, ECIS, EEP, EF, ELT, EWW, IH, I to I, Linguarama, OPU, SA, Saxoncourt, TA.

Rwanda

Pop: 7.4 m   *Area*: 26,000 sq km
Rwandan Embassy: 1 Avenue des Fleurs, Woluwe St Pierre, Brussels 1150. Tel: 00 32 2 863 0702.
Ministry of Education: BP 622, Kigali.
British Embassy: Parcelle 1017, Kimihururu, Kigali.

This former Belgian trust territory has been beset by conflict in recent years and its educational system badly disrupted. At one time the World Bank was assisting with the expansion of primary education. At the tertiary level the National University of Rwanda has campuses at Butari and Ruhengeri. Other tertiary institutions are the Institut Pédagogique, the Grand Seminaire, and the Ecole Supérieur Militaire.
Recruitment: MAM

St Helena (Atlantic)

Pop: 5,700   *Area*: 300 sq km
Dependencies: Ascension Island (Pop: 1,100); Tristan da Cunha (Pop: 300).
Government Offices: The Castle, Jamestown.

The island of St Helena boasts eight primary schools, three senior schools and one selective secondary school, and has around 71 full-time teachers. The Prince Andrew School offers vocational courses. On Ascension Island there are local schools as well as one run by Cable and Wireless for the children of its expatriate employees. Both Tristan da Cunha and St Lucia are somewhat isolated with no airlink with the outside world.
Recruitment: DFID.

St Kitts and Nevis (Caribbean)

Pop: 43,350   *Area*: 262 sq km
Easter Caribbean Commission: 10 Kensington Court, London W8 5DL. Tel: 0171 937 9522.
Ministry of Education: Cayon Street, PO Box 333, Basseterre.

Situated at the northern end of the Leeward Islands the two islands have a technical college, a teachers' training college and an extra-mural department of the University of the West Indies.
Recruitment: VSO.

St Lucia (Caribbean)

Pop: 141,000   *Area*: 616 sq km
Eastern Caribbean Commission: 10 Kensington Court, London W8 5DL. Tel: 0171 937 9522.

Ministry of Education: Laborie Street, Castries.
British High Commission: NIM Building, Waterfront, Castries.

St Lucia, the second largest of the Windward Islands, has a further education college and a branch of the University of the West Indies at Morne Fortune.

Recruitment: VSO.

St Vincent and The Grenadines (Caribbean)

Pop: 110,000   *Area*: 388 sq km

Eastern Caribbean Commission: 10 Kensington Court, London W8 5DL. Tel: 0171 937 9522.

Ministry of Education: Government Buildings, Kingstown

Most of the secondary schools are run by religious organisations with government assistance. St Vincent has a technical college and a teacher training college.

Recruitment: VSO.

Saudi Arabia

Pop: 17 m   *Area*: 2.15 m sq km

Royal Saudi Arabian Embassy: 30 Charles Street, London W1X 7PM. Tel: 0171 917 3000. Educational Office: 29 Belgrave Square, London SW1X 9QB. Tel: 0171 245 6481.

Ministry of Education: PO Box 3734, Airport Road, Riyadh.

British Council: Olaya Main Road, Al Mousa Centre, Tower B, 3rd Floor. PO Box 58012, Riyadh 11594. Branches in Jeddah, Damman and Jubail.

Saudi schools segregate the sexes at all levels of the state education-al system. There are openings for male TEFL teachers, mainly in the pri-vate sector. There are Saudi Arabian International Schools at Al Khobar, Dhahran, Jeddah, Jubail and Riyadh. Other international schools cater-ing for expatriates are: Aramco Schools (Dhahran); Continental School, Jeddah Preparatory School (Jeddah); International School (Yanbu). Foreign teachers are also used at the university level, and here there are a few opportunities for women. The country's universities are: King Abdul Aziz, Jeddah — with a branch at Taif; King Saud, Riyadh — with branches at Abha and Qaseem; King Feisal, Dammam and Hofuf; University of Petroleum and Minerals, Dhahran. The British Council operates its own language institutes and there are a number of private sector language schools as well. Foreign companies are often required to run training programmes for their Saudi staff. ARAMCO and British Aerospace are the leaders in this respect, but Saudi Airlines and hospi-tal management companies also run such programmes. Ministries, such as the Foreign Ministry, also need expatriate teachers, notably TEFL experts.

Saudi Arabia is a very conservative Muslim society, where one must take care not to give offence. European women do not have to cover their faces now, but they are expected to cover everything else. They are not allowed to drive cars. Alcohol is forbidden and opportunities to mix with the locals are very rare. Teachers are well paid, but most of the posts are bachelor status ones. Employers are responsible for obtaining work permits, etc. Among the documents you will probably have to produce is a baptismal certificate and certification that you do not suffer from AIDS.

Recruitment: British Aerospace, BC, Crown Agents, ECIS, EWW, PACES, SA, WES.

Senegal
Pop: 8 m   *Area*: 196,000 sq km
Senegalese Embassy: Norway House, 21-24 Cockspur Street, London SW1 5BN. Tel: 0171 930 7606.
Ministry of Education: BP 699, Dakar.
British Embassy: BP 6025, 30 rue du Docteur Guillet, Dakar.
British Council: 34-36 Blvd de la République, BP 6232, Dakar.

Education is based on the French system, but modified to cope with the country's present day needs. The Central Bureau recruits assistants for lycées and the British Senegalese Institutes. The American Cultural Centre and the Centre de Perfectionnement en Langue Anglaise also employ foreign TEFL teachers. International education is provided by two small establishments: the Dakar Academy (BP 3189) and the International School (c/o US Embassy) At the tertiary level there is the University of Dakar, a second university at St Louis, the Ecole Polytechnique at Thies and a Regional Management School for CEAO member states.

Recruitment: APSO, BC, CB, SIM.

Seychelles
Pop: 74,000   *Area*: 308 sq km
Seychelles High Commission: 2nd Floor, 111 Baker Street, London W1M 1FE. Tel: 0171 224 1660.
Ministry of Education: PO Box 48, Mont Fleuri.
British High Commission: Victoria House, PO Box 161, Victoria, Mahé.

Education is based on the British comprehensive system. Crown Agents recruit around ten teachers a year for government schools.

There is an International School at Victoria (PO Box 315). The islands also boast a polytechnic, technical college and a teacher training college. *Recruitment*: AIM, DFID.

Sierra Leone
Pop: 4.5 m   *Area*: 72,000 sq km
Sierra Leone High Commission: 33 Portland Place, London W1N 3AG. Tel: 0171 636 6483.
Ministry of Education: New England, Freetown.
British Council: Tower Hill, PO Box 124, Freetown.

The conflicts within the country now seem to be at an end which means that there should be a return to normality. There is an AIS in Freetown, and the Kabala Rupp Memorial School in Kabala. There are four teacher training colleges and the University of Sierra Leone which has three constituent parts: Fourah Bay College, Njala University College and the Institute of Education.
Recruitment: ACU, VSO.

Singapore
Pop: 3 m   *Area*: 581 sq km
Singapore High Commission: 9 Wilton Crescent, London SW1X 8SA. Tel: 0171 235 8315.
Ministry of Education: Kay Siang Road, Singapore 1024.
British Council: 30 Napier Road, Singapore 1025.

This prosperous island state is determined to improve educational standards, which are already high, especially in English teaching. English tends to be the medium of instruction in schools. The High Commission recruits teachers for both the secondary and the tertiary level. The international education sector is represented by the United World College of SE Asia, International School and the American School as well as some primary establishments. Tertiary level institutions include the National University of Singapore, Nanyang Technological Institute, Singapore Polytechnic, Ngee Ann Polytechnic, Institute of Education.
Recruitment: ACU, BC, IH, Contact Singapore (Charles House, Lower Ground Floor, 5-11 Regent Street, London SW1Y 4LR).

Slovakia
Pop: 4 m   *Area*: 49,000 sq km.
Slovak Embassy: 25 Kensington Palace Gardens, London W8 4QY. Tel: 0171 243 0803.
Ministry of Education: Hlboka 2, 813 30 Bratislava.

British Council: PO Box 68, Panska 17, 81499 Bratislava.

The eastern and less prosperous part of what was formerly Czechoslovakia employs a number of foreign teachers in its universities, teacher training colleges and bilingual schools. Private language schools are much in evidence. There are two international schools in Bratislava run along American lines.

Recruitment: BC, EEP, Nord Anglia.

Slovenia

Pop: 2 m   *Area*: 20,256 sq km

Slovenian Embassy: Suite 1, Cavendish Court, 11-15 Wigmore Street, London W1H 9LA. Tel: 0171 495 7775.

Ministry of Education: Zupanciceva 6, 61000 Ljubljana.

British Council: Stefanova 1/III, 61000 Ljubljana.

The most westerly and most prosperous of the former Yugoslav republics has universities at Ljubljana and Maribor. Ljubljana has an international school.

Recruitment: BC.

Solomon Islands

Pop: 350,000   *Area*: 28,000 sq km

Honorary Consulate: 17 Springfield Road, London SW19 7AL. Tel: 0171 946 5552.

Ministry of Education: PO Box 584, Honiara.

British High Commission: Telkon House, Mendana Avenue, Honiara.

The islands boast a teachers' college, Honiara Technical Institute, and the Honiara Centre of the University of the Pacific. Woodford International School is also situated in Honiara.

Recruitment: DFID, VSO.

Somalia

Pop: 8 m   *Area*: 637,000 sq km

Somali Embassy: 60 Portland Place, London W1N 3DG. Tel: 0171 580 7148 (closed).

Ministry of Education: POB 1182, Mogadishu.

British Embassy: POB 1036 Mogadishu (closed).

Somalia has been in a state of turmoil for years and very little education is taking place. Even in normal times enrolments are low: 25% receive primary education; 8% attend secondary school. In addition, the government runs ten training centres for nomads. There are two teacher training colleges and the University of Mogadishu when it is functioning.

Recruitment: BC, Concern, ECIS.

South Africa

Pop: 41.5 m   *Area*: 1.2 m sq km
South African High Commission: South Africa House, Trafalgar Square, London WC2N 5DP. Tel: 0171 930 4488.
Department of National Education: Private Bag X603, Shoeman Street, Magister Building, Pretoria 0001.
British Council: 76 Juta Street, PO Box 30637, Braamfontein 2017. Also in Cape Town and Durban.

Since the advent of majority rule the state educational system has been reorganised with a view to improving standards for all pupils. Primary and secondary education is the responsibility of the nine provincial governments: Eastern Cape, Free State, Gauteng, Kwazulu-Natal, Mpumalanga, Northern Cape, Northern Province, North West and Western Cape. Outside the state system there is a substantial private school sector which is more likely to recruit staff from abroad. Contact the following for further details: The Independent Schools Council, 31 David Road, Houghton 2196; The Catholic Institute of Education, PO Box 93239, Yeoville 2143; The SA Board of Jewish Education, PO Box 46204, Orange Grove 2119. Opportunities exist especially for specialists in science, maths, business and technical subjects at all levels of the educational system as the regime seeks to train up people from rural areas and the former homelands who are flocking into the urban areas. South Africa boasts 22 universities and 15 technikons (institutes of technology and commerce). There are American International Schools in Capetown and Johannesburg.

Reference: *South Africa News* (Outbound Newspapers).
Recruitment: AEF, APSO, BC, ECIS, ELT, LECT, SA, Skillshare, VMM, VSO, South African High Commission, Timeplan.

Spain

Pop: 40.5 m   *Area*: 505,000 sq km.
Spanish Embassy: 39 Chesham Place, London SW1X 8QA. Tel: 0171 235 5555.
Spanish Institute: 102 Eaton Square, London SW1. Tel: 0171 235 1485.
Consulates: 20 Draycott Place SW3; 21 Rodney Rd, Liverpool L1 9EF; 70 Spring Gardens, Manchester M2 2BQ.
Ministry of Education: Alcal 34, 28071 Madrid.
British Council: Paseo del General Martinez, Campos 31, 28010 Madrid. Also in Barcelona, Bilbao, Las Palmas, Murcia, Mallorca, Salamanca, Segovia, Seville, Valencia.

Until recently opportunities in state secondary schools tended to be restricted to exchange assistantships. However, the range of international schools is extensive. Such schools exist in Alicante, Barcelona (six), Bilbao, Cadiz, the Canary Islands (three), Ibiza (one), Madrid (eleven), Mallorca (five), Marbella (two), Sotogrande, Torremolinos and Valencia (two). The National Association of British Schools, Runnymede College, Arga 9, 1 Viso, Madrid 2 can provide further information. There are unlimited opportunities for TEFL teachers in Spain. The British Council has its own language institutes in Madrid, Barcelona, Valencia and Granada, and there are a number of institutes affiliated to English language teaching organisations. The British Council produces a list of these. Other opportunities exist in the tertiary sector. Since Spain is an EU member, EU nationals may work for three months without such a permit.

Recruitment: BC, Callan, CB, ELT, EWW, IH, Inlingua, Linguarama, SA, Saxoncourt, Skola, Timeplan.

Sri Lanka

Pop: 18.5 m   *Area*: 65,600 sq km
Sri Lankan High Commission: 13 Hyde Park Gardens, London W2 2LU. Tel: 0171 262 1841.
Ministry of Education and Higher Education: Isurupaya, Pelawatta, Battaramulla.
British Council: 49 Alfred House Gardens, PO Box 753, Colombo 3. Also in Kandy.

Although there has been conflict in Sri Lanka in recent years the country has always prided itself on its high levels of literacy. There are two international schools in Sri Lanka: Colombo International School and the Overseas Children's School in Battaramulla. Sri Lanka has eight universities: at Colombo, Peradinya, Jaffna, Sri Jayaawardenepura, Morutawa, Kelaniya and Ruhina. In addition there is an Open University and the University College of Baticaloa.

Recruitment: BC, ECIS, I to I, SA, VSO.

Sudan

Pop: 29 m   *Area*: 2.5 m sq km
Sudanese Embassy: 3 Cleveland Row, London SW1A 1DD. Tel: 0171 839 8080.
Ministry of Education: Khartoum.
British Council: 14 Abu Sinn Street, PO Box 1253, Khartoum East.

Sudan's education system, which was once one of the most advanced in Africa, has declined in recent years as a result of civil war, the withdrawal of British educators and the policy of Arabicisation introduced in the 1960s. The government recognises the importance of English in the development of the country, and in the mid-seventies introduced its own ELT scheme, for which the Embassy carried out recruitment. This scheme seems to have lapsed. In the past the British Council recruited for posts in the Ministry of Education and in teacher training. There are universities at Khartoum (two), Juba, Gezira Ondurman (three) and Wadi Medani. Khartoum also has a University of Science and Technology. English is the language of instruction in the south, and here a number of missionary agencies are active. There is an American School in Khartoum.

Recruitment: AIM, AP, BC, Concern, Christians Abroad, SIM, VMM, VSO.

Surinam

Pop: 407,000   *Area*: 163,000 sq km
Surinam Embassy: 2 Alexander Gogelweg, The Hague. Tel: The Hague: 00 31 70 365 0844.
Ministry of Education: Sumnel Kaffiludistraat 117-123, Paramaribo.

In this former Dutch colony in South America education was made compulsory between the ages of 6 and 12 back in 1878. It is a modified version of the Dutch system. There may be teaching opportunities at the University of Surinam in Paramaribo.

Swaziland

Pop: 908,000   *Area*: 17,000 sq km
Swaziland High Commission: 58 Pont Street, London SW1X 0AE. Tel: 0171 581 4976/7/8.
Ministry of Education: PO Box 39, Mbabane
British Council: c/o British High Commission, Alister Miller Street (Private Bag), Mbabane.

With an 85% enrolment at the primary level, Swaziland's education-al system is more impressive than those of many of its neighbours to the north. There are teaching opportunities in all subjects, including agri-culture. The capital Mbabane is home to the Waterford Kamhlaba United World College of Southern Africa and the Sifundzani International School. Tertiary level education is provided by the University of Swaziland (with campuses at Luyengo and Kwaluseni), Swaziland College of Technology and the Institute of Management and Public Administration.

Recruitment: AEF, APSO, BC, DFID, ECIS, SA, Skillshare.

Sweden

Pop: 8.9 m   *Area*: 459,000 sq km

Swedish Embassy: 11 Montagu Place, London W1H 2AL. Tel 0171 917 6400.

Ministry of Education: Mynttorget 1, 103 33 Stockholm.

British Council: Skarpogarton 6, Box 27819, 115 93 Stockholm.

In the past it has not been possible for a non-Swede to work in a Swedish state school except under an exchange scheme. However TEFL teachers are required for the adult folk universities which now do their own recruitment and sometimes for secondary schools as well. For information on posts at folk universities contact Folkuniversytet, Rehnsgatan 20, Box 7845, S-103 98 Stockholm. Tel: 00 46 8 789 4100. There are 37 university level institutions and for university posts it is best to apply direct to the university concerned. Opportunities abound in the international school sector. The main ones are: SSHL, IB-linjen, Box 8, S-193 00, Sigtuna; International School of Stockholm. Johannesgatan 18, S111 38 Stockholm; The British Primary School, Östra Valhallavägen 17, S-182 62 Djursholm; The English Junior School, Lilla danskavägen 1, S-412 74, Göteborg;

Recruitment: CB, SA.

Switzerland

Pop: 6.5 m   *Area*: 41,300 sq km

Swiss Embassy: 16-18 Montagu Place, London W1H 2BQ. Tel 0171 723 0701.

British Council: British Embassy: Sennweg, Berne 9.

Many are attracted to live and work in Switzerland, but few are chosen. State schools are the responsibility of each canton, and usually the only way into one is under an exchange scheme. The private school sector is normally overwhelmed with applications. The private schools have an association: Verband schweizersicher Privatschulen, Zeughausgasse 29, Postfach 3367, 3000 Bern 7. There are international schools and colleges galore: Basel (International); Berne (English International, International); Château d'Oex (Institut Alpin); Chesières-Villars (Aiglon College); Crans-Montana (International); Geneva (Collège du Léman, International, English); Gstaad (John F Kennedy); Hasliberg-Goldern (Ecole d'Humanité); Lausanne (Commonwealth-American, Brillantmont, Ecole Nouvelle, Inst. Dr Schmidt, Château Mont-Choisi, Le Rosey); Leysin (American); Lugano (American); Montreux (Château Beau-Cèdre, Inst. Monte Rosa, St George's); Neuchâtel (Junior, Inst. auf dem Rosenberg); Zug (American); Zürich (AIS, Inter-Community, Int'l Primary).

The restrictive immigration policy of the Swiss Government has made it difficult for foreigners to obtain residence permits with a view to taking up employment. Switzerland is not a member of the European Union. However, there are opportunities in language schools and HE. Switzerland has seven universities: Basel, Berne, Fribourg, Geneva, Lausanne, Neuchâtel and Zürich plus five other HE institutions.

Recruitment: BC, CB; ECIS, IH, SA, Timeplan.

Syria

Pop: 14.6 m   *Area*: 185,000 sq km

Syrian Embassy: 8 Belgrave Square, London SW1 8PH. Tel 0171 245 9012.

Ministry of Education: Damascus.

British Council: Abu Rumaneh, Rawda, Masr Street, Hasibi/Azem Building, PO Box 33105, Damascus.

There are two international schools of note: the Community School in Damascus and the ICARDA International School in Aleppo which serves the children of expatriates working at this research centre. The British Council has a language institute at Damascus, and there are some 25 schools offering evening classes in English. There are universities at Aleppo, Damascus, Lataki, Homs and Tishrin.

Recruitment: BC, ECIS, SA.

Taiwan (Republic of China)

Pop: 20 m   *Area*: 36,000 sq km

Taipei Representative Office in UK: 50 Grosvenor Gardens, London SW1. Tel: 0171 396 9152.

Ministry of Education: 5 Chungshan South Road, Taipei 100.

British Council: 7th Floor, Fu Key Building, 99 Jen Al Road, Section 2, Taipei 10625.

This dynamic island offers opportunities for foreign teachers especially at its international schools at Hsinchu (International), Taichung (Morrison Academy) and Taipei (Dominican Academy, American School, British School). Taiwan has many private language schools and some 28 tertiary institutions, notably the National Taiwan University, 1 Roosevelt Rd IV, Taipei.

Recruitment: Church of Scotland, SA, Saxoncourt.

Tajikistan

Pop: 6 m   *Area*: 143,000 sq km

Ministry of Education: Dunshanbe.

British Council: See Turkey: Ankara.

This landlocked state in the SE corner of the former Soviet Union has a university at Khojand and a Russian Tajik Slavonic University at Dunshanbe.

Tanzania

Pop: 30 m   *Area*: 945,000 sq km
Tanzanian High Commission: 43 Hertford Street, London W1Y 7TF. Tel: 0171 499 8951.
Ministry of Education: PO Box 9100, Dar es Salaam.
British Council: Ohio Street/Samora Avenue, PO Box 9100, Dar es Salaam.

Since independence Tanzania has striven hard to adapt its educational system to suit local conditions with mixed success. Seventy per cent of children attend primary school, and the numbers in secondary schools are increasing. There are a number of international schools including: Arusha International, Arusha; International, Dar es Salaam; Canon Andrea Mwaka, Dodoma; Morogoro International Primary School; International School, Moshi; Victoria Primary School, Mwanza. In HE there may be opportunities at the University of Dar es Salaam, Sokoine University of Agriculture or the nine other HE institutions.
Recruitment: APSO, AEF, AIM, BC, Concern, Crosslinks, ECIS, LECT, SA, SPW, VSO, VMM.

Thailand

Pop: 57 m   *Area*: 514,000 sq km
Royal Thai Embassy: 30 Queen's Gate, London SW7 5JB. Tel: 0171 589 2944.
Ministry of Education: Rajdamnern Avenue, Bangkok.
British Council: 254 Chulalongkorn Soi 64, Siam Square, Phyathai Road, Bangkok 10330.

Generally speaking Thailand is self-sufficient in teachers and lecturers, where the medium of instruction is normally Thai. However, opportunities exist for TEFL specialists in secondary education and for contract teachers in higher education and in language institutes. International education is provided along British lines by the Bangkok Patana School and the Traill Preparatory School. There are other international schools in Bangkok (including the American International, New International, Ruam Rudee, St John's), in Chiengmai (Lanna International) and Rayong (Garden International). Dulwich College and Harrow have set up British type schools for Thais on Phuket and in Nonthaburi north of Bangkok. Thailand has twenty state universities including twelve in Bangkok — notably Chulalongkorn, Medical Science, Fine Arts, Ramkhamhaeng, Kasetsart and Thammasart in Bangkok. Chiengmai, Khonkhaen and

Songkhla are the leading universities in the provinces. The international Asian Institute of Technology north of Bangkok has a substantial expatriate staff. The British Council has language teaching centres in Bangkok and Chiengmai.

Recruitment: Bell, BC, Concern, ECIS, ELT, OPU, SA, Saxoncourt, VSO, WES.

Togo

Pop: 4 m   *Area*: 57,000 sq km
Ministry of Education: BP 12175, Immeuble des Quatre Ministères, rue Colonel de Roux, Lomé.
British Consulate: BP 20050, Lomé.

Togo was originally a German colony and was held up as a model. Nowadays around 75% of the population receives a primary education, one of the highest rates in West Africa.

Half of the schools are mission establishments. Self-help is encouraged and local communities often build their own primary schools. The World Bank has helped establish two teacher training colleges and the National Institute of Agricultural Training. HE is provided by the University of Bénin at Lomé, where there are TEFL opportunities. There is an American school and the Togo British School providing international education in the capital.

Recruitment: BC, SA.

Tonga

Pop: 104,000   *Area*: 700 sq km
Tonga High Commission: 36 Molyneux Street, London W1H 6AB. Tel: 0171 724 5828.
Ministry of Education: PO Box 61, Nuku'alofa, Tonga.
British High Commission: PO Box 56, Vuna Road, Nuku'alofa.

There are a number of foreign teachers in these South Pacific islands at all levels, with science, maths, technical and business subjects being most in demand. The University of the South Pacific has an extension centre here and Tonga boasts a teacher training college and three technical institues.

Recruitment: VSO.

Trinidad and Tobago

Pop: 1.3 m   *Area*: 5,000 sq km
Trinidad and Tobago High Commission: 42 Belgrave Square, London SW1X 8NY. Tel: 0171 245 9351.
Ministry of Education: Hayes Street, St Clair, Port of Spain.

British Council: c/o British High Commission, 19 St Clair Avenue, St Clair, PO Box 778, Port of Spain.

A prosperous republic with a well developed educational system. St Andrew's School and Bishop Anstey Junior School, both in Port of Spain, offer an international curriculum. HE institutions include the East Caribbean Farm Institute, the Polytechnic Institute and the Trinidad campus of the University of the West Indies at St Augustine.

Recruitment: ACU, LECT.

Tunisia

Pop: 9 m   *Area*: 164,000 sq km

Tunisian Embassy: 29 Prince's Gate, London SW7 1QG. Tel: 0171 584 8117.

Ministry of Education: Place de la Kasbah, Tunis.

British Council: 5 Place de la Victoire, Tunis.

As a consequence of a strong interest in learning English in this former French North African colony a Lycée Pilote has been set up by the Ministry of Education, in which science subjects are taught through the medium of English. An assistantship exchange scheme is in operation at the secondary level, and other opportunities in TEFL may occur at the University of Tunis, notably the Institut Bourguiba des Langues Vivantes. Monastir and Sfax also have universities. There is a small American Co-operative School in Tunis with an international clientele.

Recruitment: BC, CB.

Turkey

Pop: 63 m   *Area*: 780,000 sq km

Turkish Embassy: 43 Belgrave Square, London SW1X 8PA. Tel: 0171 393 0202. Consulate: Rutland Lodge, Rutland Gardens, London SW7. Tel: 0171 589 0949.

Ministry of Education: Milli Eğitim Bakanliği, Ankara

British Council: Kirlangic Sokak 9, Gazi Osman Pasa, 06700 Ankara; Ors Turistik Is Merkezi, Istiklal Caddesi 251/253, Beyoğlu, 80060 Istanbul.

Over the past fifteen years there has been a boom in English teaching in Turkey at all levels from primary to adult, especially in Istanbul, Izmir and Ankara, because of the trend towards bilingual 'Anatolian' schools (using both Turkish and English as the medium of instruction) and English medium courses at universities. A large number of private 'Anatolian' schools have been set to cope with demand, while other established private schools (recognisable by the prefix 'özel') have gone over to the 'Anatolian' system, which usually involves an initial year of intensive

English. Among the leading ones are Moda, Tarhan, Marmara, Robert College, Üsküdar American Academy, British International. Science and maths teachers are also required. Salaries tend to be lower than in the UK, but so is the cost of living. The 54 state and private universities employ a sizeable number of foreign teachers, mostly in TEFL. A number of private language schools are flourishing in the main centres, but the schools run by the ITBA in Istanbul and the IBA in Ankara are the most prestigious. These are independent foundations with British Council links. The British Council in Istanbul keeps a list of language schools and 'Anatolian' schools in Western Turkey, and its counterpart in Ankara has information for the rest of the country. Several schools advertise for staff in the *TES*. The recruitment process can be a lengthy one, especially in the case of private schools, as Ministry approval has to be obtained. The Ministry's preference is for teachers with degrees in English.

Recruitment: BC, CFBT, ELT, EWW, IH, I to I, Nord Anglia, OPU, SA.

Turkmenistan

Pop: 4.5 m   *Area*: 448,000 sq km
Turkmen Embassy: 2nd Floor, 14 Wells Street. London W1P. Tel: 0171 255 1071.
Ministry of Education: Ul. Gyorogly 1, Ashgabat.
British Embassy: 301-308 Office Building, Plaza Hotel, Ashgabat.
British Council: See **Russia**.

This former Soviet republic which borders on the Caspian Sea boasts nine HE institutions. There is an AIS in Ashgabat.

Tuvalu

Pop: 8,000   *Area*: 25 sq km
Ministry of Education: Vaiaku, Funafati.
British Embassy: see **Fiji**.

Formerly the Ellice Islands, Tuvalu has an extra-mural centre of the University of the South Pacific at Funafati and a Maritime Training School which now offers technical, commercial and vocational courses.
Recruitment: DFID, VSO.

Uganda

Pop: 17 m   *Area*: 236,000 sq km
Ugandan High Commission: Uganda House, Trafalgar Square, London WC2N 5DX. Tel: 0171 839 5783.
Ministry of Education: PO Box 7063, Crested Towers, Kampala.
British Council: British High Commission, IPS Building, Parliament Avenue, PO Box 7070, Kampala.

As Uganda rebuilds its shattered infrastructure, it faces a severe shortage of teachers in most subjects. Many of the secondary schools are private or semi-private. The American style Lincoln International School functions in Kampala. The country has two universities, Makerere University (the oldest HE institution in East Africa) and the University of Science and Technology at Mbara. In addition there is a Catholic, a Christian and an Islamic University.

Recruitment: AIM, Christians Abroad, Concern, Crosslinks, MAM, Skillshare, VMM, VSO.

Ukraine

Pop: 52 m   *Area*: 603,700 sq km.
Ukrainian Embassy: 78 Kensington Park Road, London W11 2PL. Tel: 0171 727 6312.
Ministry of Education: Peremohy pr 10, 252135 Kiev.
British Embassy: 9 Desyatinna, 252025 Kiev.
British Council: 9/1 Besarabska Ploshcha, Flat 9, 252004 Kiev.

Formerly part of the Soviet Union, Ukraine boasts seven universities and an international university of science and technology. Kiev has two international schools: Kiev International and Pechersk.

Recruitment: BC, ECIS, IH, SA, TA.

United Arab Emirates (UAE)

Pop: 2.4 m   *Area*: 83,600 sq km
UAE Embassy: 30 Princes Gate, London SW7 1PT. Tel: 0171 581 1281.
Ministry of Education: PO Box 295, Abu Dhabi
British Council: Villa No 7, Al Nasr Street (near All Prints), Khalidiya, PO Box 46523, Abu Dhabi. Tariq bin Zaid Street, PO Box 1636, Dubai.

Formerly the Trucial States, this is a Federation of seven Arab emirates, each proud of its own traditions. The largest are Abu Dhabi and Dubai. UAE nationals form only a minority of the population. There is a large contingent of expatriate teachers mainly from other Arab countries, teaching in the state system. There are opportunities for foreign lecturers at the University of El Ain, the training centre of the state oil company ADMA-OPCO and the three higher colleges of technology. The British Council has its own language institutes in Abu Dhabi and Dubai, and there are private ventures, such as the Polyglot School in Dubai and the Al Bayyan Institute, Sharjah. There are a number of international schools and English medium schools employing foreign teachers. Abu Dhabi (Al Rabbeh School, Alkubairat School, American Community School, International School of Choueifat); Al Ain (English Speaking School, International School); Dubai (Cambridge

High School, Dubai College, English Speaking School, Jebel Ali School, Jumairah American School, Jumairah English Speaking School, Rashid School for Boys); Ras El Kahimah (English Speaking School); Sharjah (Al Qasinia Private School, International School, English School).
Recruitment: BC, Crown Agents, ECIS, EWW, ELT, PACES, SA, WES, UAE Embassy.

United States of America
Pop: 237,000   *Area*: 9 m sq km
American Embassy: Grosvenor Square, London W1A 1AE. Tel: 0171 499 9000; Consulate: 5 Upper Grosvenor Street, London W1A 2JB Tel: 0171 499 3443. And in Edinburgh and Belfast.
British Embassy: 3100 Massachusetts Avenue NW, Washington DC 20008.

The USA is more than self-sufficient in secondary school teachers, except in maths and science. The situation is slightly more promising in primary schools, particularly in the areas of bilingual education and special education. Public education is the responsibility of each individual state, and their certification requirements can differ considerably from one state to another. Some may require teachers to be American citizens while others may require prospective teachers to have received a job offer from a state school before they can apply for certification. Private and parochial schools, however, are not usually bound by the requirements laid down by the state education authorities. There are three courses of action you can take:

● Apply to the appropriate State Board of Education, Division of Teacher Certification, to check the status of your qualifications and enquire about vacancies.

● Write to the local Superintendent of Schools of the city or district where you would like to teach to enquire about vacancies.

● Apply direct to the principals of private or parochial schools.

Appointments are usually made between Christmas and the spring. There are a few international schools which prepare for British examinations and the International Baccalaureate. They include: The Anglo-American School, 18 W 89th St, New York NY 10024; United Nations International School, 24-50 East River Drive, New York, NY 10010; Washington International School, 2735 Olive St, Washington, DC 20007; Dwight School, 402 E 67th St, New York, NY 10021.

Teacher exchanges are handled by the Central Bureau and the British

American Exchange Foundation, 34 Belgrave Rd, Seaford, E Sussex. A useful source of information and addresses is the US-UK Educational Commission, 62 Doughty Street, WC1N 2LS. Tel: 0171 404 6994.

If you wish to work on a more permanent basis in the USA you will need to apply for an immigrant visa (or a temporary visa), the processing of which can be lengthy.

Internet: Try http://www.careerpath com or http://volvo.gslis.utexas.edu /~acadres/geographic.html for academic vacancies.

Reference: *Getting a job in America* (How To Books); *Going USA* (Outbound Newspapers).

Recruitment: CB, ECIS.

Upper Volta
(See **Burkino Faso**)

Uruguay
Pop: 3.2 m   *Area*: 176,000 sq km
Uruguayan Embassy: 140 Brompton Road, London SW3 1HY. Tel: 0171 589 8735.
Ministry of Education: Sarandi 440, Montevideo.
British Embassy: Calle Marco Bruto 1073, PO Box 16024, Montevideo 11300.

This compact country with scenery reminiscent of the Cotswolds boasts only one sizeable city — Montevideo. There are a number of international schools, notably the Crandon Institute, the American School, St Catherine's and St Andrew's. The Anglo Uruguayan Cultural Institute has 25 regional branches teaching English and the American supported Alianza Cultural Uruguay-USA has 30. There are four universities, including the Universidad de la Republica.

Recruitment: BC, CB, SA, Skola.

Uzbekistan
Pop: 22 m   *Area*: 447,400 sq km
Uzbekistan Embassy: 41 Holland Park, London W11 2PP. Tel: 0171 229 7679.
Ministry of Education: Alleya Paradov 5, Tashkent.
British Council: University of World Languages Building, 11 Kounoev Street, Tashkent.

There are universities and medical schools in Tashkent and Samarkand. Tashkent has two international schools: Tashkent International and Tashen Ulugbek International. The British Council has been helping with the development of new English textbooks and has

run courses for teachers. It plans to offer language teaching to private students and company staff in the future.
Recruitment: BC, I to I.

Vanuatu
Pop: 160,000   *Area*: 14,800 sq km
Ministry of Education: P O Box 028, Port Vila.
British High Commission: PO Box 567, KPMG House, Rue Pasteur, Port Vila.

Formerly the Anglo-French condominium of the New Hebrides, both French and English are used as the medium of instruction. There are ten secondary schools on the islands, together with a technical college and a teacher training college. The University of the South Pacific has a centre at Port Vila.
Recruitment: DFID, VSO.

Venezuela
Pop: 20.5 m   *Area*: 912,000 sq km
Venezuelan Embassy: 1 Cromwell Road, London SW7 2HW. Tel: 0171 581 4206.
Ministry of Education: Edif Educación, Esq El Conde, Caracas.
British Council: Torre La Noria, Piso 6, Paseo Enrique Eraso, Las Mercedes/Sector San Román, Apartado 65131, Caracas 1065.

This oil producing country operates a teacher exchange programme with the UK. International schools include: Caracas (AIS, British School, Escuela Campo Alegre, Leap); Maracaibo (Escuela Bella Vista); Valencia (Colegio International). The British Council has its own language institutes in Caracas, Ciudad Guyana and Maracaibo; the USA has two Bi-national Centres; and there are private language schools as well. Venezuela has sixteen state universities, thirteen private sector ones, two Roman Catholic universities and a technical university.
Recruitment: BC, CB, Inlingua, SA.

Vietnam
Pop: 74 m   *Area*: 333,000 sq km
Vietnamese Embassy: 12 Victoria Road, London W8 5RD. Tel: 0171 937 1912.
Ministry of Education: 21 Le Thanh Tong, Hanoi.
British Council: 18b Cao Ba Quat, Ba Dinh District, Hanoi; 25 Le Duan Street, District 1, Ho Chi Minh City (Saigon).

There are now opportunities for foreigners here, particularly in the TEFL field. The British Council has language centres in Hanoi and Ho

Chi Minh City (Saigon). A sign of the times is that a private college has been set up in Hanoi, the first since 1954. There are international schools in Hanoi (Hanoi International, UN International) and Ho Chi Minh City (Saigon International).
Recruitment: BC, I to I, SA, VSO.

West Bank and Gaza (Palestinian administered territories)
Pop: 1.9 m   *Area*: 6,242 sq km.
Ministry of Education: Ramallah.
Ministry of HE: Gaza.
British Council: Al Nuzha Building, 2 Abu Obeida Street, PO Box 19136, Jerusalem. Also in Gaza City, Hebron and Nablus.

Aid is flowing in to develop educational facilities in this area which has an uneasy relationship with the Israeli authorities.
Recruitment: BC, UNAIS, UNRWA (PO Box 484, Amman, Jordan)

Yemen
Pop: 16 m   *Area*: 472,000 sq km
Yemeni Embassy: 57 Cromwell Road, London SW7 2ED. Tel: 0171 584 6607.
Ministry of Education: Sana'a
British Council: House 7, Street 70, PO Box 2157, Sana'a. Ho Chi Minh Street, PO Box 6170, Khormasksar, Aden.

The country is making a considerable effort to develop its educational system with help from its rich Arab neighbours. With the highest adult illiteracy rate in Asia (86.3%) it has a tremendous task on its hands. Opportunities exist in the Sana'a International School and the bilingual Mohammed Ali Othman School in Taiz. There are two universities, at Sana'a and Aden, and the British Council has language centres in both cities.
Recruitment: BC, SA, WES.

Yugoslavia
Pop: 10.5 m   *Area*: 102,000 sq km
Yugoslav Embassy: 5 Lexham Gardens, London W8 5JU. Tel: 0171 370 6105.
British Council: General Zdanova 34, 11001 Belgrade.

During the nineties Bosnia-Herzegovina, Croatia, Macedonia and Slovenia separated from Yugoslavia leaving two individual republics (Serbia, Montenegro) and two autonomous provinces (Kosovo and Metohija, Vojvodina) each responsible for their own educational

matters. Belgrade has an international school and the country has six universities.
Recruitment: BC, ECIS, EEP.

Zaire
(see **Congo, Democratic Government of**)

Zambia
Pop: 9 m   *Area*: 853,000 sq km
High Commission: 2 Palace Gate, London W8 5NG. Tel: 0171 589 6555.
Ministry of Education: PO Box RW 50093, 15102 Ridgeway, Lusaka.
British Council: PO Box 34571, Heroes Place, Cairo Road, Lusaka.

Zambia has more or less achieved its aim of universal primary education, and the next objective is to completely Zambianise the teaching corps. At the moment there is still expatriate involvement in schools. Opportunities exist at Kitwe (Lechwe School), Lusaka (International School), and Ndola (Nsansa School). There may be training opportunities with the mining companies of the Copper Belt as well as opportunities for lecturers at the University of Zambia at Lusaka, the Copperbelt University at Ndola or the 14 teacher training colleges.
Recruitment: ACU, AEF, APSO, BC, ECIS, VSO

Zimbabwe
Pop: 11.5 m   *Area*: 390,500 sq km
High Commission: 429 Strand, London WC2R 0SA. Tel: 0171 836 7755.
Ministry of Education: PO Box CY121, Union Avenue, Causeway, Harare. (*Ministry of Higher Education*: PO Box UA 275)
British Council: PO Box 664, 23 Jason Moyo Avenue, Harare.

There are a number of opportunities here for expatriates, but they tend now to be offered on contract rather than permanent terms. Education is non-racial at all levels, and virtually universal. Among the leading private schools are Falcon College at Esigodini, Arundel School in Harare, Peterhouse at Marondera. In HE expatriates are employed at the University of Zimbabwe (Harare) and the University of Science and Technology at Bulawayo. There are also two private universities: Africa University at Mutari and Solusi University at Figtree.
Recruitment: ACU, AEF, APSO, BC, CA, Crosslinks, SA, SPW, VMM, VSO.

Teacher Recruitment Organisations

This is a select list of organisations most of which were either actively recruiting for the overseas education sector in 1998 or have connections with organisations that were. Abbreviations after the name are used in the preceding country reference section.

The fact that an organisation is listed here should not be taken to imply recommendation on the part of either the author or the publisher. It should be borne in mind that recruitment priorities are apt to change and there is no guarantee that the current details will remain in force indefinitely.

Action Partners (AP)
Bawtry Hall, South Parade, Bawtry, Doncaster DN10 6JH.
Tel: 01302 710750.
Fax: 01302 719399.
E-mail: actionpartners.org.uk.
A missionary organisation which recruits teachers on missionary and volunteer terms mainly for Ghana, Nigeria, Sudan and Egypt.

Africa Evangelical Fellowship (AEF)
6 Station Court, Station Approach, Borough Green, Sevenoaks TN15 8AD.
Tel: 01732 885590. Fax: 01732 882990.
Website: www.netaccess.on.ca/~sma/gallery/aef/display/display.htm.
E-mail: 100635.2043@compuserve.com.
Missionary organisation recruiting teachers for primary and secondary schools in Africa including TEFL and theological teachers.

Africa Inland Mission (AIM)
2 Vorley Road, London N19 5HE.
Tel: 0181 281 1184.
E-mail: africa.mission@ukonline.co.uk.
Missionary organisation which recruits teachers for East and Central Africa, Madagascar, the Comores Islands and the Seychelles.

Agency for Personal Service Overseas (APSO)
29-30 Fitzwilliam Square, Dublin 2, Ireland.
Tel: 00 353 1 661 4411.
Fax: 00 353 1 661 4202.
E-mail: apso@iol.ie.
Ireland's national voluntary organisation recruits primary and secondary teachers for Africa and Asia; lecturers for Africa, Asia and Central America; TEFL teachers for Africa, Asia, Central America and Eastern Europe; and special education teachers for Africa.

Association of Commonwealth Universities (ACU)
John Foster House, 36 Gordon Square, London WC1H 0PF.
Tel: 0171 387 8572.
Fax: 0171 383 0368.
Website: www.acu.ac.uk.
E-mail: appts@acu.ac.uk.
Advertises over 1,000 academic, administrative and library posts on behalf of some 470 universities within the Commonwealth. Contracts up to five years. Unable to deal with speculative applications.

Baptist Missionary Society
PO Box 49, 129 Broadway, Didcot, OX11 8XA
Tel: 01235 512077.
Fax: 01235 511265.
Recruits a few teachers of maths, science and EFL for primary and secondary mission schools in Africa and SE Asia.

Bell Educational Trust
(Overseas Schools), Hillscross, Red Cross Lane, Cambridge CB2 2QX.
Tel: 01223 246644.
Fax: 01223 410282.
Website: www.bell-schools.ac.uk.
E-mail: lizc@bell-schools.ac.uk.
Recruits qualified graduate EFL teachers with at least two years' experience for its own schools in Italy, Poland and Thailand.

British Aerospace
Saudi Arabian Support Department, Warton Aerodrome, Preston, Lancs PR4 1LA.
Tel: 01772 634317.
Fax: 01772 852096.
Recruits EFL teachers and trainers in aircraft related technical skills for the Saudi Arabian Airforce.

British Council (BC)
Central Management of Direct Teaching, 10 Spring Gardens, London
SW1A 2BN.
Tel: 0171 389 4914.
Fax: 0171 389 6347.
Website: www.britcoun.org.
E-mail: calice.miller@britcoun.org.
Recruits 300 EFL teachers and supervisory staff annually to work at its
120 or so English Language centres in 51 countries. Diploma or PGCE
in TEFL plus two years' experience usually required; MA or MBA for
managerial posts.

British Council (BC)
Overseas Appointments Services, Bridgewater House, 58 Whitworth
Street, Manchester M1 6BB.
Tel: 0161 957 7383.
Fax: 0161 957 7397.
Website: www.britcoun.org.
E-mail: mark-hepworth@britcoun.org.
Recruits teachers and specialists in ELT and other subjects mainly for
public sector posts and projects which often form part of Britain's aid
programme. The Division advertises posts and operates a candidate
database.

Callan School of English
Berwick House, 139 Oxford Street, London W1R 1TD.
Tel: 0171 437 4573.
Fax: 0171 494 3204
E-mail: 100345.3077@compuserve.com.
Recruits EFL teachers for private schools in Italy, France, Poland, Brazil
and Spain that use the Callan method. Age limits: 18-30. All candidates
receive a free intensive training course before appointment.

Central Bureau for Educational Visits & Exchanges (CB)
The British Council, 10 Spring Gardens, London SW1A 2BN .
Tel: 0171 389 4004.
Fax: 0171 389 4426.
Website: www.britcoun.org/cbeve.
E-mail: info@centralbureau.org.uk and
101472.2264@compusserve.com.
Recruits English language assistants aged 20-30 for Europe, Latin
America, Canada (Quebec), Eastern Europe, China and Senegal. Posts
are also available for intending teachers in all EU countries. Arranges

post to post exchanges (on secondment) for qualified and experienced modern language teachers to Austria, Denmark, France, Germany, Spain, and Switzerland and Bulgaria. Also arranges exchanges for teachers of all disciplines with the USA. Offices in Edinburgh and Belfast.

CFBT Education Services (Centre for British Teachers)
1 The Chambers, East Street, Reading RG1 4JD.
Tel: 0118 952 3900.
Fax: 0118 952 3924.
Website: www.cfbt.com.
E-mail: intrecruit@cfbt-hq.org.uk.
Recruits graduate TEFL and IT teachers on a regular basis for Brunei, Oman and Turkey. Minimum qualification TEFL certificate. Opportunities also arise elsewhere in teacher training, curriculum development, etc. Operates an international recruitment database for which CVs should be submitted on disc or e-mail in Word or WordPerfect format.

Christians Abroad (CA)
1 Stockwell Green, London SW9 9HP.
Tel: 0171 346 5951.
Fax: 0171 346 5955.
E-mail: wsp@cabroad.org.uk.
Recruits teachers of English, EFL, science, maths, engineering, etc for Cameroon, China, Jamaica, Japan, Malawi, Sudan, Tanzania, Uganda, Zimbabwe for educational or health establishments or non-governmental organisations.

Church of Scotland, (World Mission and Unity)
121 George Street, Edinburgh EH2 4YN.
Tel: 0131 225 5722.
Fax: 0131 226 6121.
E-mail: kirkworldlink@gn.apc.org.
Recruits teachers of maths, science, EFL and other subjects for various church affiliated educational establishments in Kenya, Malawi, Zambia, Nepal, Pakistan, Taiwan, China, Israel, Egypt, Mozambique.

Concern Worldwide
248-250 Lavender Hill, London SW11 1LJ.
Tel: 0171 738 1033.
Fax: 0171 738 1032.
Recruits educational consultants for its own educational programmes (usually primary, vocational, non-formal) in Angola, Bangladesh,

Ethiopia, Somalia, Tanzania, Uganda, Mozambique, Cambodia, Laos. Well qualified teachers (usually primary) needed for programme design, curriculum development, administration and programme implementation.

Council on International Educational Exchange (CIEE)
52 Poland Street, London W1V 4JQ.
Tel: 0171 478 2000/2010.
Fax: 0171 734 7322.
E-mail: info@ukciee.org and jetinfo@ciee.org.
Recruits 550 graduate EFL teaching assistants for high schools in Japan under the Japan Exchange and Teaching (JET) programme in collaboration with the Japanese government. No teaching qualifications required, but salary paid. Also recruits 100 graduates to teach EFL in universities and colleges in Eastern China. No qualifications required, but a fee is payable.

Crosslinks
251 Lewisham Way, London SE4 1XF.
Tel: 0181 691 6111.
Missionary organisation which recruits primary, secondary and EFL teachers for Africa (Kenya, Tanzania, Uganda, Zimbabwe), Europe (France, Portugal, Russia and Spain), Latin America (Bolivia, Peru).

Crown Agents
International Recruitment Division, St Nicholas House, St Nicholas Road, Sutton SM1 1EL.
Tel: 0181 643 3311.
Fax: 0181 643 9331.
E-mail: crownagents@attmail.com.
Recruits teachers and lecturers in EFL (DFEE qualified) and technical subjects (at least HND and Cert Ed) for education ministries, secondary schools, technical colleges and industrial training centres mainly on the Arabia Peninsula (Saudi Arabia, Bahrain, UAE). Upper age limit: 57. Previous experience in region preferred.

Department for Education and Employment (DFEE)
(European Schools Section), Sanctuary Buildings, Great Smith Street, London SW1P 3BT.
Tel: 0171 273 5764.
Fax: 0171 273 5890.
Recruits nursery, primary and secondary school teachers for the nine European schools in Luxembourg, Brussels (two), Mol (Belgium), Varese (Italy), Karlsruhe, Munich, Bergen (Netherlands), Culham (UK). Recruitment normally takes place in January and February through

advertisements in the *Times Educational Supplement*. Five years' relevant experience required and a working knowledge of at least one other EU language.

Department for International Development (DFID)
(Appointments Officer), Abercrombie House, Eaglesham Road, East Kilbride G75 8EA.
Tel: 01355 844000.
Website: www.oneworld.org/dfid.
E-mail: recruitment-enqs@dfid.gtnet.gov.uk.
Maintains a register of qualified people interested in working for the aid programme to whom it forwards details of suitable vacancies. Most educational appointments are in advisory roles.

East European Partnership (EEP)
Carlton House, 27A Carlton Drive, London SW15 2BS.
Tel: 0181 780 7555.
Fax: 0181 780 7550.
E-mail: depstein@vso.org.uk.
The East European division of Voluntary Services Overseas (VSO). Recruits qualified professionals with a minimum of two years' post-qualification experience for Eastern Europe and the former Soviet Union, notably Albania, Bulgaria, Czech Republic, Kazakhstan, Latvia, Lithuania, Macedonia, Slovakia, Yugoslavia.

ELT International
49 Oxford Road, Banbury, Oxon OX16 9AH.
Tel: 01295 263480/263502.
Fax: 01295 271658.
E-mail: 100760.2247@compuserve.com.
Recruits TEFL teachers for its affiliated schools in France, Germany, Indonesia, Italy, Kuwait, Malaysia, Portugal, Spain, South Africa, Thailand, Turkey, UAE and Vietnam, and other institutions in other countries (including Russia and China).

English First Recruitment, (EF)
c/o Annika Hammargen, Box 5761, 114 87 Stockholm, Sweden.
Tel: 00 7 095 937 3887.
Fax: 00 46 8 768 1812 & 00 7 095 937 3889.
Website: www.ef.com or www.englishtown.com.
E-mail: e1teacher@ef.com or bernard_shearer@ef.com.
A worldwide organisation which recruits TEFL teachers with a degree, TEFL qualification and one year's experience for English First language schools in China, Indonesia, Lithuania, Mexico, Poland and Russia.

Work involves contact with children aged 5 upwards, teenagers and adults using mainly English First materials and computer-aided language learning programmes. Candidates for academic co-ordinator posts need a diploma or equivalent plus two or three years' teaching experience.

English Worldwide (EWW)
The Italian Building, Dockhead, London SE1 2BS.
Tel: 0171 252 1402.
Fax: 0171 231 8002.
E-mail: info.eww@pop3.hiway.co.uk.
Recruits teachers of EFL and all primary and secondary school subjects for language schools, international schools, state schools and private colleges in Europe, the Middle East, Far East and Latin America. Age range: 21-50. Teachers must be qualified and have experience for most of the posts.

European Council of International Schools (ECIS)
21 Lavant Street, Petersfield, Hants GU32 3EW.
Tel: 01730 268244.
Fax: 01730 267914.
Website: www.ecis.org.
E-mail: ecis@ecis.org.
Recruits teachers of all disciplines and senior administrators for international schools worldwide. Publishes the annual *ECIS Directory,* organises twice-yearly recruitment fairs and operates candidates register.

Gabbitas Educational Consultants
Carrington House, 126-130 Regent Street, London W1R 6EE.
Tel: 0171 439 2071.
Fax: 0171 437 1764.
Recruits teachers of all GCSE, A Level and IB subjects for British schools overseas which follow a British style curriculum (South America, Africa, Middle East, Far East, Europe). Holds a register of candidates.

Hilderstone College
St Peter's Road, Broadstairs, Kent CT10 2AQ.
Tel: 01843 869171.
Fax: 01843 603877.
Website: www.hilderstone.ac.uk.
E-mail: info@hilderstone.ac.uk.
Recruits secondary school teachers with TEFL qualifications for Shumei Schools in Greater Tokyo.

Inlingua Teacher Training & Recruitment
Rodney Lodge, Rodney Road, Cheltenham GL50 1JF.

Tel: 01242 253171.
Fax: 01242 253181.
Website: www.inlingua-cheltenham.co.uk.
E-mail: training@inlingua-cheltenham.co.uk.
Recruits around 200 qualified EFL teachers per year for affiliated and non-affiliated language schools in Germany, Italy, Indonesia, Poland, Russia, Spain, Singapore, Venezuela and elsewhere. Preference given to Inlingua-trained teachers.

International House (IH)
Staffing Unit, 106 Piccadilly, London W1V 9FL.
Tel: 0171 491 2410.
Fax: 0171 491 2679.
Website: www.international-house.org.
E-mail: 100645.1547@compuserve.com.
Recruits 350 EFL teachers for private affiliated language schools in Argentina, Australia, Austria, Argentina, Belarus, Brazil, Czech Republic, Egypt, Estonia, Finland, France, Georgia, Germany, Greece, Hungary, Italy, Lithuania, Macedonia, Poland, Portugal, Romania, Russia, Singapore, South Africa, Spain, Switzerland, Turkey, Ukraine, USA. Minimum requirement Cambridge RSA Certificate in TEFLA.

Interserve
325 Kennington Road, London SE11 4QH.
Tel: 0171 735 8227.
Fax: 0171 587 5362.
E-mail: 100014.2566@compuserve.com.
A missionary organisation which sends teachers to India, Pakistan and Nepal.

i to i International Projects Ltd
1 Cottage Road, Headingley, Leeds LS6 4DD.
Tel: 0113 217 9800.
Fax: 0113 217 9801.
Website: www.i-to-i.com/iventure.
E-mail: info@i-to-i.com.
A charity which trains and sends volunteers to teach English (TEFL) to India, Russia, Sri Lanka, Turkey, Vietnam typically for three months, but longer and shorter placements are possible. Recruits range from gap year students to experienced people who wish to have a working holiday with a difference. A fee is payable. Publishes a quarterly newsletter *Inspired* .

Language Solutions Ltd
Dilke House, Malet Street, London WC1E 7JA.

Tel: 0171 323 0585.
Fax: 0171 323 0586.
Recruits qualified TEFL teachers with some ESP expertise for in-house training with oil companies and other businesses in Baku, Azerbaijan.

League for the Exchange of Commonwealth Teachers (LECT)
Commonwealth House, 7 Lion Yard, Tremadoc Road, London SW4 7NQ.
Tel: 0171 498 1101.
Fax: 0171 720 5403.
E-mail: 100745.1501@compuserve.com.
Arranges exchanges (on secondment) for teachers with at least five years' experience for various Commonwealth countries, notably Canada, Australia and New Zealand but also Africa (Gambia, Ghana, Kenya, Tanzania, South Africa), Asia (Bangladesh, India, Pakistan) and the Caribbean (Guyana, Jamaica, Trinidad).

Linguarama
Oceanic House, 89 High Street, Alton, Hants GU34 1LG.
Tel: 01420 80899.
Fax: 01420 80856.
Website: www.linguarama.com.
E-mail: linguarama_alt@compuserve.com.
Recruits EFL teachers for its schools in Austria, Czech Republic, Finland, France, Germany, Holland, Hungary, Italy, Poland, Romania, Russia and Spain. Applicants without a Cambridge/RSA Cert TEFLA or a Trinity College TESOL Cert must take one-week intensive course before appointment.

Methodist Church
World Church Office, 25 Marylebone Road, London NW1 5JR.
Tel: 0171 486 5502.
Fax: 0171 935 1507.
Recruits maths, science, music, PE and EFL teachers for posts in Bangladesh, China, Japan, Nepal, Poland and other countries. Minimum appointment usually two years.

Mid Africa Ministry (MAM)
157 Waterloo Road, London SE1 8UU.
Tel: 0171 261 1370.
Fax: 0171 406 2910.
E-mail: mid_africa_ministry@compuserve.com.
A missionary organisation which recruits Christian mission partners and self-funded volunteer teachers to work under the auspices of the Anglican Church in Rwanda, Burundi, Congo, Uganda.

Network Overseas (NO)
34 Mortimer Street, London W1N 8JR.
Tel: 0171 580 5151.
Fax: 0171 580 6242.
Website: www.sonnet.co.uk/network
E-mail: network@network.sonnet.co.uk.
Network's education division recruits for TEFL, science, engineering training and instruction posts on Kuwait, Qatar, Saudia Arabia and the UAE.

Nord Anglia International (NA)
10 Eden Place, Cheadle, Stockport, Cheshire SK8 1AT.
Tel: 0161 491 4191.
E-mail: 100532.40@compuserve.com.
Recruits EFL teachers for language schools worldwide, especially Eastern Europe.

OMF International (UK)
Station Approach, Borough Green, Sevenoaks, Kent TB15 8BG.
Tel: 01732 887299.
Fax: 01732 887224.
Website: www.omf.org.uk.
E-mail: omf@omf.org.uk.
A Christian organisation which recruits primary and secondary school teachers for East and SE Asia.

Overseas Placing Unit (OPU)
Level 1, Rockingham House, 123 West Street, Sheffield S1 4ER.
Tel: 0114 259 6051/6052.
Fax: 0114 259 6040.
A specialist branch of the Employment Service (DFEE) which recruits for vacancies abroad (including teaching posts) through local Jobcentres.

PACES Recruitment Consultants
PO Box 232, Redhill, Surrey RH1 8YP.
Tel: 01833 744558.
Fax: 01833 744588.
Recruits qualified teachers for British schools mainly on the Arabian peninsula. Please send SAE for latest details.

Recruitment International
International House, PO Box 300, Harrogate, North Yorks HG1 5XL.
Tel: 01423 530533.
Fax: 01423 530558.
E-mail: ri_group@compuserve.com.

Recruits physics, maths and EFL teachers for schools, colleges, oil companies, and industrial training institutes in the Middle East. Postgraduate qualifications plus five years' experience required.

St Giles College
51 Shepherds Hill, Highgate, London N6 5QP.
Tel: 0181 340 0828.
Fax: 0181 348 9389.
Website: www.stgiles.co.uk.
E-mail: lonhigh@stgiles.u-net.com.
Not a recruitment agency as such but can help its trainees and former trainees to obtain positions abroad.

Saxoncourt Recruitment
Norman House, 105-109 The Strand, London WC2R 0AA.
Tel: 0171 836 1567.
Fax: 0171 836 1789.
Website: www.saxoncourt.com.
E-mail: recruit@saxoncourt.com.
Recruits 300 EFL teachers each year to more than 20 different countries in Asia, Europe, Latin America and the Middle East. Vacancies at all levels from newly qualified teachers to senior posts. Minimum qualifications: Cambridge/RSA Cert TEFLA or Trinity College CTESOL.

Search Associates (SA)
PO Box 168, Chieng Mai 5000, Thailand.
Tel: 00 66 53 244322.
Fax: 00 66 53 260118.
Website: www.search-associates.com.
E-mail: deelman@loxinfo.co.th.
An agency which recruits qualified teachers with at least two years' experience and school administrators for international schools worldwide (nursery, pre-school, primary, secondary). Part of a North American based organisation founded by John Magagna in 1991 the Chieng Mai branch of SA specialises in assisting British and International Baccalaureate schools with their recruitment needs. Interviews are conducted in the UK, Australia and other countries. North American teachers should contact a US or Canadian associate (eg Search Associates, PO Box 922, Jackson, MI).

Service Childrens Education (SCE)
Ministry of Defence (Germany), Bldg 5, BFPO 40.
Tel: 00 49 2161 908 ext 2432.
Fax: 00 49 2161 908 ext 2396.

Recruitment for the schools on British military bases abroad is now done from an office in Germany. SCE recruits mainly primary and some secondary school teachers for schools there and in Belgium, Belize, Brunei, Cyprus, Denmark, Falklands, Gibraltar and Italy.

SIM UK
Ullswater Crescent, Colsdon, Surrey CR5 2HR.
Tel: 0181 660 7778.
Fax: 0181 660 7778.
Website: www.sim.org.
E-mail: postmaster@sim.co.uk.
A missionary organisation which recruits teachers for West, Central and East Africa, Asia (Bangladesh, Pakistan, Philippines) and Latin America (Bolivia, Chile, Peru).

Skillshare Africa
126 New Walk, Leicester LE1 7JA.
Tel: 0116 254 1862.
Fax: 0116 254 2614.
E-mail: skillshare-uk@geo2.poptel.org.uk.
Recruits volunteer basis TEFL teachers and nursing trainers for Mozambique, educational advisers for Lesotho, Swaziland and Botswana. Also recruits teacher trainers and educational experts on behalf of the development charity Link Africa for South Africa.

Skola Recruitment
21 Star Street, London W2 1QB.
Tel: 0171 387 0656.
Fax: 0171 724 2219.
Recruits qualified EFL teachers for private language schools in China, Greece, Italy, Russia. Spain and Uruguay.

South American Missionary Society (SAMS)
Unit 1, Prospect Business Park, Langston Road, Loughton IG10 3TZ.
Tel: 0181 502 3504.
Fax: 0181 502 3504.
E-mail: 101607.507@compuserve.com.
A missionary organisation which recruits secondary school teachers (especially TEFL) for Chile and Paraguay.

Specialist Language Services (SLS)
7 Marsden Business Park, Clifton, York YO3 4XG.
Tel: 01904 691313.
Fax: 01904 691102.

E-mail: admin@slsyork.co.uk.
Recruits specialists in English for Special Purposes (ESP) for Europe (especially Germany and Italy), the Middle East and occasionally for the Far East.

Students Partnership Worldwide (SPW)
17 Dean's Yard, London SW1P 3PB.
Tel: 0171 222 0138.
Fax: 0171 233 0008.
E-mail: spwuk@gn.apc.org.
Established in 1985 SPW organises educational, environmental and social programmes lasting up to nine months for young people aged 18-25 to work with local volunteers in Namibia, Tanzania, Uganda, Zimbabwe, Nepal and India. Participants are required to cover the cost of their placement.

Teaching Abroad Ltd (TA)
Gerrard House, Rustington, West Sussex BN16 1AW.
Tel: 01903 859911.
Fax: 01903 785779.
Website: www.teaching-abroad.co.uk.
E-mail: teaching_abroad@garlands.uk.com.
Recruits volunteer EFL teaching assistants of all ages (from 17 to 70) to work in Brazil, China, Ghana, India, Mexico, Russia (Moscow, St Petersburg, Siberia), Ukraine. No teaching qualifications are required at present and contract arrangements are flexible ranging from one month to one year. Substantial local back up. Minimum qualification: university entrance qualifications. Possibly a good way of gaining TEFL experience.

Timeplan Education Group Ltd
20/21 Arcadia Avenue, London N3 2JU.
Tel: 0181 371 8030.
Fax: 0141 204 5900.
Website: www.timeplan.com.
Glasgow office: 307 West George Street, Glasgow G2 4LF.
Tel: 0141 204 5800.
Education specialists who recruit teachers (especially at secondary level) on behalf of the New Zealand Ministry of Education; also teachers from pre-school to secondary level for schools (mainly international) worldwide, especially Brunei, Colombia, Italy, Netherlands, South Africa, Spain and Switzerland.

United Nations Association International Service (UNAIS)
Hunter House, 57 Goodramgate, York YO1 2LS.

Tel: 01904 647799.
Fax: 01904 652353.
Website: www.oneworld.org/is.
E-mail: unais-uk@geo2.poptel.org.uk.
Recruits a small number of people annually to work in health education, community education and skills training projects.

United World Colleges (UWC)
International Office, Lynton House, Tavistock Square, London WC1H 9LT.
Tel: 0171 388 2066
Fax: 0171 388 3166.
Co-ordinates the ten member colleges in Canada, India, Italy, Hong Kong, Norway, Singapore, USA, Venezuela and Wales. Most are international schools which prepare pupils for the International Baccalaureate; the Venezuelan one is an agricultural and rural development college. Each college does its own recruitment.

Volunteer Missionary Movement (VMM)
1 Stockwell Green, London SW9 9JF.
Tel: 0171 737 3678.
Fax: 0171 737 3237.
E-mail: vmmevago@iol.ie.
Also in Glasgow (Tel: 0141 550 8283)
Dublin (Tel: 00 353 1 837 6565) and
Greendale, USA (Tel: 00 1 414 423 8660).
Recruits teachers of English, science, maths, geography, history, etc as well as teacher trainers, and technical and health instructors for Eastern and Southern Africa.

Voluntary Service Overseas (VSO)
317 Putney Bridge Road, London SW15 2PN.
Tel: 0181 780 7500.
Fax: 0181 780 7576.
Website: www.oneworld.org/vso/.
E-mail: enquiries@vso.co.uk.
Recruits over 400 volunteer teachers a year over a wide range of disciplines for many countries in Africa, Asia, the Caribbean and Pacific, Belize and Guyana.

World Church and Mission (WCM)
United Reformed Church, 86 Tavistock Place, London WC1H 9RD.
Tel: 0171 916 2020.
Fax: 0171 916 2021.

Recruits secondary teachers and theological lecturers for Africa, Bangladesh and India, Jamaica, the Far East and the Pacific. Also EFL lecturers for tertiary institutions in China.

Worldwide Educational Service (WES)
Canada House, 272 Field End Road, Eastcote, Ruislip HA4 9NA.
Tel: 0181 582 0317.
Fax: 0181 582 0320.
Website: www.wesworldwide.com.
E-mail: wes@wesworldwide.com.
Recruits qualified teachers at all levels for primary and secondary schools worldwide, especially the Middle East, Far East and Africa.

Useful Addresses

Animal Aunts, 45 Fairview Road, Headley Down, Hants GU35 3HQ. Tel: 01428-712611.

Association for Language Learning, 150 Railway Terrace, Rugby CV21 3HN. Tel: 01788-546443. Fax: 01788 544149. E-mail:langlearn@aol.com.

Association for Recognised English Language Services, 2 Pontypool Place, Valentine Place, London SE1 8QF. Tel: 0171-242 3136.

Association of Language Excellence Centres, PO Box 178, Manchester M60 1LL. Tel: 0161-228 1366. Fax: 0161-236 8667.

Audio Forum, Microworld House, 2-6 Foscope Mews, London W9 2HH. Tel: 0171-266 2202.

Avalon Overseas, Drury Way, Brent Park, London NW10 0JN. Tel: 0181-451 6336. Fax: 0181-451 6419. E-mail: avalon @transeuro.com. International removers.

Blair Consular Services, 9 City Business Centre, Lower Road, London SE16 2XB. Tel: 0171-252 1451. Visas.

Bone & Co Insurance Brokers, 69A Castle Street, Farnham, Surrey GU9 7LP. Tel: 01252-724140.

British Airways Travel Clinic, 156 Regent Street, London W1R 5TA. Also at other locations. Tel: 0171-831 5333.

British Association for Counselling, 1 Regent Place, Rugby CV21 2PJ. Tel: 01788-578328.

British Association of State Colleges in English Language Teaching, Cheltenham and Gloucester College of Higher Education, The Lodge, Francis Close Hall, Swindon Road, Cheltenham, GL50 4AZ. Tel: 01242-227099.

British Association of Removers, 3 Churchill Court, 58 Station Road, North Harrow HA2 7SA. Tel: 0181-861 3331.

BBC Publications, Woodlands, 80 Wood Lane, London W12 0TT. Tel: 0181-743 5588. Publishers of language courses.

BBC World Service, PO Box 76, Bush House, Strand, London WC2B 4PH. Tel: 0171-240 3456.

Bishops Move, Overseas House, Stewarts Road, London SW8 4UG.

Tel: 0171-498 0300. Fax: 0171-498 0749. E-mail: www.bishops-move.co.uk. International removers.

Britannia, Unit 3, Wyvern Estate, Beverley Way, New Malden, Surrey KT3 4PH. Tel: 0181-336 0220. Fax 0181-336 0961. E-mail: www.britannia_movers.co.uk. International removers.

BUPA International, Russell Mews, Brighton BN7 2NE. Tel: 01273-208181. Fax: 01273-866583. E-mail:www.bupa.com/int. Health insurance.

Brown Shipley Lomond Ltd, 84 Coombe Road, New Malden, Surrey KT3 4QS. Tel: 0181-949 8811. Financial advisers.

Career Analysts, 90 Gloucester Place, London W1H 4BL. Tel: 0171-935 5452.

Career Counselling Services, 46 Ferry Road, London SW13 9PW. Tel: 0181-741 0335.

Career Development Centre for Women, 97 Mallard Place, Twickenham, Middlesex. Tel: 0171-892 3806.

Career Relocations, 7 Chester Street, London SW1X 7BB. Tel: 0171-235 0106. Careers advice for spouses.

Career Select, 2 Strangeways Villas, Truro, Cornwall TR1 2PA. Tel: 01872-41355. Careers guidance by post.

Centre for International Briefing, Farnham Castle, Surrey GU9 0AG. Tel: 01252-720416. Website: www.cibfarnham.com. E-mail:cibfarnham@dial.pipex.com.

Christians Abroad, 1 Stockwell Green, London SW9 9HP. Tel: 0171-737 7811. Also 121 George Street, Edinburgh EH2 4YN.

City Business Library, 1 Brewers' Hall Garden, London Wall, London EC2V 5BX Tel: 0171-638 8215.

Commonwealth Information Centre, Commonwealth Institute, Kensington High Street, London W8 6NQ. Tel: 0171-603 4535.

Consyl Publishing, 3 Buckhurst Road, Town Hall Square, Bexhill on Sea, Sussex TN40 1QF. Tel: 01424-223111. Publishers of (I)Australian Outlook(P) and (I)New Zealand Outlook(P).

Copsey Removals, 178 Crow Lane, Romford, Essex RM7 0ES. Tel: 0181-592 1003. Fax: 01708-727305. International removers.

CV Services International, Wellfield, Rainford, St Helens, Merseyside WA11 8PY. Tel: 0744-883894. Fax: 0744-882121.

Dean Associates, 51 High Street, Emsworth, Hants PO 10 7AN. Tel: 01243-378022. Education advisers.

Department of Health Leaflets Unit, PO Box 21, Honeypot Lane, Stanmore, Middlesex HA7 1AY. Tel: 0800-555777.

Department of Social Security, Overseas Branch, Benton Park Road, Newcastle upon Tyne NE98 1YX. Tel: 0191-225 7341.

ECCTIS 2000, Oriel House, Oriel Road, Cheltenham GL50 1XP. Tel: 01242-252627.

Employment Conditions Abroad, Anchor House, 15 Britten Street, London SW3 3TY. Tel: 0171-351 7151.

European Commission Office, 8 Storey Gate, London SW1P 3AT. Tel: 0171-973 1992. Fax: 0171 973 1900. Also in Belfast, Cardiff, Edinburgh, Dublin.

European Council for International Schools (ECIS), 21 Lavant Street, Petersfield, Hants GU32 3EW. Tel: 01230-268244.

Expat Network, International House, 500 Purley Way, Croydon, Surrey CR0 4NZ. Tel: 0181-760 5100. Fax: 0181-760 0469.

Expat Tax Consultants, Churchfield House, North Drive, Hebburn, Tyne & Wear NE31 1ES. Tel: 0191-483 7805.

Expatriate Advisory Services, 14 Gordon Road, West Bridgeford, Nottingham NG2 5LN. Tel: 01602-816572. Financial advisers.

Expats International, 29 Lacon Road, London SE22 9HE. Tel: 0181-229 2484.

FCO Travel Advice Unit, Consular Dept, Clive House, Petty France, London SW1H 9HD. Tel: 0171-270 4129.

Wilfred T Fry Ltd, Crescent House, Crescent Road, Worthing BN11 1RN. Tel: 01903-231545. Fax: 01903-200868. Financial advisers.

Gabbitas Educational Consultants, Carrington House, 126-130 Regent St, London W1R 6EE. Tel: 0171-439 2071.

GJW Education & Guardianship Services, Southcote, Coreway, Devon EX10 9SD. Tel: 01395-515614.

Golden Arrow Shippers, Horsford Kennels, Lydbury North, Shropshire SY7 8AY. Tel: 015888-240. Pet transport specialists.

Good Book Guide, 24 Seward Street, London EC1V 3PS. Tel: 0171-490 0900. Book mail order.

Grant & Cutler, 55 Great Marlborough Street, London W1V 2AY. Tel: 0171-834 2012. Language bookshop.

Hall-Godwins Overseas, Briarcliff House, Kingsmead, Farnborough, Hants GU14 7TE. Tel: 01252-521701. Financial advisers, including pensions.

Harley Medical Services, 177A Harley Street, London W1N 1DH. Tel: 0171-935 1536. Visas, Medicals.

Healthsearch Ltd, 9 Newland Street, Rugby CV22 7BJ. Tel: 01788-541855. Impartial advice on medical insurance.

Higher Education Advice and Planning Service, 200 Greyhound Road, London W14 9RY. Tel: 0181-385 3377. Fax: 0181-381 3377.

Homesitters Ltd, The Old Bakery, Western Road, Tring, Herts HP23 4BB. Tel: 01442-891188. Caretaking service.

Independent Assessment and Research Centre, 17 Portland Place, London W1 3AF. Tel: 0171-935 2373.

Independent Schools Information Service (ISIS), 56 Buckingham Gate, London SW1E 6AG. Tel: 0171-630 8793.

IFA Promotion, 17–119 Emery Road, Bristol BS4 5PF. Tel: 0117-971 1177. Information on independent financial advisers.

Inland Revenue Claims Branch, Foreign Division, Merton Road, Bootle L69 9BL. Tel: 0151-922 6363.

Institute of Education Library, University of London, 20 Bedford Way, London WC1H 0AL. Tel: 0171-637 1682.

Institute of Freight Forwarders, Redfern House, Browells Lane, Feltham, Middlesex. Tel: 0181-844 2266.

Institute of Linguists, Saxon House, 48 Southwark St, London SE1 1UN. Tel: 0171-340 3100. Fax: 0171-340 3101. E-mail: info@iol.org.uk.

Institution of Professional Managers and Specialists, 75 York Road, London SE1 7AQ. Tel: 0171-928 9951.

International Association of Teachers of English as a Foreign Language (IATEFL), 3 Kingsdown Park, Tankerton, Whitstable, Kent CT5 2DJ. Tel: 01227-276528.

International Baccalaureat: European Office, 15 Route des Morillons, CH1218 Grand Saconnex, Geneva. Tel: 0041 22 791 0274.

International Educators' Institute, 102A Popes Lane, London W5 4NS. Tel and Fax: 0181-840 2587. US Headquarters: PO Box 513, Cummaquid, MA 02637, USA. Tel + 1 508 362 1414. Fax: + 1 508 362 1411. Website: www.tieonline.com. E-mail: tie@capecod.net.

International Private Healthcare Ltd (IPH), PO Box 488, IPH House, Borehamwood, Herts WD6 6AN. Tel: 0181-905 28888.

International Teachers Benefit Portfolio, Bone & Co Insurance Brokers, 69A Castle Street, Farnham, Surrey GU9 7LP. Tel: 01252-724140.

Kays Overseas Division, Northwith Avenue, Babourne, Worcester WR3 7AX. Fax: 01905-615233. Mail order.

Kings Barn Export Ltd, Unit 29, Station Road, Southwater Industrial Estate, West Sussex RH13 7HQ. Tel: 01403-732020. Mail order.

LCL, 104 Judd Street, London WC1H 9NF. Tel: 0171-837 0487. Language bookshop.

Linguaphone, 50 Poland Street, London W1V 4AX. Tel: 0171-734 0574.

Manor Car Storage, PO Box 28, Clavering, Saffron Walden, Essex CB11 4RA. Tel: 01799-550021.

Medical Advisory Services for Travellers Abroad Ltd (MASTA), Bureau of Hygiene & Tropical Medicine, Keppel Street, London WC1E 7HT. Tel: 0171-631 4408 and 0891 600350.

Mercers College, Ware, Herts SG12 9BU. Tel: 01920-465926.

Mid-Career Development Centre, 429 Brighton Road, Croydon CR2 6UD. Tel: 0181-763 1973.

Ministry of Agriculture, Animal Health Division IC, Hook Rise South, Tolworth, Surbiton, Surrey KT6 7NF. Tel: 0181-330 4441. Advice on taking pets abroad.

National Business Language Information Service, CILT, 20 Bedfordbury, London WC2N 4LB. Tel: 0171-359 5131.

Open University, PO Box 71, Walton Hall, Milton Keynes MK7 6AG. Tel: 01908-74066.

Outbound Newspapers Ltd, 1 Commercial Road, Eastbourne BN21 3XQ. Tel: 01323-412001. Publishers of *Australian News*, *Canada News*, *South Africa News*, *Destination New Zealand*, *Going USA* (P).

Overseas Resettlement Secretary, Church of England Board for Social Responsibility, Church House, Dean's Yard, London SW1P 3NX. Tel: 0171-222 9011. Contacts at overseas destination.

Par Air Services, Warren Lane, Stanway, Colchester, Essex. Tel: 01206-330332. Fax: 01206-331277. Pet transport specialists.

SATCO, 69 Kilravock Street, London W10 4HY. Tel: 0181-968 8543. Visas.

SFIA Educational Trust, SFIA House, 15 Forlease Road, Maidenhead SL6 1JA. Tel: 01628-34291. Information on private schools in UK.

School of Oriental & African Studies (External Services Division), Thornhaugh Street, Russell Square, London WC1H 0XG. Tel: 0171-637 2388. Briefings and language training.

Seatax Ltd, 100 East Iaith Gate, Doncaster DN1 1JA. Tel: 01302-364673. Tax advisers.

Spratts Animal Travel Service, 756 High Road, Goodmayes, Ilford, Essex IG3 8SY. Tel: 0181-597 2415.

Dave Tester Expatriate Insurance Services, 18a Hove Park Villas, Hove BN3 6HG. Tel: 01273-703469. Fax: 01273-777723. E-mail:dave.tester@compuserve.com. Insurance broker.

Thames Consular Services, 363 Chiswick High Road, London W4 4HS. Tel: 0181-995 2492. Visas.

TraQs Consulting, Riding Court, Riding Court Road, Datchet, Berks SL3 9LE. Tel: 01753-582020. Fax: 01753-582737. Tax planning software.

Trinity College, External Examinations Department, 16 Park Crescent, London W1N 4AH. Tel: 0171-323 2328. Fax: 0171-323 5201.

TSW Tax Consultants Ltd, 66 New Bond Street, London W1Y 9DF.. Tel: 0171-491 2535.

UK Expatriates Professional Advisory Services Ltd, 84 Grange Road, Middlesborough TS1 2LS. Tel: 01642-221211. Tax advisers.

University of Cambridge Local Examination Syndicate (UCLES), 1 Hills Road, Cambridge CB1 2EU. Tel: 01223 553789.

University of London, Secretary for External Students, Senate House, Malet Street, London WC1E 7HU.

Vocational Guidance Association, 7 Harley House, Upper Harley Street, London NW1 4RP. Tel: 0171-935 2600.

Women's Corona Society, c/o Commonwealth Institute, Kensington High Street, London W8 6NQ. Tel: 0171-610 4407. Briefings and country reports.

WES Home School, Blagrave House, 17 Blagrave Street, Reading, Berks RG1 1QA. Tel: 0118-958 9993. Fax: 0118-958 9994.
Website: www.weshome.demon.co.uk.
E-mail: office@weshome.demon.co.uk.

Further Reading

COUNTRIES & REGIONS

Culture Shock (Kuperard). A series of country profiles which includes Argentina, Australia, Bolivia, Borneo, Burma, Canada, Chile, China, Cuba, Czech Republic, Denmark, Egypt, France, Germany, Greece, Hong Kong, India, Indonesia, Iran, Israel, Italy, Japan, Korea, Laos, Malaysia, Mauritius, Mexico, Morocco, Nepal, Netherlands, Norway, Pakistan, Philippines, Singapore, South Africa, Spain, Sri Lanka, Sweden, Switzerland, Syria, Taiwan, Thailand, Turkey, UAE, USA, Vietnam.

Getting a Job in Europe, P Riley (Northcote House).

Getting a Job in America, Roger Jones (How To Books, 5th edition 1998).

Getting a Job in Australia, Nick Vandome (How To Books, 3rd edition).

How to Get a Job in Europe, Mark Hemphsell (How To Books, 3rd edition).

Living & Working in America, Steve Mills (How To Books, 4th edition).

Living & Working in Australia, Laura Veltman (How To Books, 6th edition).

Live and Work in Central America, Avril Harper (Grant Dawson, 1991).

Living and Working in France, Alan Hart (How To Books, 1998).

How to Live & Work in Germany, Christine Hall (How To Books, 2nd edition).

How to Live and Work in Hong Kong, Jeremy Gough (How To Books).

How to Live & Work in Italy, Amanda Hinton (How To Books, 1993).

Living and Working in New Zealand, Joyce Muirhead (How To Books, 4th edition).

Living and Working in Saudi Arabia, R. Rayburn & K. Bush (How To Books, 2nd edition).

Living and Working in Spain, Robert A C Richards (How To Books, 2nd edition 1998).

Jobs in Japan, J Wharton (Global Press — distr. Vacation Work).

Live and Work in Belgium, The Netherlands and Luxembourg, A de Vries (Vacation Work, 1992).

Live and Work in Canada, Avril Harper (Grant Dawson).

Live and Work in France, Mark Hempshell (Vacation Work, 1991).

Live and Work in Germany, Victoria Pybus (Vacation Work, 1992).

Live and Work in Germany, Mark Hempshell (Grant Dawson, 1991).

Live and Work in Italy, Victoria Pybus and Rachael Robinson (Vacation Work).

Live and Work in Scandinavia, Victoria Pyb us (Vacation Work, 1995).

Living and Working in Europe, E Cobbe and J MacCarthaigh (Gill & Macmillan, 1992).

Living and Working in Switzerland, D Hampshire (Survival Books).

Living and Working in the USA, David Hampshire (Survival books).

Living in France, P Holland (Robert Hale, 1990).

Living in Italy, K Menzies (Robert Hale, 1991).

Living in Portugal, Susan Thackeray (Robert Hale).

Living in Spain, John Reay-Smith (Robert Hale, 1989).

Long Stays in Belgium and Luxembourg, J. Hazlewood (David & Charles, 1986).

Long Stays in France, R Mazzawi and D Philpott (David & Charles, 1990).

Long Stays in Germany, J A S Abecasis-Philips (David & Charles, 1990).

Long Stays in Spain, Peter Davey (David & Charles, 1991).

Setting up in Italy, Sebastian O'Kelly (Merehurst, 1990).

Setting up in Spain, David Hewson (Merehurst, 1990).

Working in the European Community, A J Raban (Hobsons).

Working in France, Carol Pineau and Maureen Kelly (Franc Books, BP 29, 94301 Vincennes, France).

EDUCATION

Adult Education in Developing Countries, E.K. Townsend Coles (Pergamon, 1977).

An African School: A Record of Experience, K. Elliot (Cambridge University Press, 1970).

Canadian Education in the 1980s, J Donald Wilson (Detselig, Calgary, 1981).

China Learns English Heidi Ross (Yale UP).

A Critical Analysis of School Science Teaching in Arab Countries, J.E. Arrayed (Longman, 1980).

The Development of Modern Education in the Gulf, S. Al-Misnad (Ithaca Press, London, 1985).

Developments in Technical & Vocational Education: A Comparative Survey (UNESCO, 1998).

Educating & Training Technicians, A. MacLennan (Commonwealth Secretariat, 1975).

Education & Development, Ed: R. Garrett (Croom Helm, 1984).

Education & Japan's Modernization, Makoto Aso & Ikuo Amano (Japan Times, 1983 — available from the Japanese Embassy).

Education & Schooling in America, G.L. Gutek (Prentice Hall, 1998).

Education and Schooling in Australia, Gerald L. Gutek (Prentice Hall, 1988).

Education & Society in Africa, Mark Bray, Peter B. Clarke & David Stephens (Edward Arnold, 1986).

Education & Society in the Muslim World, Ed: Mohammed Wasiullah Khan (Hodder & Stoughton, 1981).

Education for a Changing Spain, John M. McNair (Manchester University Press, 1984).

Education in a future South Africa, E. Unterhalter, H. Wolpe, Thozamile Botha — eds (Heinemann, 1991).

Education in Africa: A Comparative Survey, A.B. Fafunwa & J.U. Aisuku (Allen & Unwin, 1982).

Education in Asia & The Pacific, R.R. Singh (UNESCO, PO Box 1425, Bangkok, 1986).

Education in Australia, Phillip E. Jones (David & Charles, 1974).

Education in Central America and the Caribbean, Colin Brock and Donald Clarkson — eds (Routledge, 1990).

Education, Industrialisation & Technical Progress in Mexico, Jorge Padua (IIEP Paris, 1986).

Education in Korea: A Third World Success Story, J.E. Jayasuriya (Korean National Commission for UNESCO, 1983).

Education in Latin America, Eds: Colin Brock & Hugh Lawlor (Croom Helm, 1985).

Education in Latin America & The Caribbean: Trends & Prospects 1970-2000, J.B. Gimeno (UNESCO, 1983).

Education in Modern Egypt: Ideals & Realities, G.D.M. Hyde (Routledge & Kegan Paul, 1978).

Education in Northern Nigeria, A. Ozigi & L. Ocho (Allen & Unwin, 1981).

Education in the Arab World, B.G. Massialas & S.A. Jarrar (Praeger, 1983).

Education in the Soviet Union, Mervyn Matthews (Allen & Unwin, 1982).

Education Policy & Development Strategy in the Third World, M.K. Bacchus (Avebury Gower Publishing Co, 1987).

Educational Innovation in China, Keith Lewin et al (Longman, 1994).

English in Asia, John Wharton (Global Press). Deals mainly with Japan, Korea and Taiwan.

Essays on Canadian Education, Nick Kach (Detselig, 1986).

A Handbook for Teaching English at Japanese Colleges and Universities, Paul Wadden (OUP, 1993).

How Chinese Managers Learn, Malcolm Warner (Macmillan, 1992).

International Handbook of Education Systems, Brian Holmes, J Cameron, et al — eds (Wiley 1983). Vol I: Europe and Canada; Vol II: Africa and the Middle East; Vol III: Asia, Australasia and Latin America.

An Introduction to Education in American Society, E.F. Provenzo Jnr (Charles E. Merrill, 1986).

Islam: Continuity & Change in the Modern World, John Obert Voll (Longman, 1982).

Japan and Education, Michael D Stephens (Macmillan, 1991).

The Japanese School, Benjamin Duke (Praeger, 1986).

Jobs in Japan, John Wharton (Global Press, 1989).

Little England on the Veld, Peter Randall (Ravan Press, Johannesburg, 1982).

Making Science Laboratory Equipment: A Manual for Students & Teachers in Developing Countries, X.F. Carelse (John Wiley, 1983).

Other Schools & Ours, Edmund King (Holt Rinehart & Winston, 1979).

Pacific Universities, Ron Crocombe and Malama Meleisa (Pacific Studies Institute, University of the South Pacific, 1998).

People Development in Developing Countries, Ross Matheson (Associated Business Programmes, 1978).

Recent Trends in Eastern European Education, Wolfgang Mitter et al — eds (German Institute for International Educational Research).

Rethinking Education in Ethiopia, Tekste Negash (Norkiska Afrikainstitutet, Uppsala, Sweden).

Rural Development: Putting the Last First, Robert Chambers (Longman, 1983).

School Education in India, H S Singha (Sterling Publishers New Delhi, 1991).

Schooling in East Asia, Eds: R. Murray Thomas & T. Neville Postlethwaite (Pergamon, 1983).

Schooling in the ASEAN Region, T Neville Postlethwaite and R Murray Thomas — eds (Pergamon, 1980).

Schooling in the Pacific Islands, R. Murray Thomas (Pergamon, 1984).

Schools in New Zealand Society, Eds: Graham H. Robinson & Brian T. O'Rourke (Longman Paul, 1980).

Secondary Education in Fiji, Helen Tavola (Pacific Studies Institute, University of the South Pacific, 1991).

Secondary Education in Nigeria, S. Adesina & S. Ogunsagu (University of Ife Press, 1984).

Singapore's New Education System, Soon Teck Wong (Institute of SE Asia Studies, 1988).

Society, Schools & Progress in E. Europe, Nigel Grant (Pergamon, 1969).

Teacher Education in ASEAN, Ed: Frances Wong (Heinemann, 1976).

Teaching Tactics for Japan's English Classrooms, John Wharton (Global Press, 1989).

The Schooling of China, John Cleverley (Allen & Unwin, 1991).

The French Educational System, H D Lewis (Croom Helm, 1985).

Teaching English Abroad, Susan Griffith (Vacation Work, 1997).

Teaching English in Eastern and Central Europe, Robert Lynes (In Print Publishing, 1995).

Teaching English in Italy, Martin Penner (In Print, 1994).

Teaching English in South East Asia, Nuala O'Sullivan (In Print, 1997).

The Teaching Nation: Prospects for Teachers in the European Community, Guy Neave (Pergamon).

Tradition & Change in Swedish Education, Leon Boucher (Pergamon 1992).

World Education Series (American Association of Collegiate Registrar & Admissions Officers — up-to-date reviews of education in individual countries). Including Algeria, Australia, Austria, Belgium, Colombia, Commonwealth Caribbean, Dominican Republic, Germany, Greece, Haiti, Indonesia, Iran, Italy, Korea, Malaysia, Mexico, Netherlands, New Zealand, Peru, Southern Africa, Switzerland.

World Yearbook of Education 1991: International Schools and International Education, Patricia L Jonietz — ed (Evans Bros, 1991).

GENERAL & REFERENCE

Commonwealth Universities Yearbook (Association of Commonwealth Universities, annual).

The Commonwealth Yearbook (HMSO — annual).

The Directory (European Council for International Schools: ECIS).

The EARLS Guide to Language Schools in Europe (EARLS)

EFL Guide (EL Gazette).

The ECIS Higher Education Directory (John Catt Educational, annual).

The ECIS International Schools Directory (John Catt Educational, annual).

Getting a Job Abroad, Roger Jones (How To Books, 5th edition 1998).

How to Master Languages, Roger Jones (How To Books 1993).

Independent & Boarding Schools World Yearbook, Nexus Business

Communications, Inter-Nation Education Division, Warwick House, Swanley, Kent BR8 8HY. Tel: 01322 660070.

International Directory of Voluntary Work, David Wordsworth (Vacation Work 1989).

Learning Languages: Where and How (Wie and Wo Verlag).

Living and Working Abroad — A wife's guide, (Kuperard, 1997).

Living and Working Abroad — A parent's guide, (Kuperard, 1997).

Obtaining Visas and Work Permits, Roger Jones (How To Books, 1996).

Riding the Waves of Culture, Fons Trompenaars (Economist Books).

Teach Abroad (Central Bureau).

Teaching English Abroad, Susan Griffith (Vacation Work, 1991).

The Third World Directory (Directory of Social Change).

Traveller's Handbook, J Gorman (ed) (WEXAS 1992).

Traveller's Health, Richard Dawood (OUP).

Traveller's World Guides (Trade & Travel Publications): Caribbean; Indonesia, Malaya, Singapore; Mexico and Central America; North Africa; South America; South Asia.

Travelling Alone: A Guide for Working Women, R Bailey (Macdonald Optima 1988).

The Tropical Traveller, John Hatt (Pan 1982).

What can a teacher do except teach?, Barbara Onslow (COIC 1983).

Working Abroad: Essential Financial Planning for Expatriates, Jonathan Golding (International Venture Handbooks 1993).

Working Holidays (Central Bureau — annual).

Working Overseas Resource Pack (Returned Volunteer Action).

The World of Learning (Europa — annual).

PERIODICALS

Comparative Education Review (Carfax Publishing Co, PO Box 25, Abingdon, Oxon OX14 3UE). This is a scholarly publication which appears three times a year. It includes articles on educational developments both at home and abroad and reviews of recent books.

EL Gazette, Dilke House, 1 Malet Street, London WC1E 7AJ. Tel: 0171-255 1969. Fax: 0171-255 1972. E-mail: 100130,2037@compuserve.com. This is a monthly newspaper for TEFL teachers both in the UK and abroad. Together with the *Times Educational Supplement* and the *Guardian* it is the main advertising medium for TEFL posts. The organisation also publishes the *Careers Handbook for English Language Teaching*.

Home and Away (Expats International), 29 Lacon Road, London SE22 9HE. Tel: 0181-299 4986. The monthly magazine of Expats

International, an organisation with 8,000 members, dealing with all matters of concern to expatriates, including finance, family matters and overseas jobs markets. Subscribers, who are generally on overseas contracts, also receive an extensive list of vacancies in the UK and abroad, and can have their details circulated to employers registered with the organisation.

Jobfinder (Overseas Consultants, PO Box 152, Isle of Man). A fortnightly jobs bulletin which includes some teaching vacancies.

Nexus, Expat Network (See Useful Addresses). A monthly magazine which contains articles on job opportunities and job advertisements, though not usually many teaching posts.

Overseas Jobs Express, Island Publishing, Premier House, Shoreham Airport BN43 5FF. Tel: 01273 440220. Fax: 01273 440229. Website: www.overseasjobs.com. A fortnightly newspaper which contains articles on overseas jobs and extensive job advertising.

Pay Away, Ransom Publications, 57 Dafforne Road, Tooting Bec, London SW17 8TY. Tel: 0181-767 4169. Magazine which includes advice and contacts for teaching abroad.

Resident Abroad, Greystoke Place, Fetter Lane, London EC4A 1ND. Tel: 0171-405 6969. A magazine concentrating on expatriate financial matters and carrying extensive financial advertising and analysis.

TIE (The International Educator), 102A Popes Lane, London W5 4NS. Tel & Fax: 0181-840 2587. US Headquarters: PO Box 513, Cummaquid, MA 02637, USA. Tel: 00 1 508 362 1414. Fax: 00 1 508 362 1411. Website: www.tieonline.com. E-mail: tie@capecod.net. The official quarterly publication of the International Educator's Institute, a division of the Overseas Schools Assistance Corporation, a private non-profit making corporation which contain news, articles and job vacancies in international schools. There is a summer 'jobs only' supplement.

Times Educational Supplement, Admiral House, 66–68 East Smithfield, London E1 9XY. Tel: 0171-782 3000. Fax: 0171-782 3200. A weekly publication which includes educational news from other countries and an extensive overseas appointments section. The major agencies advertise here, and there are usually plenty of advertisements placed by overseas establishments, too.

Times Higher Education Supplement, Admiral House, 66–68 East Smithfield, London E1 9XY. Tel: 0171-782 3000. Fax: 0171-782 3200. A weekly publication which concentrates on the HE sector of education. In each issue there are usually a number of advertisements for lecturing posts abroad, most of them in Commonwealth countries.

PUBLISHERS

American Association of Collegiate Registrar & Admissions Officers, 1 Dupont Circle NW, Suite 330, Washington DC 20036, USA.

Associated Business Programmes, Ludgate House, 107-111 Fleet Street, London EC4A 2AB.

Association of Commonwealth Universities, John Foster House, 26 Gordon Square, London WC1H 0PF.

Commonwealth Secretariat, Marlborough House, Pall Mall, London SW1Y 5HX.

Detselig, distributed by Lavis Marketing, 73 Lime Walk, Headington, Oxford OX3 7AD.

Directory of Social Change, Radius Works, Back Lane, London NW3 1HL.

Directory Profiles Ltd, 51A George Street, Richmond, Surrey TW9 1HJ.

EARLS (European Affiliation of Registered Language Schools), 43 Gowrie Road, London SW11 5NN.

ECIS (European Council of International Schools), 21 Lavant Street, Petersfield, Hants GU32 3EW.

Employment Conditions Abroad, Anchor House, 15 Britten Street, London SW3 3TY.

German Institute for International Educational Research, Schlossstrasse 29, Frankfurt am Main.

Global Press, distributed by Vacation Work Publications.

Institute for SE Asian Studies, Heng Mui Ken Terrace, Pasir Panjang, Singapore 0511.

IIEP (International Institute for Education Planning), 7-9 rue Eugäne Delacroix, 75116 Paris, France).

Charles E. Merrill Publishing International, Finsbury Business Centre, 40 Bowling Green Lane, London EC1R 0NE.

Pacific Studies Institute, University of the South Pacific, Suva, Fiji.

Praeger Publishers, 521 Fifth Avenue, New York, NY 10175, USA.

Ravan Press, PO Box 31134, Berea, Johannesburg 2001, South Africa.

Sterling Publishers, L-10 Green Park Extension, New Delhi 110016.

Trade & Travel Publications, 6 Riverside Court, Lower Bristol Rd, Bath BA2 3DZ.

University of California Press Ltd, 126 Buckingham Palace Road, London SW1W 9SD.

University of Ife Press Ltd, Ife, Nigeria.

Vacation Work Publications, 9 Park End Street, Oxford OX1 1HJ.

Wie & Wo Verlag, Postfach 464, D-5300 Bonn 1, Germany.

WEXAS, 45 Brompton Road, London SW3 1DE.

Index

LIVING & WORKING IN AMERICA
How to obtain entry and settle in successfully

Steve Mills

Now in its fifth updated edition, this highly readable and informative handbook explains America's rules and regulations on immigration, a jungle of quotas, green cards and special categories; plus work and lifestyle prospects in this ultimate land of opportunity. 'The scope and presentation of the material is excellent, well worth buying.' *Nexus Expatriate Magazine*. 'Very useful and informative . . . It contains much information about the rules and regulations on immigration, normally difficult to obtain from official sources . . . A mine of information and a must for potential US visitors.' *The Expatriate.* Steve Mills lectures at the David Bruce Centre for American Studies at the University of Keele and has himself spent five years living and working in the USA.

272pp illus. 1 85703 377 9. 5th edition.

HOW TO GET A JOB IN EUROPE
A guide to employment opportunities and contacts

Mark Hempshell

This book sets out exactly what opportunities exist in Europe. 'A very useful book . . . a valuable addition to any careers library – well written clear and interesting.' *Phoenix* (Association of Graduate Careers Advisory Services). 'I learned a lot from the book and was impressed at the amount of information that it contained.' *Newscheck* (Careers Service Bulletin). Mark Hempshell is a freelance writer who specialises in overseas employment topics.

208pp illus. 1 85703 177 6. 3rd edition.

LIVING & WORKING IN NEW ZEALAND
How to prepare for a successful long or short-term stay

Joy Muirhead

A highly informative and up-to-date guide explaining how to enter New Zealand in the wake of the newly liberalised laws relating to immigration, plus everything you need to know about accommodation, getting around, employment, education, health, lifestyles and more. 'Authoritative information.' *New Zealand Outlook.* 'Essential reading.' *Destination New Zealand.* Joy Muirhead is also author of *Finding a Job in New Zealand.*

202pp illus. 1 85703 474 0. 4th edition.

DOING VOLUNTARY WORK ABROAD
How to combine foreign travel with valuable work experience helping others

Mark Hempshell

Doing voluntary work abroad offers a great chance to combine foreign travel and valuable work experience, while helping others and learning about a different way of life. Here's the book that shows you the way — checking out the qualifications, skills and experience you may need, and finding the opportunities, whether in the UK or the rest of Europe, North and South America, or the countries of Africa and Asia. The book details the variety of opportunities available from working in conservation or technological development, to working with the disabled or other disadvantaged groups. Complete with typical case histories, and checklists of essential information about each type of assignment. Mark Hempshell is a specialist writer on international employment topics.

160pp illus. 1 85703 469 4. 2nd edition.

GETTING A JOB IN AUSTRALIA
A guide to employment opportunities and contacts

Nick Vandome

This handbook provides a complete step-by-step guide to all aspects of job-finding in Australia, for both casual and permanent employment. 'Very helpful, with details of entry requirements, samples of forms that may be needed, and details on employment law and conditions ranging from national holidays to sexual harassment . . . Indispensable.' *TNT Magazine.* 'Packed with information which is well presented and easily accessible.' *Bulletin* (National Association of Careers & Guidance Teachers). 'Provides a complete step-by-step guide.' *Australian Outlook.*

190pp illus. 1 85703 280 2. 3rd edition.

GETTING A JOB IN AMERICA
How and where to find the right employment opportunities and contacts

Roger Jones

This is an essential handbook for everyone planning to work in the US, whether on a short-term vacation assignment, on secondment or contract, or on a permanent basis. Roger Jones is a freelance author specialising in careers and expatriate matters and has himself worked overseas. 'Essential for anyone who is thinking of working in the US.' *Going USA.* 'Outlines with some thoroughness the procedures a future immigrant or temporary resident would have to undertake. . . For young people considering a US exchange or summer employment, the section on vacation jobs is particularly worthwhile.' *Newscheck* (Careers Service Bulletin). 'Very good value for money.' *School Librarian Journal.*

224pp illus. 1 85703 464 3. 4th edition.

OBTAINING VISAS & WORK PERMITS
How and where to obtain the services of immigration lawyers and consultants worldwide

Roger Jones

Today more people than ever are keen to put down roots in foreign countries on either a temporary or long-term basis. But many need advice on how to surmount the many legal obstacles to taking up residence in a foreign land. This unique guide and directory by the author of *How to Emigrate*, lists experts in immigration law and procedures who can guide you through the pitfalls and help you obtain the necessary visas.

140pp. illus. 1 85703 414 7.

LIVING & WORKING IN AUSTRALIA
How to prepare for a successful short or long-term stay

Laura Veltman

Millions of people worldwide apply every year to enter Australia — and less than 1 in 10 are permitted to live there on a permanent basis. This lively and easy-to-use handbook, now in its sixth edition, explains how the latest changes in the law affect your chances, and provides a complete practical guide to relocating Down Under, whether for three months, three years, or on a permanent basis. 'Meets a genuine long-stand need for inside information . . . almost obligatory reading . . . A bonza book.' *Australian Outlook.* 'Lively and uncompromising.' *Australian News.* Laura Veltman is a British expat herself, and is a specialist writer and researcher on Australian migration and business matters.

250pp illus. 1 85703 257 8. 6th edition.

LIVING & WORKING IN FRANCE
How to prepare for a successful visit, be it short, long-term, or forever

Alan Hart

To really enjoy the full experience of living in this varied and exciting country, you need to understand not only the language, but also the people, customs and society of France. This book will help you to adjust rapidly and successfully to the French way of life, to integrate, make friends, and avoid the worst mistakes and experiences of the unprepared and unsuspecting foreigner in France. Alan Hart moved to France in 1991. He has extensive experience of helping newcomers, ranging from students to executives, to adjust and establish themselves in France. He is an executive member of The British Community Committee in Paris.

208pp. illus. 1 85703 439 2.

LIVING & WORKING IN SPAIN
How to prepare for a successful visit, be it short, long-term, or forever

Robert A. C. Richards

Spain has been popular as a holiday and retirement destination and has become important as a focus for commercial life. The second edition of this popular guide has now been updated and revised to provide vital information for everyone planning to live in Spain, either on a temporary or permanent basis and whether for business, professional purposes, study, leisure or retirement. The book gives a fascinating account of Spain's variegated lifestyles and how to cope. Robert Richards has lived in Spain since 1963, working as a teacher and then as a foreign press correspondent. He has lived in Valencia and Santander and is now a resident of Madrid.

144pp. illus. 1 85703 278 0. 2nd edition.

HOW TO GET A JOB ABROAD
A handbook of opportunities and contacts

Roger Jones

Now in a fourth fully revised edition, this top-selling title is essential for everyone planning to spend a period abroad. 'A highly informative book . . . containing lots of hard information and a first class reference section.' *The Escape Committee Newsletter.* 'An excellent addition to any careers library . . . Compact and realistic . . . There is a wide range of reference addresses covering employment agencies, specialist newspapers, a comprehensive booklist and helpful addresses . . . All readers, whether careers officers, young adults or more mature adults, will find use for this book.' *Newscheck* (Careers Services Bulletin). Roger Jones is a specialist writer on expatriate and employment matters.

272pp illus. 1 85703 182 2. 4th edition.

How To Books

How To Books provide practical help on a large range of topics. They are available through all good bookshops or can be ordered direct from the distributors. Just tick the titles you want and complete the form on the following page.

___ Achieving Personal Well-being (£8.99)
___ Applying for a Job (£8.99)
___ Arranging Insurance (£9.99)
___ Awakening the Writer Within (£8.99)
___ Backpacking Round Europe (£8.99)
___ Be a Freelance Journalist (£8.99)
___ Be a Freelance Secretary (£8.99)
___ Become a Freelance Sales Agent (£9.99)
___ Becoming a Father (£8.99)
___ Building Self-Esteem (£8.99)
___ Buy & Run a Shop (£8.99)
___ Buy & Run a Small Hotel (£8.99)
___ Buying a Personal Computer (£9.99)
___ Career Networking (£8.99)
___ Career Planning for Women (£8.99)
___ Cash from your Computer (£9.99)
___ Choosing a Nursing Home (£9.99)
___ Choosing a Package Holiday (£8.99)
___ Claim State Benefits (£9.99)
___ Collecting a Debt (£9.99)
___ Communicate at Work (£7.99)
___ Conduct Staff Appraisals (£7.99)
___ Conducting Effective Interviews (£8.99)
___ Controlling Anxiety (£8.99)
___ Coping with Self Assessment (£9.99)
___ Copyright & Law for Writers (£8.99)
___ Creating a Twist in the Tale (£8.99)
___ Creative Writing (£9.99)
___ Critical Thinking for Students (£8.99)
___ Dealing with a Death in the Family (£9.99)
___ Dealing with Your Bank (£8.99)
___ Do Your Own Advertising (£8.99)
___ Do Your Own PR (£8.99)
___ Doing Business Abroad (£10.99)
___ Doing Business on the Internet (£12.99)
___ Doing Voluntary Work Abroad (£9.99)
___ Employ & Manage Staff (£8.99)
___ Find Temporary Work Abroad (£8.99)
___ Finding a Job in Canada (£9.99)
___ Finding a Job in Computers (£8.99)
___ Finding a Job in New Zealand (£9.99)
___ Finding a Job with a Future (£8.99)
___ Finding Work Overseas (£9.99)
___ Freelance DJ-ing (£8.99)
___ Freelance Teaching & Tutoring (£9.99)
___ Get a Job Abroad (£10.99)
___ Get a Job in Europe (£9.99)
___ Get a Job in France (£9.99)
___ Get a Job in Travel & Tourism (£8.99)
___ Get into Radio (£8.99)
___ Getting a Job in America (£10.99)
___ Getting a Job in Australia (£9.99)
___ Getting into Films & Television (£10.99)
___ Getting That Job (£8.99)
___ Getting your First Job (£8.99)
___ Going to University (£8.99)

___ Having a Baby (£8.99)
___ Healing the Hurt Within (£8.99)
___ Helping your Child to Read (£8.99)
___ How to Study & Learn (£8.99)
___ Investing in People (£9.99)
___ Investing in Stocks & Shares (£9.99)
___ Know Your Rights at Work (£8.99)
___ Learning to Counsel (£9.99)
___ Live & Work in Germany (£9.99)
___ Live & Work in Greece (£9.99)
___ Live & Work in Italy (£8.99)
___ Living & Working in America (£12.99)
___ Living & Working in Australia (£12.99)
___ Living & Working in China (£9.99)
___ Living & Working in France (£9.99)
___ Living & Working in Hong Kong (£10.99)
___ Living & Working in New Zealand (£9.99)
___ Living & Working in Spain (£8.99)
___ Living & Working in the Netherlands (£9.99)
___ Living Away From Home (£8.99)
___ Making a Complaint (£8.99)
___ Making a Video (£9.99)
___ Making a Wedding Speech (£8.99)
___ Making Money from Letting (£8.99)
___ Making Money from Writing £8.99)
___ Manage a Sales Team (£8.99)
___ Manage an Office (£8.99)
___ Manage Computers at Work (£8.99)
___ Manage Your Career (£8.99)
___ Managing Budgets & Cash Flows (£9.99)
___ Managing Credit (£8.99)
___ Managing Meetings (£8.99)
___ Managing Projects (£8.99)
___ Managing Through People (£8.99)
___ Managing Your Personal Finances (£8.99)
___ Managing Yourself (£8.99)
___ Market Yourself (£8.99)
___ Mastering Book-Keeping (£8.99)
___ Mastering Business English (£8.99)
___ Mastering Public Speaking (£8.99)
___ Maximising Your Memory (£8.99)
___ Migrating to Canada (£12.99)
___ Obtaining Visas & Work Permits (£9.99)
___ Organising Effective Training (£9.99)
___ Passing Exams Without Anxiety (£8.99)
___ Passing That Interview (£8.99)
___ Plan a Wedding (£8.99)
___ Planning Your Gap Year (£8.99)
___ Preparing a Business Plan (£8.99)
___ Publish a Newsletter (£9.99)
___ Publishing a Book (£9.99)
___ Rent & Buy Property in Italy (£9.99)
___ Research Methods (£8.99)
___ Researching for Writers (£8.99)
___ Retire Abroad (£8.99)
___ Run a Voluntary Group (£8.99)

How To Books

___ Securing a Rewarding Retirement (£8.99)
___ Self-Counselling (£8.99)
___ Selling Your House (£8.99)
___ Setting up Home in Florida (£9.99)
___ Setting Up Your Own Limited Company (£9.99)
___ Spending a Year Abroad (£8.99)
___ Start a Business from Home (£7.99)
___ Start a New Career (£6.99)
___ Starting to Manage (£8.99)
___ Starting to Write (£8.99)
___ Start Word Processing (£8.99)
___ Start Your Own Business (£8.99)
___ Study Abroad (£8.99)
___ Study & Live in Britain (£7.99)
___ Studying at University (£8.99)
___ Studying for a Degree (£8.99)
___ Successful Grandparenting (£8.99)
___ Successful Mail Order Marketing (£9.99)
___ Successful Single Parenting (£8.99)
___ Survive Divorce (£8.99)
___ Surviving Redundancy (£8.99)
___ Taking in Students (£8.99)
___ Taking on Staff (£8.99)
___ Taking Your A-Levels (£8.99)
___ Teach Adults (£8.99)
___ Teaching Abroad (£8.99)
___ Teaching Someone to Drive (£8.99)
___ Thriving on Stress (£8.99)
___ Travel Round the World (£8.99)
___ Unlocking Your Potential (£8.99)
___ Understand Finance at Work (£8.99)
___ Using the Internet (£9.99)
___ Winning Consumer Competitions (£8.99)
___ Winning Presentations (£8.99)
___ Work from Home (£8.99)
___ Work in Retail (£8.99)
___ Working Abroad (£14.99)
___ Working as a Holiday Rep (£9.99)
___ Working as an Au Pair (£8.99)
___ Working in Japan (£10.99)
___ Working in Photography (£8.99)
___ Working in Hotels & Catering (£9.99)
___ Working on Contract Worldwide (£9.99)
___ Working on Cruise Ships (£9.99)
___ Write a Press Release (£9.99)
___ Write & Sell Computer Software (£9.99)
___ Writing a CV that Works (£8.99)
___ Writing a Non Fiction Book (£9.99)
___ Writing a Pantomime (£8.99)
___ Writing a Report (£8.99)
___ Writing a Textbook (£12.99)
___ Writing an Assignment (£8.99)
___ Writing an Essay (£8.99)
___ Writing & Publishing Poetry (£9.99)
___ Writing & Selling a Novel (£8.99)
___ Writing Business Letters (£8.99)
___ Writing for Publication (£9.99)
___ Writing for Radio (£8.99)
___ Writing for Television (£8.99)
___ Writing Humour (£8.99)
___ Writing Reviews (£9.99)
___ Writing Romantic Fiction (£9.99)
___ Writing Science Fiction (£9.99)
___ Writing Short Stories & Articles (£8.99)
___ Writing Your Dissertation (£8.99)

To: Plymbridge Distributors Ltd, Plymbridge House, Estover Road, Plymouth PL6 7PZ. Customer Services Tel: (01752) 202301. Fax: (01752) 202331.

Please send me copies of the titles I have indicated. Please add postage & packing (UK £1, Europe including Eire, £2, World £3 airmail).

☐ I enclose cheque/PO payable to Plymbridge Distributors Ltd for £ _____

☐ Please charge to my ☐ MasterCard, ☐ Visa, ☐ AMEX card.

Account No. ☐☐☐☐☐☐☐☐☐☐☐☐☐☐☐☐

Card Expiry Date ☐ 19 ☎ **Credit Card orders may be faxed or phoned.**

Customer Name (CAPITALS) ....

Address ....

.... Postcode ....

Telephone .... Signature ....

Every effort will be made to despatch your copy as soon as possible but to avoid possible disappointment please allow up to 21 days for despatch time (42 days if overseas). Prices and availability are subject to change without notice.

Code BPA

CW00373623

COOK'S COLLECTION

STUDENT EATS

Fuss-free and tasty recipe ideas
for the modern cook

CONTENTS

INTRODUCTION

Whether you're an experienced cook or totally new to cooking, as a student living away from home for the first time you'll want to have a few recipes up your sleeve. While occasional takeaways are all part of student life, in between those quick and often expensive fixes you'll want to refuel with good food that you've made yourself from fresh and nutritious ingredients.

For anyone who's found themselves away from home for the first time, knowing how and what to cook can seem a bit daunting. Suddenly, those familiar home-cooked dishes seem a distant memory, and recreating them in a new and unfamiliar kitchen, with limited equipment, can feel a bit overwhelming. But help is at hand with *Student Eats*! This is a great first cookbook – for students cooking for themselves at college or university, for those moving out of home for the first time, or for anyone developing an interest in cooking. It will become your culinary companion for life, that favourite cookbook you turn to time and again when you want to prepare something delicious and interesting for yourself or your friends.

When you're first moving away from home you'll want to stock up on some basic storecupboard essentials. You'll always be able to put a meal together if you keep a few staples on standby: flour, pasta, rice, quinoa; canned pulses, tomatoes and tuna; olive oil and sunflower or groundnut oil, vinegar, mustard, soy sauce, chilli sauce, Worcestershire sauce, tomato purée, tahini; seeds and nuts, ground spices, dried herbs, ready-made stocks and honey. You won't need all of these things at the start, but as you work through this cookbook and begin to make more recipes, you'll naturally build up a storecupboard of these ingredients.

Next you'll want to think about fresh ingredients. Try to eat a variety of fresh fruit and vegetables throughout the week as this will provide you with the widest range of nutrients. Frozen fruit and veggies come in handy as these can be stored and used as when you need them. Meat and fish can be bought fresh or frozen – and you'll often find these on offer in the supermarkets, so make use of the promotions you come across and use your freezer to keep what you won't use immediately. Do make sure you always allow enough time for thawing – take meat, fish etc. out of the freezer the night before and leave it in the fridge overnight to thaw completely.

Organisation is the key when you're a student or taking your first steps living away from home. In order to save time and money it's a good idea to plan meals at the beginning of the week by looking at the ingredients you already have, what your budget is and how much time you'll have to cook each meal. Knowing what you need will mean you'll only need to make one trip to the supermarket each week, which is going to be a massive time-saver and will likely save you a bit of money too.

You'll also want to make sure you have enough equipment to get started with. Three saucepans – small, medium and large will ensure you can cook a couple of things at the same time. A wok and a frying pan are also useful to have for stir-fries, sautéing and general frying. A blender will come in handy for soups or smoothies and a food processor will make light work of chopping, but these aren't essential for every recipe. A couple of baking sheets, muffin tin, roasting tin and a baking dish are handy for oven-cooked dishes.

You'll also want a set of sharp knifes, a mixing bowl, a chopping board, a rolling pin, a box grater, some wooden spoons, a fish slice or spatula, a tin opener and a garlic press. However, many pieces of equipment can easily be substituted: if a recipe asks for a sauté pan, you can improvise with a frying pan or saucepan. If you're moving into a house share it might be worth checking what equipment other people already have or might be willing to share.

Other kitchen essentials you might find useful are things like kitchen foil for lining baking trays, plastic wrap for keeping food fresh, clips to seal open bags of pasta or rice, sandwich bags for snacks and lunch, and plastic containers to freeze leftovers in. Freezing leftovers is a great way to save time and money as it often doesn't take much longer or cost much more to cook a double portion of chilli and freeze a portion for another day.

To ensure success every time, always read through the recipe before you start cooking. You don't want to discover halfway through that you're missing a vital ingredient or that someone has helped themselves to an all-important rasher of bacon, the last handful of pasta or the remains of the butter without your knowledge! Get all the ingredients and equipment you'll need ready, line them up in the order in which you'll be using them and then begin. You'll find it much easier to multi-task in the kitchen if everything is to hand. A tidy kitchen is also easier to work in than a messy one, so make sure you avoid any housemate squabbles by clearing up after every cooking session.

So, to help fuel study, work or socialising, why not try starting your day with a Kale Coco Bomb Smoothie (see page 20). Lunch can be made in advance and eaten on the go with Quinoa Salad in a Jar (see page 88) and dinner is made easy with Lemon Chicken Courgetti (see page 137).

With this book on your shelf you can enjoy cooking a wide range of meals from quick and healthy to occasional treats and impressive dinners for friends, with confidence.

CHAPTER ONE

BREAKFAST

MORNING POWERBOWL
SMOOTHIE

SERVES: *1* | **PREP:** *10 mins* | **COOK:** *No cooking*

INGREDIENTS

50 g/1¾ oz strawberries
50 g/1¾ oz blackberries
50 g/1¾ oz raspberries
1 banana, peeled
150 ml/5 fl oz hemp milk
1 tbsp coconut oil
1 tbsp ground almonds
1 kiwi fruit, peeled and sliced
2 tsp chia seeds
1 small mango, stoned, peeled and
  chopped
1 tbsp chopped walnuts
2 tsp toasted sesame seeds

1. Place the strawberries, blackberries, raspberries, half the banana, the hemp milk, coconut oil and ground almonds in a blender and blend until smooth.

2. Pour the mixture into a bowl. Place the kiwi slices on top, in a row running down the centre of the bowl. Scatter the chia seeds in a row to the left of the kiwi slices.

3. Place the chopped mango next to the chia seeds on the far left-hand side of the bowl.

4. Next add the chopped walnuts to the bowl, on the far right-hand side.

5. Slice the remaining banana and add in a row next to the chopped walnuts. Finish with a row of the toasted sesame seeds next to the kiwi slice. Serve immediately.

HEALTHY FRUIT
& NUT BOWL

SERVES: *4* | **PREP:** *15 mins, plus chilling* | **COOK:** *No cooking*

INGREDIENTS

1 orange

*2 mangoes, peeled, stoned and
    chopped*

4 tbsp chia seeds

4–5 tbsp milk

2 tbsp goji berries

seeds from 2 passion fruits

55 g/2 oz pineapple, cut into chunks

2 tbsp sunflower seeds

2 tbsp pumpkin seeds

55 g/2 oz redcurrants

2 kiwi fruits, peeled and sliced

2 tbsp flaked almonds, toasted

1. Grate the orange rind, then peel the orange and put the flesh into a food processor with the chopped mango. Process for a few seconds to break everything down.

2. Add the orange rind, chia seeds and milk and process again for 20–30 seconds, scraping down any mixture from the side of the bowl. Leave to stand for 5 minutes.

3. Process the mixture again, then divide between four bowls and chill in the refrigerator for 10 minutes.

4. Top with the remaining ingredients and serve.

BIRCHER MUESLI

INGREDIENTS

250 g/9 oz rolled oats
1 tbsp wheatgerm
200 ml/7 fl oz milk
2 tbsp honey, plus extra to serve
(optional)
2 tbsp natural yogurt
1 apple, peeled
150 g/5½ oz chopped nuts, such as
macadamia nuts, cashew nuts or
hazelnuts
mixed berries and fruit purée, to
serve (optional)

1. The night before serving, mix together the oats, wheatgerm and milk in a large mixing or serving bowl, cover with clingfilm and chill overnight.

2. To serve, stir the oat mixture and add the honey and yogurt. Halve, core and grate the apple and add to the mixture. Mix well with a large spoon to combine.

3. Spoon into serving bowls and top with the nuts and berries, if using.

4. Drizzle over a little more honey or some fruit purée, if liked, and serve immediately.

APPLE & SPICE PORRIDGE

SERVES: *4* | **PREP:** *10 mins* | **COOK:** *15 mins*

INGREDIENTS

600 ml/1 pint milk or water
1 tsp salt
115 g/4 oz rolled oats
2 large apples
½ tsp ground mixed spice
clear honey, to serve (optional)

1. Put the milk in a large saucepan and bring to the boil. Add the salt and sprinkle in the oats, stirring constantly.

2. Reduce the heat to low and simmer, stirring occasionally, for 10 minutes.

3. Meanwhile, halve, core and grate the apples. When the porridge is creamy and much of the liquid has evaporated, stir in the apple and mixed spice.

4. Spoon into bowls and drizzle with honey, if using. Serve immediately.

MUESLI

SERVES: *4* | **PREP:** *10–15 mins* | **COOK:** *No cooking*

INGREDIENTS

115 g/4 oz jumbo oats
55 g/2 oz ready-to-eat dried
  apricots
25 g/1 oz pecan nuts
55 g/2 oz sultanas
40 g/1½ oz dried cranberries
15 g/½ oz pumpkin seeds
15 g/½ oz sunflower seeds
1 tbsp sesame seeds
1 apple
milk or natural yogurt, to serve

1. Place the jumbo oats in a large mixing bowl.

2. Dice the dried apricots and roughly chop the pecan nuts.

3. Add the diced apricots, chopped pecan nuts, sultanas, cranberries, pumpkin seeds, sunflower seeds and sesame seeds to the bowl, mixing well to combine.

4. Core, thinly slice and chop the apple and mix again to combine.

5. Serve with milk or natural yogurt. Store any leftover muesli in an airtight container.

SUMMER BERRY
PANCAKE STACKS

SERVES: *4* | **PREP:** *10 mins, plus standing* | **COOK:** *10 mins*

INGREDIENTS

150 g/5½ oz plain white flour
1½ tsp baking powder
pinch of salt
1 tbsp caster sugar
250 ml/9 fl oz milk
1 large egg
2 tbsp melted butter
2 tbsp finely chopped fresh mint
sunflower oil, for oiling
icing sugar, for dusting

TO SERVE

200 g/7 oz Greek-style natural
  yogurt
350 g/12 oz mixed berries, such
  as blackberries, raspberries,
  redcurrants and blueberries

1. Sift the flour, baking powder, salt and sugar into a bowl. Add the milk, egg, butter and mint and beat until smooth. Leave to stand for 5 minutes.

2. Lightly grease a griddle pan or frying pan and heat over a medium heat. Spoon tablespoons of batter into the pan and cook until bubbles appear on the surface.

3. Turn over with a palette knife and cook on the other side until golden brown. Repeat this process using the remaining batter, while keeping the cooked pancakes warm.

4. Stack the pancakes with the yogurt and berries, dust with icing sugar and serve.

CRANBERRY
GRANOLA

SERVES: *8* | **PREP:** *10–15 mins, plus cooling* | **COOK:** *30 mins*

INGREDIENTS

2 tbsp vegetable oil

125 ml/4 fl oz maple syrup

2 tbsp clear honey

1 tsp vanilla extract

280 g/10 oz rolled oats

2 tbsp sesame seeds

4 tbsp sunflower seeds

4 tbsp pumpkin seeds

150 g/5½ oz dried cranberries

1. Preheat the oven to 150°C/300°F/Gas Mark 2. Thoroughly mix together all the ingredients in a large bowl.

2. Divide the mixture between two baking sheets and spread out evenly. Bake in the preheated oven for 15 minutes.

3. Stir the mixture thoroughly, then return to the oven and bake for a further 15 minutes. Leave to cool completely on the baking sheets before serving. Store any leftover granola in an airtight container.

KALE COCO
BOMB SMOOTHIE

SERVES: *1* | **PREP:** *10–15 mins* | **COOK:** *No cooking*

INGREDIENTS

40 g/1½ oz green curly kale,
  shredded
200 ml/7 fl oz chilled water
1 tsp hemp seeds or hempseed oil
100 g/3½ oz frozen banana
1 tsp raw cacao powder
¼ vanilla pod, seeds scraped
small pinch of raw cacao powder,
  to garnish

1. Put the kale in a blender with the water and blend until smooth.

2. Add the hemp seeds, banana, cacao powder and vanilla seeds and blend again until smooth and creamy.

3. Pour into a glass and serve immediately, garnished with a pinch of raw cacao.

SKIN-SOOTHER
SMOOTHIE

SERVES: *1* | **PREP:** *10 mins* | **COOK:** *No cooking*

INGREDIENTS
BANANA LAYER

1 banana, peeled and roughly
*   chopped*
1 tbsp smooth peanut butter
1 tbsp natural yogurt

BLUEBERRY LAYER

150 g/5½ oz blueberries
juice of ½ lemon

KIWI LAYER

3 kiwi fruits, peeled and roughly
*   chopped*
1 tbsp milled linseeds

1. Put all the ingredients for the banana layer in a blender and blend until smooth. Transfer to a jug and rinse the blender goblet.

2. To make the blueberry layer, put the blueberries and lemon juice into the blender and blend until smooth. Transfer to a separate jug and rinse the blender goblet.

3. To make the kiwi layer, place the kiwi in the blender with the linseeds and blend until smooth.

4. Layer the three smoothie mixtures into a large glass and serve immediately.

SUPER-POWERED MANGO

INGREDIENTS

2 clementines, zest and a little
  pith removed
1 mango, stoned and peeled
2 apples, halved
small handful of crushed ice,
  to serve (optional)
chilled water, to taste
1 tsp clear honey

1. Feed the clementines, mango and apples through a juicer.

2. Half-fill a glass with crushed ice, if using. Pour in the juice, top up with water to taste, stir in the honey and serve immediately.

BERRY BREAKFAST SMOOTHIE

SERVES: *1* | **PREP:** *10 mins* | **COOK:** *No cooking*

INGREDIENTS

175 g/6 oz blueberries

115 g/4 oz cranberries

150 ml/5 fl oz natural yogurt

2 tsp clear honey

4 tbsp chilled water

1. Put the blueberries and cranberries in a blender and whizz until smooth.

2. Add the yogurt, honey and water and whizz again.

3. Pour into a glass and serve.

CRANBERRY & PINEAPPLE SMOOTHIE

INGREDIENTS

25 g/1 oz chia seeds
½ small pineapple, peeled and
roughly chopped
115 g/4 oz cranberries
small handful of crushed ice
(optional)

1. Put the chia seeds in a blender and blend until finely ground.

2. Add the pineapple and cranberries and blend until smooth.

3. Half-fill a glass with crushed ice, if using, then pour in the juice and serve immediately.

BACON BUTTIES WITH
HOME-MADE TOMATO SAUCE

SERVES: *2* | **PREP:** *20–25 mins* | **COOK:** *30 mins*

INGREDIENTS

4 rashers smoked back bacon
25 g/1 oz butter, softened
4 thick slices brown or white bread
pepper (optional)

TOMATO SAUCE

2 tbsp olive oil
1 red onion, chopped
2 garlic cloves, chopped
250 g/9 oz plum tomatoes, chopped
250 g/9 oz canned chopped
   tomatoes
½ tsp ground ginger
½ tsp chilli powder
40 g/1½ oz dark brown sugar
100 ml/3½ fl oz red wine vinegar
salt and pepper (optional)

1. To make the tomato sauce, heat the oil in a large saucepan and add the onion, garlic and tomatoes. Add the ginger and chilli and season to taste with salt and pepper, if using. Cook for 15 minutes, or until soft.

2. Pour the mixture into a food processor and blend well. Sieve thoroughly to remove all the seeds. Return the mixture to the pan and add the sugar and vinegar. Bring back to the boil and cook until it has the consistency of ketchup. Bottle quickly in airtight bottles or jars and store in the refrigerator until ready to serve.

3. Preheat the grill to high. Place the bacon under the preheated grill and cook, turning frequently, until the bacon is crisp and golden brown. Spread the butter over the slices of bread.

4. Place two rashers on each of two slices of bread, season with pepper to taste, if using, and spoon or pour the sauce over the bacon. Top with the remaining slices of bread and serve immediately.

BREAKFAST
BURRITO

SERVES: *1* | **PREP:** *15–20 mins* | **COOK:** *8–10 mins*

INGREDIENTS

2 egg whites

pinch of salt

¼ tsp pepper

1 spring onion, thinly sliced

½ tsp vegetable oil

25 g/1 oz red or green pepper,
*   deseeded and diced*

2 tbsp canned black beans, drained
*   and rinsed*

1 wholemeal flour tortilla, warmed

15 g/½ oz feta cheese, crumbled

2 tbsp salsa

1 tsp finely chopped fresh coriander,
*   plus extra leaves to garnish*

1. In a small bowl, combine the egg whites, salt, pepper and spring onion and stir well.

2. Heat the oil in a non-stick frying pan over a medium–high heat. Add the red pepper and cook, stirring, for about 3 minutes, or until it begins to soften. Reduce the heat to medium, pour in the egg mixture and cook, stirring frequently, for a further 1–2 minutes, or until the egg sets.

3. Put the beans in a microwave-safe bowl and microwave on High for about 1 minute, or until heated through.

4. Spoon the cooked egg mixture onto the tortilla. Top with the beans, cheese, salsa and coriander. Serve immediately, garnished with whole coriander leaves.

AVOCADO TOASTS

SERVES: *4* | **PREP:** *10 mins* | **COOK:** *10 mins*

INGREDIENTS

8 slices granary bread
4 tbsp tahini
4 large avocados, peeled, stoned
  and sliced

DUKKAH

100 g/3½ oz hazelnuts
80 g/2¾ oz sesame seeds
2 tbsp cumin seeds
2 tbsp coriander seeds
2 tsp pepper
1 tsp salt

1. To make the dukkah, preheat the oven to 180°C/350°F/Gas Mark 4.

2. Spread the hazelnuts over a baking sheet and bake in the preheated oven for 3–4 minutes. Rub them in a clean tea towel to remove the skins.

3. Place the hazelnuts in a food processor and process until they are roughly chopped.

4. Dry-fry the sesame seeds in a frying pan over a medium heat for 1–2 minutes, until golden. Place the sesame seeds and hazelnuts in a bowl.

5. Add the cumin seeds and coriander seeds to the pan and dry-fry for 1–2 minutes, then crush in a pestle and mortar, or spread between two sheets of baking paper and crush with a rolling pin. Add to the nuts and seeds with the pepper and salt and mix well.

6. Toast the bread and spread each slice with tahini.

7. Top each toast with half an avocado, mashing it lightly with a fork, then sprinkle with the dukkah to serve.

BOILED EGGS
WITH SOLDIERS

SERVES: *2* | **PREP:** *5 mins* | **COOK:** *8–10 mins*

INGREDIENTS

4 large eggs
salt and pepper (optional)

SOLDIERS

4 slices crusty white bread, buttered
and cut into thick fingers

1. Bring a small saucepan of water to the boil – the water should be deep enough to cover the eggs.

2. Gently lower the eggs into the water using a long-handled spoon. Keep the water at a gentle simmer and cook for 3–4 minutes for a runny yolk and set white, or 4–5 minutes for a firmer egg.

3. Remove the eggs from the pan using a slotted spoon, drain quickly on kitchen paper and place in egg cups.

4. Serve immediately with the soldiers and salt and pepper, if using.

FRENCH TOAST

INGREDIENTS

6 eggs

175 ml/6 fl oz milk

¼ tsp ground cinnamon

pinch of salt

12 slices day-old white bread

55 g/2 oz butter or margarine, plus
  extra to serve

½–1 tbsp sunflower oil or corn oil

warmed syrup, to serve

1. Break the eggs into a large, shallow bowl and beat together with the milk, cinnamon and salt.

2. Add the bread slices and press them down so that they are covered on both sides with the egg mixture. Leave to stand for 1–2 minutes to soak up the egg mixture, turning the slices over once.

3. Melt 25 g/1 oz of the butter with ½ tablespoon of the oil in a large frying pan. Add as many bread slices to the pan as will fit in a single layer and cook for 2–3 minutes until golden brown.

4. Turn the bread slices over and cook on the other side until golden brown. Repeat this process with the remaining bread, adding extra butter and oil to the pan if necessary, while keeping the cooked French toast warm.

5. Serve the French toast in stacks with butter and warmed syrup.

SAUSAGE FRITTATA

SERVES: *2* | **PREP:** *15–20 mins, plus cooling* | **COOK:** *20 mins*

INGREDIENTS

4 pork sausages

sunflower oil, for frying

4 boiled potatoes, cooled and diced

8 cherry tomatoes

4 eggs, beaten

salt and pepper (optional)

1. Preheat the grill to medium–high. Arrange the sausages on a foil-lined grill pan and cook under the preheated grill, turning occasionally, for 12–15 minutes, or until cooked through and golden brown. Leave to cool slightly, then slice into bite-sized pieces.

2. Meanwhile, add a little oil to a 25-cm/10-inch heavy-based frying pan with a heatproof handle and heat over a medium heat. Add the potatoes and cook until golden brown and crisp all over, then add the tomatoes and cook for a further 2 minutes. Arrange the sausages in the pan so that there is an even distribution of potatoes, tomatoes and sausages.

3. Add a little more oil to the pan if it seems dry. Season the beaten eggs with salt and pepper to taste, if using, then pour the mixture over the ingredients in the pan. Cook for 3 minutes, without stirring or disturbing the eggs. Place the pan under the preheated grill for 3 minutes, or until the top is just cooked. Cut into wedges to serve.

HAM & EGG CUPS

SERVES: *4* | **PREP:** *20 mins* | **COOK:** *15–20 mins*

INGREDIENTS

olive oil, for oiling
8 wafer-thin slices of ham
15 g/½ oz butter
4 spring onions, thinly sliced
4 large hen eggs or duck eggs
pepper (optional)
4 slices hot buttered toast, to serve

1. Preheat the oven to 200ºC/400ºF/Gas Mark 6. Lightly oil four holes in a muffin tin. Line each hole with 2 slices of ham, laying the slices across one another and ruffling them around the sides to make cups. There will be some ham protruding above the top of the tin.

2. Melt the butter in a small frying pan. Add the spring onions and gently fry for 2 minutes until soft. Remove from the heat. Divide two thirds of the onions and their buttery juice between the ham cups.

3. Crack the eggs one at a time into a small bowl. Slide into the ham cups, taking care not to let the eggs run down the sides. Season to taste with pepper, if using. Spoon over the remaining spring onions and bake in the preheated oven for 12–15 minutes until the whites of the eggs are just set. Serve immediately with hot buttered toast.

BREAKFAST
OMELETTE

SERVES: *1* | **PREP:** *15–20 mins* | **COOK:** *20–25 mins*

INGREDIENTS

2 tsp sunflower oil

2 pork sausages

55 g/2 oz closed-cup mushrooms,
*   sliced*

2 back bacon rashers

2 large eggs

2 tbsp milk

large knob of butter

1 tomato, cut into wedges

pinch of dried thyme

salt and pepper (optional)

buttered toast, to serve

1. Preheat the grill to high. Heat the oil in a frying pan, add the sausages and fry for 8–10 minutes, turning frequently, until golden brown and cooked through. Remove from the pan, set aside and keep warm. Add the sliced mushrooms to the pan and fry over a high heat until golden brown. Set aside with the sausages.

2. Preheat the grill to high. Cook the bacon under the preheated grill, turning frequently, until crisp. Do not switch off the grill.

3. Meanwhile, whisk together the eggs and milk in a jug and season to taste with salt and pepper, if using. Wipe the pan clean and add the butter. Pour in the egg mixture and cook for 1–2 minutes until the egg is beginning to set. Using a fork, draw the cooked egg into the centre of the pan to allow the runny egg to run to the edges. Remove the pan from the heat when omelette is almost set.

4. Thickly slice the sausages. Place the sausages, bacon, mushrooms and tomato on one side of the omelette. Sprinkle with the thyme and pop under the grill for 1–2 minutes until sizzling. Slide the omelette onto a warmed plate, folding half of the omelette over the filling. Serve immediately with buttered toast.

CHAPTER TWO

SIDES &
SNACKS

COLOURFUL COLESLAW

SERVES: *4* | **PREP:** *25 mins* | **COOK:** *No cooking*

INGREDIENTS

4 tbsp natural yogurt

½ tsp Dijon mustard

juice of 1 lime

½ tsp clear honey

2 tsp tahini

100 g/3½ oz red cabbage, shredded

100 g/3½ oz white cabbage, shredded

2 carrots, grated

1 small red onion, thinly sliced

1 red pepper, deseeded and thinly sliced

1 yellow pepper, deseeded and thinly sliced

1 fennel bulb, trimmed and shredded

4 radishes, thinly sliced

1 tbsp chopped fresh basil

1 tbsp chopped fresh parsley

1 tbsp chopped fresh mint

3 tbsp pine nuts, toasted

2 tbsp hemp seeds, toasted

1. Put the yogurt, mustard, lime juice, honey and tahini into a large bowl and mix to combine.

2. Add the red cabbage, white cabbage, carrots, onion, red and yellow peppers, fennel, radishes, basil, parsley, mint, pine nuts and hemp seeds.

3. Toss well to coat with the dressing and serve.

CAULIFLOWER FLATBREADS

MAKES: *8 flatbreads* | **PREP:** *45 mins, plus cooling and resting* | **COOK:** *30–45 mins*

INGREDIENTS

225 g/8 oz wholemeal flour

100 g/3½ oz plain flour, plus extra for dusting

1 tsp freshly ground cardamom seeds

2 tsp salt

250 ml/9 fl oz lukewarm buttermilk

150 g/5½ oz butter, melted

FILLING

2 tbsp vegetable oil

2 tsp cumin seeds

1 tbsp hot curry powder

4 garlic cloves, crushed

2 tsp finely grated fresh ginger

150 g/5½ oz cauliflower florets, very finely chopped

2 tsp salt

2 potatoes, boiled, peeled and roughly mashed

6 tbsp finely chopped fresh coriander

1. To make the filling, heat the oil in a large frying pan over a medium heat. Add the cumin seeds, curry powder, garlic, ginger and cauliflower and stir-fry for 8–10 minutes. Add the salt and the potatoes and stir well to mix evenly. Remove from the heat and stir in the coriander. Set aside and leave to cool.

2. Meanwhile, sift together the wholemeal flour, plain flour, cardamom seeds and salt into a large bowl, adding in any bran remaining in the sieve. Make a well in the centre and pour in the buttermilk and 2 tablespoons of melted butter. Work into the flour mixture until soft. Turn out onto a floured work surface and knead for 10 minutes. Shape into a ball and put into a large bowl, cover with a damp cloth and leave to rest for 20 minutes. Divide the dough into eight balls, then roll out each ball into a 15-cm/6-inch round. Place a little of the filling in the centre of each round and fold up the edges of the dough into the centre to enclose the filling. Press down lightly and roll out with a rolling pin to a diameter of 15 cm/6 inches. Repeat with the remaining dough and filling.

3. Heat a non-stick griddle pan or heavy-based frying pan over a medium heat. Brush each flatbread with a little of the remaining melted butter. Brush the pan with a little melted butter. Put a flatbread on the pan and cook for 1–2 minutes, pressing down with a spatula. Turn, brush with a little more butter and cook for a further 1–2 minutes, or until flecked with light brown spots. Remove from the pan, transfer to a plate, cover with foil and keep warm while you cook the remaining flatbreads. Serve warm.

PASTA SALAD WITH CHARGRILLED PEPPERS

SERVES: *4* | **PREP:** *20 mins* | **COOK:** *15 mins*

INGREDIENTS

1 red pepper

1 orange pepper

280 g/10 oz dried conchiglie

5 tbsp extra virgin olive oil

2 tbsp lemon juice

2 tbsp pesto

1 garlic clove, crushed

3 tbsp shredded fresh basil leaves

salt and pepper (optional)

1. Put the whole peppers on a baking sheet and place under a preheated grill, turning frequently, for 15 minutes until charred all over. Remove with tongs and place in a bowl. Cover with crumpled kitchen paper and set aside.

2. Meanwhile, add a little salt, if using, to a large saucepan of water and bring to the boil. Add the pasta, bring back to the boil and cook for 8–10 minutes until tender but still firm to the bite.

3. Combine the oil, lemon juice, pesto and garlic in a large bowl, whisking well to mix. Drain the pasta, add it to the pesto mixture while still hot and toss well. Set aside.

4. When the peppers are cool enough to handle, peel off the skins, then cut open and remove the seeds. Roughly chop the flesh and add to the pasta with the basil. Season to taste with salt and pepper, if using, and toss well. Serve at room temperature.

HERBY POTATO SALAD

SERVES: *4* | **PREP:** *20 mins, plus cooling* | **COOK:** *15 mins*

INGREDIENTS

500 g/1 lb 2 oz new potatoes
16 cherry tomatoes, halved
55 g/2 oz black olives, stoned and
*   roughly chopped*
4 spring onions, finely sliced
2 tbsp chopped fresh mint
2 tbsp chopped fresh parsley
2 tbsp chopped fresh coriander
juice of 1 lemon
3 tbsp extra virgin olive oil
salt and pepper (optional)

1. Add a little salt, if using, to a large saucepan of water and bring to the boil. Add the potatoes, bring back to the boil and cook for 15 minutes, or until tender. Drain, then leave to cool slightly before peeling. Cut into halves or quarters, depending on size.

2. Combine the potatoes with the tomatoes, olives, spring onions, mint, parsley and coriander in a serving bowl.

3. Mix the lemon juice and oil together in a small bowl or jug and pour over the potato salad. Season to taste with salt and pepper, if using, before serving.

JUMBO POTATO
WEDGES WITH DIPS

SERVES: *4* | **PREP:** *30 mins, plus cooling* | **COOK:** *35 mins*

INGREDIENTS

6 large baking potatoes
6 tbsp olive oil
1 tbsp paprika
1 tsp dried oregano
small bunch of fresh thyme
3 garlic bulbs, tops cut off
4 tbsp mayonnaise
4 tbsp soured cream
2 tbsp creamed horseradish
small bunch of fresh chives, snipped
salt and pepper (optional)

1. Preheat the oven to 200°C/400°F/Gas Mark 6.

2. Cut each potato in half lengthways, then cut each half into three wedges and place in a large bowl. Season to taste with salt and pepper and add the oil, paprika, oregano, thyme and garlic bulbs. Gently mix until all of the potatoes and garlic are covered.

3. Line a large baking sheet with baking paper and add the potatoes and garlic, making sure that you scrape everything out of the bowl. Cook in the preheated oven for 20 minutes, or until the garlic feels soft when pressed. Remove the garlic and set aside and turn the wedges over. Return the wedges to the oven and cook for a further 15 minutes. When the potatoes are cooked, remove from the oven and leave to cool for 5 minutes.

4. Meanwhile, put the mayonnaise and soured cream into separate bowls. Add the creamed horseradish and chives to the soured cream and mix well, then set aside. Place the slightly cooled garlic bulbs on a clean surface and scrape out the cooked flesh with a knife, discarding the skin, then roughly chop and add to the mayonnaise.

5. Serve the potato wedges with the dips.

CRUNCHY PARMESAN
& KALE CRISPS

SERVES: *4* | **PREP:** *10 mins* | **COOK:** *15 mins*

INGREDIENTS

200 g/7 oz kale, woody stalks
 removed
1 tbsp olive oil
pinch of cayenne pepper
100 g/3½ oz Parmesan cheese,
 finely grated
sea salt (optional)

1. Preheat the oven to 180°C/350°F/Gas Mark 4. Put the kale and oil in a bowl, season with the cayenne pepper and salt, if using, then toss.

2. Arrange the kale in a single layer on a large baking sheet. Sprinkle the cheese over the kale. Bake for 10–15 minutes, or until the leaves are dry and crisp but just a little brown at the edges.

3. Leave to cool and crisp up for 5 minutes, then serve.

GARLIC & HERB LABNEH

SERVES: *4* | **PREP:** *20 mins, plus chilling* | **COOK:** *No cooking*

INGREDIENTS

300 g/10½ oz Greek-style natural yogurt

1 garlic clove, crushed

2 tbsp finely chopped fresh herbs, such as coriander, parsley and mint

2 tbsp extra virgin olive oil

2 tbsp pistachio nuts, chopped

400 g/14 oz freshly cut vegetable crudités, including asparagus, red pepper, cucumber, baby courgette, baby corn, carrots and broccoli florets

salt and pepper (optional)

1. The labneh needs to be made the day before serving – line a sieve with a piece of muslin and place the sieve over a bowl.

2. Pour in the yogurt and chill in the refrigerator for 24 hours. Squeeze the muslin occasionally to help it along. The yogurt, or labneh, remaining in the muslin will have a cheese-like consistency.

3. Stir the garlic and herbs into the labneh and season with salt and pepper, if using.

4. Divide between four bowls, drizzle with oil and sprinkle with chopped nuts. Serve with the vegetable crudités for dipping.

SPICED BEETROOT &
CUCUMBER TZATZIKI

SERVES: *4* | **PREP:** *15–20 mins* | **COOK:** *No cooking*

INGREDIENTS

*115 g/4 oz cooked beetroot in
    natural juices, drained and diced*
150 g/5½ oz cucumber, diced
40 g/1½ oz radishes, diced
1 spring onion, finely chopped
12 Little Gem lettuce leaves

DRESSING

*150 g/5½ oz 2% fat Greek-style
    natural yogurt*
¼ tsp ground cumin
½ tsp clear honey
2 tbsp finely chopped fresh mint
salt and pepper (optional)

1. To make the dressing, put the yogurt, cumin and honey in a bowl, stir in the mint and season to taste with salt and pepper, if using.

2. Add the beetroot, cucumber, radishes and spring onion, then gently toss together.

3. Arrange the lettuce leaves on a plate. Spoon a little of the salad into each leaf and serve immediately.

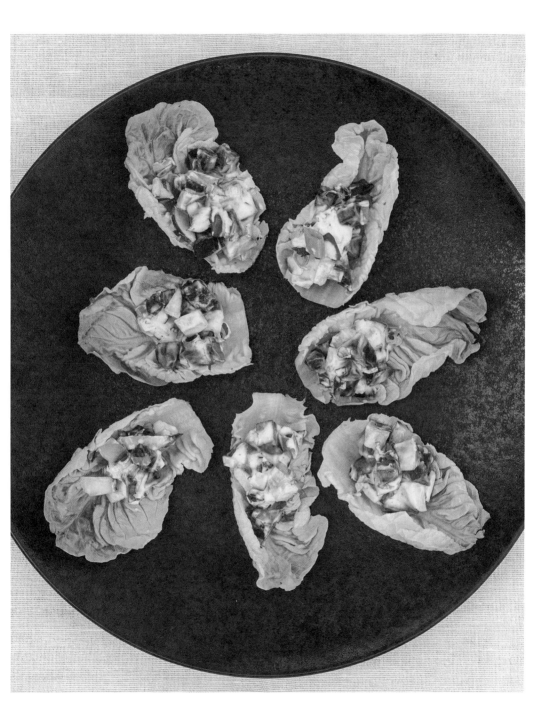

BABA GHANOUSH

SERVES: 6 | **PREP:** 20–25 mins, plus cooling | **COOK:** 1 hour

INGREDIENTS

2 large aubergines
1 garlic clove, chopped
2 tsp ground cumin
4 tbsp tahini
2 tbsp lemon juice
4 tbsp natural yogurt
2 tbsp chopped fresh coriander, plus
extra to garnish

1. Preheat the oven to 220°C/425°F/Gas Mark 7. Prick the aubergine skins and place them on a baking sheet. Bake for 1 hour, or until very soft. Remove from the oven and set aside to cool.

2. Peel off and discard the aubergine skins. Coarsely chop the flesh and place it in a food processor. Add the garlic, cumin, tahini, lemon juice, yogurt and chopped coriander and process until smooth and combined, scraping down the sides as necessary.

3. Transfer to a serving dish, sprinkle with a little chopped coriander and serve.

CHORIZO & CHEESE QUESADILLAS

SERVES: *4* | **PREP:** *20 mins* | **COOK:** *25–30 mins*

INGREDIENTS

115 g/4 oz mozzarella cheese,
  grated
115 g/4 oz Cheddar cheese, grated
225 g/8 oz cooked chorizo sausage
  (outer casing removed), diced
4 spring onions, finely chopped
2 fresh green chillies, deseeded and
  finely chopped
8 flour tortillas
vegetable oil, for brushing
salt and pepper (optional)
guacamole and salsa, to serve

1. Place the mozzarella cheese, Cheddar cheese, chorizo, spring onions, chillies, and salt and pepper to taste, if using, in a bowl and mix well to combine. Divide the mixture between four of the tortillas, then top with the remaining tortillas.

2. Brush a large non-stick or heavy-based frying pan with oil and heat over a medium heat. Add one quesadilla and cook, pressing it down with a spatula, for 4–5 minutes until the underside is crisp and lightly browned. Turn over and cook on the other side until the cheese is melting. Remove from the pan and keep warm. Cook the remaining quesadillas in the same way.

3. Cut each quesadilla into quarters and serve immediately with guacamole and salsa.

GOAT'S CHEESE TRUFFLES WITH HONEY & PISTACHIO CRUMB

MAKES: *12 truffles* | **PREP:** *15 mins* | **COOK:** *No cooking*

INGREDIENTS

150 g/5½ oz French rindless soft
goat's cheese
1 tsp clear honey
40 g/1½ oz pistachio nuts, finely
chopped
sea salt (optional)
pepper (optional)

1. Mix the cheese and honey with a little salt and pepper in a bowl.

2. Scoop heaped teaspoons of the mixture onto a plate to make about 12 mounds.

3. Scatter the nuts over a separate, smaller plate, then roll one mound of cheese at a time in the nuts until evenly coated and shaped like a ball. Place on a plate and chill in the refrigerator for 1 hour before serving. Pack any leftover truffles into a small plastic container and store in the refrigerator for up to 3 days.

HUMMUS

SERVES: 6 | **PREP:** *20 mins* | **COOK:** *No cooking*

INGREDIENTS

*400 g/14 oz canned chickpeas,
    drained and rinsed*

*1 garlic clove, crushed to a paste
    with ¼ tsp salt*

3–4 tbsp tahini

2–4 tbsp lemon juice

¼ tsp ground cumin

*extra virgin olive oil (optional), plus
    extra to serve*

salt (optional)

*paprika and chopped fresh parsley,
    to garnish*

1. Put all but 1 tablespoon of the chickpeas into a food processor. Add the garlic and process to a thick, coarse paste. Add 3 tablespoons of the tahini and process again until blended. Add 2 tablespoons of the lemon juice, the cumin, and salt to taste, if using, and process until creamy. Taste and add extra tahini and/or lemon juice, if liked. For a thinner dip, with the motor running, drizzle in a little oil, if using, or water until you reach the desired consistency.

2. To serve, transfer to a serving bowl, then use the back of a spoon to make an indentation in the centre of the dip. Put the reserved chickpeas in the indentation and drizzle with oil. Sprinkle with paprika and chopped parsley to garnish.

SPICE-ROASTED EDAMAME
& CRANBERRIES

SERVES: *4* | **PREP:** *15 mins* | **COOK:** *15 mins, plus cooling*

INGREDIENTS

350 g/12 oz frozen edamame (soya)
  beans
5-cm/2-inch piece fresh ginger,
  peeled and finely grated
1 tsp Sichuan peppercorns, roughly
  crushed
1 tbsp soy sauce
1 tbsp olive oil
3 small star anise
40 g/1½ oz dried cranberries

1. Preheat the oven to 180°C/350°F/Gas Mark 4. Place the beans in a roasting tin, then sprinkle over the ginger and peppercorns, drizzle with soy sauce and oil, and mix together.

2. Tuck the star anise in among the beans, then roast, uncovered, in the preheated oven for 15 minutes.

3. Stir in the cranberries and leave to cool. Spoon into a small jar and eat within 12 hours.

ROOT VEGETABLE CRISPS
WITH HERBY YOGURT DIP

SERVES: *4* | **PREP:** *30 mins, plus chilling* | **COOK:** *15–20 mins, plus cooling*

INGREDIENTS

1 kg/2 lb 4 oz mixed root vegetables,
such as carrots, parsnips or sweet
potatoes and golden beetroot,
very thinly sliced
4 tbsp virgin olive oil

HERBY YOGURT DIP

200 g/7 oz Greek-style natural
yogurt
2 garlic cloves, finely chopped
4 tbsp finely chopped fresh herbs,
such as flat-leaf parsley, chives,
basil and oregano
salt and pepper (optional)

1. Preheat the oven to 200°C/400°F/Gas Mark 6. To make the herby yogurt dip, spoon the yogurt into a jug, then stir in the garlic and herbs and season to taste with salt and pepper, if using. Cover and chill in the refrigerator.

2. Put the vegetables in a large bowl. Slowly drizzle over the oil, gently turning the vegetables as you go, until they are all coated.

3. Arrange the vegetables over three baking sheets in a single layer, then season with salt and pepper, if using. Bake for 8–10 minutes, then check – the slices in the corners of the trays will cook more quickly, so transfer any that are crisp and golden to a wire rack. Cook the remainder for a further 2–3 minutes, then transfer any cooked crisps to the wire rack. Cook the remaining slices for a further 2–3 minutes if needed, then transfer to the wire rack and leave to cool.

4. Arrange the crisps in a bowl, then spoon the dip into a smaller bowl and serve.

FROZEN YOGURT-COATED BERRIES

SERVES: *4* | **PREP:** *20–25 mins, plus freezing* | **COOK:** *No cooking*

INGREDIENTS

225 g/8 oz fat-free Greek-style natural yogurt
1 tbsp clear honey
¼ tsp natural vanilla extract
115 g/4 oz blueberries
125 g/4½ oz raspberries

1. Line two baking sheets or trays with non-stick baking paper, checking first that they will fit into the freezer.

2. Put the yogurt, honey and vanilla extract in a medium-sized bowl and stir together. Drop a few blueberries into the yogurt, then use two forks to coat the berries in a thin layer of yogurt. Lift out, one berry at a time, draining off the excess yogurt, and transfer to one of the lined trays.

3. Continue dipping and coating until all the blueberries are on the tray. Repeat with the raspberries. Freeze, uncovered, for 2–3 hours until frozen hard.

4. Lift the berries from the trays and pack into polythene bags or covered plastic containers. Seal and freeze for up to 1 month.

5. Remove as many as you need from the freezer and leave to thaw for 10 minutes before serving so that the fruit can soften slightly.

ORANGE & DATE BARS

MAKES: *10 bars* | **PREP:** *12 mins, plus chilling* | **COOK:** *No cooking*

INGREDIENTS

butter, for greasing
400 g/14 oz canned chickpeas,
    drained and rinsed
7 dates, stoned
1 tbsp milled linseeds
2 tbsp almond butter
½ tsp ground cinnamon
grated rind of 1 orange
2 tbsp chopped mixed peel

1. Grease a 15-cm/6-inch square baking tin.

2. Place the chickpeas, dates, linseeds, almond butter, cinnamon and orange rind in a food processor and blitz until the mixture breaks down and starts to come together.

3. Stir the mixed peel into the processor.

4. Spoon the mixture into the prepared tin and smooth the top. Chill in the refrigerator for 1 hour, then remove from the tin and cut into 10 bars.

APRICOT FLAPJACKS

MAKES: *12 flapjacks* | **PREP:** *20 mins, plus cooling* | **COOK:** *25–30 mins*

INGREDIENTS

250 g/9 oz butter
250 g/9 oz golden caster sugar
175 g/6 oz golden syrup
425 g/15 oz rolled oats
55 g/2 oz large raisins
*55 g/2 oz ready-to-eat dried
   apricots, chopped*
50 g/1¾ oz chopped walnuts
25 g/1 oz flaked almonds
grated rind of 1 orange

1. Preheat the oven to 180°C/350°F/Gas Mark 4. Line a 30 x 20-cm/ 12 x 8-inch baking tin with baking paper. Melt the butter, sugar and golden syrup in a large saucepan over a low heat, stirring constantly, until combined.

2. Remove the pan from the heat and stir in the oats, raisins, apricots, walnuts, almonds and orange rind. Stir well to combine. Spoon the mixture into the prepared tin and spread to the corners, flattening the mixture evenly.

3. Bake in the preheated oven for 20–25 minutes, or until golden on top. Leave in the tin to cool completely, then remove and cut into 12 pieces with a sharp knife.

MAPLE & CINNAMON CASHEW BUTTER

MAKES: *375 g/13 oz of nut butter* | **PREP:** *5 mins* | **COOK:** *No cooking*

INGREDIENTS

250 g/9 oz roasted, unsalted
*   cashew nuts*
3 tbsp maple syrup
1 tsp vanilla extract
¾ tsp cinnamon
pinch of salt
2 tsp coconut oil

1. Place the nuts in a food processor and process for 1 minute. Scrape down the side of the bowl and process again for 1–2 minutes. Repeat until you have a smooth paste.

2. Add the maple syrup, vanilla extract, cinnamon and salt and continue processing until the mixture is very smooth. With the processor running, add the oil and process until well combined.

3. Serve immediately or store in a covered container in the refrigerator for several weeks.

CHOCOLATE & PEANUT BUTTER ENERGY BALLS

MAKES: *8 balls* | **PREP:** *15 mins, plus chilling* | **COOK:** *No cooking*

INGREDIENTS

50 g/1¾ oz blanched almonds

60 g/2¼ oz unsweetened peanut butter

20 g/¾ oz unsalted peanuts, roughly chopped

3 tbsp linseeds

25 g/1 oz plain chocolate with 85% cocoa solids, finely chopped

1 tsp cocoa powder

sea salt (optional)

1. Put the almonds in a food processor and process for a minute, until you have the texture of rough flour.

2. Put the peanut butter, peanuts, linseeds, chocolate and a small pinch of salt, if using, into a bowl and mix to combine. Add the almond flour, reserving 1½ tablespoons. Mix until you have a texture resembling chunky clay.

3. Sprinkle the remaining almond flour and the cocoa powder onto a plate and mix with a teaspoon. Using the palms of your hands, shape a tablespoon-sized blob of the peanut mixture into a ball. Roll it in the cocoa powder mixture, then transfer to a plate. Make a further seven balls in the same way.

4. Cover and chill in the refrigerator for at least 30 minutes, or up to 2 days.

PEANUT BUTTER S'MORES

MAKES: *3 s'mores* | **PREP:** *10 mins, plus cooling* | **COOK:** *1 min*

INGREDIENTS

115 g/4 oz smooth peanut butter

6 graham crackers or digestive biscuits

85 g/3 oz plain chocolate, broken into squares

1. Preheat the grill to high. Spread the peanut butter on one side of each cracker.

2. Place the chocolate pieces on three of the crackers and invert the remaining crackers on top.

3. Toast the s'mores under the preheated grill for about 1 minute, until the filling starts to melt. Turn carefully using tongs. Leave to cool slightly, then serve.

NUT &
BERRY BARS

MAKES: *12 bars* | **PREP:** *12 mins* | **COOK:** *24–26 mins*

INGREDIENTS

butter, for greasing
100 g/3½ oz coconut oil
90 g/3¼ oz black treacle
20 g/¾ oz light muscovado sugar
20 g/¾ oz agave syrup
235 g/8½ oz rolled oats
10 g /¼ oz milk powder
50 g/1¾ oz pecan nuts, roughly
  chopped
25 g/1 oz Brazil nuts, roughly
  chopped
20 g/¾ oz goji berries

1. Preheat the oven to 180°C/350°F/Gas Mark 4. Grease an 18-cm/7-inch square tin and set aside.

2. In a large saucepan, melt the coconut oil over a medium heat with the treacle, sugar and agave syrup. Stir until the sugar has dissolved.

3. Pour the remaining ingredients into the pan and mix well together.

4. Pour the mixture into the prepared tin and level the top.

5. Bake in the preheated oven for 18–20 minutes. Remove from the oven and leave to cool completely before cutting into bars.

CHAPTER THREE

LUNCH

• • •

CHICKEN NOODLE SOUP

SERVES: *4* | **PREP:** *20 mins* | **COOK:** *20 mins*

INGREDIENTS

1 litre/1¾ pints chicken stock

1 tbsp soy sauce

1 garlic clove, crushed

1 red chilli, deseeded and finely chopped

3-cm/1¼-inch piece fresh ginger, peeled and grated

500 g/1 lb 2 oz skinless, boneless chicken breasts

4 eggs

400 g/14 oz soba noodles

100 g/3½ oz sweetcorn

4 pak choi, cut lengthways into quarters

1 tbsp sesame oil, for drizzling

1. Place the stock, soy sauce, garlic, chilli and ginger in a saucepan and bring to the boil. Add the chicken and simmer for 10–12 minutes until the chicken is tender and the juices run clear when a skewer is inserted into the thickest part of the meat. Remove from the heat, take the chicken out with a slotted spoon, reserving the stock, and keep warm until needed.

2. Meanwhile, bring a small saucepan of water to the boil, add the eggs and cook for 4–5 minutes. Refresh under cold water. Drain and peel the eggs.

3. Return the stock to the heat, bring to a simmer and add the noodles. Cook for 2 minutes, or according to the packet instructions. Add the sweetcorn and pak choi and simmer for a further 2 minutes.

4. Shred or thickly slice the chicken and return to the pan with the stock and noodles to heat through for 1 minute.

5. Serve the soup in four warmed bowls with halved soft-boiled eggs on top, drizzled with the sesame oil.

JERK TURKEY SOUP

SERVES: *4* | **PREP:** *25 mins* | **COOK:** *45 mins*

INGREDIENTS

1 tbsp olive oil

1 onion, finely chopped

2 garlic cloves, finely chopped

2 -cm/¾-inch piece fresh ginger, peeled and finely chopped

¼ tsp freshly grated nutmeg

¼ tsp ground allspice

½ tsp dried crushed red chillies

2 tsp ground cumin

2 tsp fresh thyme leaves

450 g/1 lb tomatoes, peeled and roughly chopped

600 ml/1 pint turkey stock

1 tbsp tomato purée

1 tbsp dark muscovado sugar

400 g/14 oz canned black-eyed beans, drained

280 g/10 oz turkey breast fillet portions

2 tbsp chopped fresh coriander

salt and pepper (optional)

1. Heat the oil in a saucepan over a medium heat, add the onion and fry, stirring, for 5 minutes until just beginning to colour. Sprinkle over the garlic and ginger, then add the nutmeg, allspice, chillies and cumin. Add the thyme and tomatoes and mix together well.

2. Pour in the stock, add the tomato purée, sugar, beans and turkey pieces and bring to the boil. Cover and simmer for 30 minutes or until the turkey pieces are cooked through with no hint of pink juices when pierced in the thickest parts with a knife. Lift the turkey pieces out of the pan, transfer to a plate and tear into shreds with two forks.

3. Stir the coriander into the soup with salt and pepper to taste, if using. Ladle into warmed bowls, then top with the shreds of turkey and serve immediately.

HAM & LENTIL SOUP

SERVES: *2* | **PREP:** *15 mins* | **COOK:** *25 mins*

INGREDIENTS

200 g/7 oz cooked ham

1 tbsp vegetable oil

1 onion, finely chopped

1 garlic clove, finely chopped

1 carrot, finely diced

1 celery stick, thinly sliced

*400 g/14 oz canned green lentils,
   drained and rinsed*

*1 tsp finely chopped fresh rosemary
   leaves*

*600 ml/1 pint vegetable stock or
   ham stock*

pepper (optional)

1. Using two forks, finely shred the ham and set aside.

2. Heat the oil in a saucepan over a medium–high heat. Add the onion, garlic, carrot and celery and sauté for 4–5 minutes, or until beginning to soften.

3. Add the lentils, rosemary, ham and stock and season to taste with pepper, if using. Cover and simmer for 20 minutes, or until the vegetables are just tender. Serve immediately.

CHUNKY VEGETABLE SOUP

SERVES: *4* | **PREP:** *15 mins* | **COOK:** *20–25 mins*

INGREDIENTS

1 red onion

1 celery stick

1 courgette

2 carrots

2 tbsp sunflower oil

400 g/14 oz canned chopped plum tomatoes

300 ml/10 fl oz chicken stock or vegetable stock

large fresh thyme sprig, plus extra chopped thyme to garnish

salt and pepper (optional)

1. Cut the onion, celery, courgette and carrots into 1-cm/½-inch cubes.

2. Heat the oil in a large saucepan over a medium heat. Add the vegetables and sauté, stirring, for 5 minutes without browning.

3. Add the tomatoes, stock and the thyme sprig. Bring to the boil, then reduce the heat. Cover and simmer for 10–15 minutes until the vegetables are just tender. Remove the thyme sprig and season to taste with salt and pepper, if using.

4. Transfer the soup to warmed serving bowls. Garnish with chopped thyme and serve immediately.

QUINOA SALAD
IN A JAR

MAKES: *12 small jars or 6 large jars* | **PREP:** *15 mins* | **COOK:** *15 mins*

INGREDIENTS

250 g/9 oz red or golden quinoa
4 spring onions, thinly sliced
325 g/11½ oz fresh strawberries,
    sliced
115 g/4 oz fresh goat's cheese,
    crumbled
85 g/3 oz roasted unsalted
    pistachio nuts, chopped
handful of fresh mint leaves,
    chopped

DRESSING

6 tbsp lemon juice
1 tsp clear honey
1 tsp Dijon mustard
½ tsp salt
½ tsp pepper
150 ml/5 fl oz olive oil

1. Cook the quinoa according to the packet instructions and leave to cool until needed.

2. To make the dressing, combine the lemon juice, honey, mustard, salt and pepper in a small jar or bowl and shake or whisk to combine. Add the oil and shake or whisk vigorously until emulsified.

3. Toss 3 tablespoons of the dressing with the quinoa.

4. To compose the salads, place 1 tablespoon of the dressing in each of twelve 225-ml/8-fl oz wide-mouthed preserving jars, or place 2 tablespoons of the dressing in each of six 450-ml/16-fl oz wide-mouthed preserving jars. Add a layer of quinoa to each jar. Sprinkle over the spring onions, add a layer of strawberries, a layer of cheese and a layer of nuts, then top with mint. Spoon a little more dressing over the top and serve immediately.

LENTIL & TUNA SALAD

SERVES: *4* | **PREP:** *20 mins* | **COOK:** *No cooking*

INGREDIENTS

2 ripe tomatoes

1 small red onion

small bunch of fresh coriander

400 g/14 oz canned green lentils,
*   drained*

185 g/6½ oz canned tuna in spring
*   water, drained*

pepper (optional)

DRESSING

3 tbsp virgin olive oil

1 tbsp lemon juice

1 tsp wholegrain mustard

1 garlic clove, crushed

½ tsp ground cumin

½ tsp ground coriander

1. Using a sharp knife, deseed the tomatoes and chop them into small dice. Finely chop the onion and the fresh coriander.

2. To make the dressing, whisk together the oil, lemon juice, mustard, garlic, cumin and ground coriander in a small bowl until thoroughly combined. Set aside until required.

3. Mix the onion, tomatoes and lentils together in a large bowl.

4. Flake the tuna with a fork and stir it into the onion, tomato and lentil mixture. Stir in the coriander and mix well to combine.

5. Pour the dressing over the salad and season to taste with pepper, if using. Serve immediately.

THAI CHICKEN &
SOBA NOODLE SALAD

SERVES: *4* | **PREP:** *15 mins* | **COOK:** *10 mins*

INGREDIENTS

225 g/8 oz dried soba noodles

*350 g/12 oz cooked chicken,
  shredded*

*1 cucumber, peeled, deseeded and
  cut into matchsticks*

140 g/5 oz cabbage, shredded

*1 red pepper, deseeded and cut into
  matchsticks*

*3 spring onions, thinly sliced, to
  garnish*

*70 g/2½ oz crushed roasted
  unsalted peanuts, to garnish*

DRESSING

juice of 1 lime

1 tbsp Thai fish sauce

1 tbsp soft light brown sugar

2 tbsp smooth peanut butter

1 garlic clove, finely chopped

*1–2 small hot red chillies, deseeded
  and finely chopped*

3 tbsp vegetable oil

*15 g/½ oz fresh coriander leaves,
  chopped*

*15 g/½ oz fresh mint leaves,
  chopped*

1. Cook the noodles according to the packet instructions. Drain and rinse with cold water. Set aside to cool completely.

2. Meanwhile, to make the dressing, combine the lime juice, fish sauce, sugar, peanut butter, garlic and chillies in a small bowl and whisk to mix well. Whisk in the oil until well combined and emulsified. Stir in the coriander and mint.

3. Combine the cooked noodles, chicken, cucumber, cabbage and red pepper in a large bowl and toss to combine. Add the dressing and toss again to coat well. Garnish with spring onions and peanuts and serve.

RAINBOW POWER ROLLS

SERVES: *4* | **PREP:** *15 mins* | **COOK:** *No cooking*

INGREDIENTS

4 granary rolls

4 tbsp hummus

1 large carrot, grated

6 radishes, thinly sliced

½ red pepper, deseeded and sliced

½ yellow pepper, deseeded and sliced

2 tbsp frozen sweetcorn, thawed

2 tbsp frozen peas, thawed

2 tbsp alfalfa seed sprouts

1. Slice each roll across the middle horizontally and spread the bottom half with hummus.

2. Divide the carrot, radishes, red and yellow peppers, sweetcorn, peas and alfalfa sprouts between the rolls.

3. Replace the tops of the rolls and serve.

TURKEY & RAINBOW CHARD ROLL-UPS

SERVES: *8* | **PREP:** *30 mins* | **COOK:** *No cooking*

INGREDIENTS

*8 rainbow chard leaves and stems
(choose leaves that are about the
same size as the slices of turkey)*

1 avocado, halved and stoned

juice of 1 lemon

8 thin slices of cooked turkey

150 g/5½ oz hummus

*2 spring onions, trimmed and cut
into very fine strips*

1 carrot, cut into matchstick strips

*100 g/3½ oz courgettes, cut into
matchstick strips*

1. Cut the stems from the chard leaves, then cut the stems into very thin matchstick strips and set aside. Peel the avocado and cut into long, thin slices, then toss in the lemon juice and set aside.

2. Separate the chard leaves and arrange, shiny-side down, on a large chopping board. Cover each one with a slice of turkey, then spread the turkey with a little hummus.

3. Divide the chard stems, spring onions, carrot and courgettes between the chard leaves, making a little pile on each leaf that runs in the centre of the leaf from long edge to long edge.

4. Top the little mounds with the avocado slices, then roll up from the base of the leaf to the tip and put on a plate, join downwards. Continue until all the leaves have been rolled.

5. Cut each roll into thick slices and transfer to individual plates, or wrap each roll in clingfilm and chill for up to 1 hour. Don't keep them for longer as the avocado will begin to discolour.

FRIED HAM &
CHEESE SANDWICH

SERVES: *1* | **PREP:** *10–15 mins* | **COOK:** *6–8 mins*

INGREDIENTS

2 thin slices crusty bread
20 g/¾ oz butter, softened
55 g/2 oz Gruyère cheese, grated
1 slice cooked ham, trimmed to fit
   the bread, if necessary

1. Thinly spread each slice of bread on one side with butter, then put one slice on a board, buttered side down.

2. Sprinkle half the cheese over the unbuttered side, taking it to the edge. Add the ham and the remaining cheese, then top with the remaining slice of bread, buttered side up, and press down.

3. Heat a heavy-based frying pan over a medium–high heat. Reduce the heat to medium, add the sandwich and fry on one side for 2–3 minutes until golden brown.

4. Flip the sandwich over and fry on the other side for 2–3 minutes until all the cheese is melted and the bread is golden brown.

5. Cut the sandwich in half diagonally and serve immediately.

TUNA & SWEETCORN MELTS

SERVES: *2* | **PREP:** *15 mins* | **COOK:** *5–6 mins*

INGREDIENTS

2 wholemeal pittas

5 tbsp ready-made tomato pizza sauce

100 g/3½ oz canned tuna in water or oil, drained

50 g/1¾ oz canned, drained sweetcorn kernels

100 g/3½ oz mozzarella cheese, thinly sliced

1. Preheat the grill to medium. Lightly sprinkle the pittas with water and toast one side until piping hot and springy to the touch.

2. Remove the pan from the grill, turn the pittas and spread them evenly with the tomato sauce, followed by the tuna and sweetcorn. Top with the cheese slices.

3. Return to the grill and cook until the cheese is bubbling and melted. Serve immediately.

MIGHTY
MEATBALL SUBS

SERVES: 4 | **PREP:** 25 mins, plus chilling | **COOK:** 25–30 mins

INGREDIENTS

groundnut oil, for shallow-frying
1 tbsp olive oil
1 small onion, sliced
4 sub rolls or small baguettes
4 tbsp mayonnaise
55 g/2 oz sliced jalapeños (from a jar)
2 tbsp American mustard

MEATBALLS

450 g/1 lb fresh lean beef mince
1 small onion, grated
2 garlic cloves, crushed
25 g/1 oz fine white breadcrumbs
1 tsp hot chilli sauce
wholemeal flour, for dusting
salt and pepper (optional)

1. To make the meatballs, place the beef, onion, garlic, breadcrumbs and chilli sauce in a bowl. Season to taste with salt and pepper, if using, and mix thoroughly. Shape the mixture into 20 small equal-sized balls using floured hands. Cover and chill in the refrigerator for 10 minutes, or until required.

2. Heat a shallow depth of groundnut oil in a wok or heavy frying pan until very hot, then add the meatballs in batches and fry for 6–8 minutes, turning frequently, until golden brown and firm. Remove with a slotted spoon, drain on kitchen paper and keep hot.

3. Heat the olive oil in a clean frying pan, add the onions and fry over a medium heat, stirring occasionally, until soft and golden brown.

4. Split the rolls lengthways, without cutting all the way through, and spread with the mayonnaise. Arrange the onions, meatballs and jalapeños down the centre of the rolls and squeeze over the mustard. Serve immediately.

STEAK & ENGLISH MUSTARD SANDWICHES

SERVES: 2 | **PREP:** 15–20 mins, plus resting | **COOK:** 25–30 mins

INGREDIENTS

15 g/½ oz butter

2 tbsp olive oil

1 onion, halved and thinly sliced

½ tsp brown sugar

2 rump steaks, each about 175 g/
    6 oz and 2 cm/¾ inch thick

1 tsp crushed black peppercorns

4 tbsp mayonnaise

2 tsp ready-made English mustard

4 slices thick crusty bread

25 g/1 oz rocket leaves

salt and pepper (optional)

1. Heat the butter and half the oil in a frying pan add the onion and fry gently for 10 minutes until soft. Season to taste with salt and pepper, if using, and sprinkle over the sugar. Increase the heat a little and continue cooking for a further 5 minutes until the onion is golden and caramelized.

2. Heat a griddle pan until very hot. Drizzle the remaining oil over the steaks, coat with the crushed peppercorns and lightly season with salt, if using. Add the steaks to the pan and cook over a high heat for 3–5 minutes on each side until cooked to your liking. Remove the steaks from the pan, cover and leave to rest in a warm place for 10 minutes.

3. Meanwhile, mix the mayonnaise and mustard together and spread thickly over two slices of the bread. Top with the rocket leaves. Using a sharp knife, thinly slice the steaks at an angle. Pile the steak on top of the rocket leaves and top with the caramelized onions. Sandwich with the remaining slices of bread and serve immediately.

BULGAR WHEAT BALLS
WITH HUMMUS

SERVES: *4* | **PREP:** *20 mins, plus chilling* | **COOK:** *25–30 mins*

INGREDIENTS

200 g/7 oz bulgar wheat
1 small red onion, peeled and diced
2 tsp ground cumin
2 tsp ground turmeric
½ tsp smoked paprika
15 g/½ oz fresh coriander, chopped
2 eggs
2 tbsp olive oil, for frying
2 tbsp sesame seeds, toasted, to
garnish
4 small handfuls fresh watercress
(about 15 g/½ oz each), to serve

HUMMUS

400 g/14 oz canned chickpeas,
drained and rinsed
60 g/2¼ oz walnuts, toasted
1 garlic clove, crushed
juice of 1 lemon
7 tbsp extra virgin olive oil
salt and pepper (optional)

1. Bring a large saucepan of water to the boil. Add the bulgar wheat and cook for 20 minutes until very soft. Drain and refresh under cold running water.

2. Put the bulgar wheat, onion, spices, coriander and eggs into a bowl and mix together.

3. Shape the mixture into 12 walnut-sized balls using your hands. Place them on a plate and chill in the refrigerator for 30 minutes.

4. Meanwhile, make the hummus. Place the chickpeas and walnuts in a food processor and blitz until they resemble breadcrumbs. Add the garlic and lemon juice to the processor and blitz again.

5. With the machine running, gradually add the extra virgin olive oil until you have a smooth consistency. Season to taste with salt and pepper, if using. Transfer the hummus to a bowl and set aside.

6. Heat the olive oil in a frying pan, add the bulgar wheat balls and cook over a medium heat for 3–4 minutes, turning occasionally, until brown all over.

7. Serve the bulgar wheat balls on a bed of watercress, topped with a dollop of hummus and sprinkled with toasted sesame seeds.

CHICKEN SLIDERS

SERVES: *4* | **PREP:** *15–20 mins* | **COOK:** *8 mins*

INGREDIENTS

4 chicken breast fillets (about 1 cm/½ inch thick)
225 ml/8 fl oz buttermilk
125 g/4½ oz plain flour
1 tbsp sweet paprika or smoked paprika
2 tsp garlic powder
1 tsp pepper
1 tsp salt
½ tsp cayenne pepper
125 ml/4 fl oz vegetable oil

TO SERVE

4 tbsp mayonnaise
4 soft burger buns, split
tomato slices
lettuce leaves
coleslaw

1. Place the chicken breasts in a bowl with the buttermilk and toss to coat.

2. Put the flour into a shallow bowl and add the paprika, garlic powder, pepper, salt and cayenne pepper. Stir to combine. Remove the chicken fillets from the buttermilk, one at a time, and dip them in the flour mixture. Return to the buttermilk and dip in the flour mixture again.

3. Heat the oil in a large frying pan over a medium–high heat until very hot. Add the chicken fillets in a single layer and cook for about 3 minutes on each side until golden brown and cooked through.

4. To serve, spread 1 tablespoon of the mayonnaise on the top half of each bun. Place tomato slices and lettuce leaves on the base of each bun. Top with a chicken fillet and finish with the bun tops. Serve immediately with coleslaw on the side.

SUPER-SIZED FISH FINGER SANDWICHES

SERVES: *2* | **PREP:** *15 mins* | **COOK:** *15 mins*

INGREDIENTS

oil, for deep-frying
20 fish fingers
4 large slices white bread
100 g/3½ oz rocket

RUSSIAN DRESSING

2 tbsp mayonnaise
1 tbsp creamed horseradish
1 tbsp tomato ketchup
1 tbsp soured cream
1 tbsp sriracha hot chilli sauce
1 tsp Worcestershire sauce
½ tsp smoked paprika

1. Mix all of the Russian dressing ingredients together in a small bowl and set aside until needed.

2. Heat enough oil for deep-frying in a large saucepan or deep-fryer to 180–190°C/350–375°F, or until a cube of bread browns in 30 seconds.

3. Add the fish fingers to the pan in batches of 10 and cook for 5 minutes, or until golden. Remove them with a slotted spoon, drain on kitchen paper, then set aside and keep warm while you cook the remaining fish fingers.

4. Spread the dressing over one side of each slice of bread. Divide the fish fingers between two of the slices, then top with the rocket and the remaining slices of bread. Serve immediately.

ROASTED VEGETABLE & FETA CHEESE WRAPS

SERVES: *4* | **PREP:** *20–25 mins, plus cooling* | **COOK:** *20–25 mins*

INGREDIENTS

1 red onion, cut into eighths

1 red pepper, deseeded and cut into eighths

1 small aubergine, cut into eighths

1 courgette, cut into eighths

4 tbsp extra virgin olive oil

1 garlic clove, crushed

100 g/3½ oz feta cheese, crumbled

small bunch of fresh mint, shredded

4 flour tortillas

salt and pepper (optional)

1. Preheat the oven to 220°C/425°F/Gas Mark 7. Mix the vegetables, oil and garlic together with salt and pepper to taste, if using, in a non-stick baking tray and roast in the preheated oven for 15–20 minutes, or until golden and cooked through.

2. Remove from the oven and leave to cool, then mix in the cheese and mint.

3. Preheat a non-stick frying pan over a high heat until almost smoking. Add the tortillas and warm for a few seconds on each side. Remove from the pan.

4. Divide the vegetable and cheese mixture between the tortillas. Fold the bottoms and tops of the tortillas over the filling, then roll up and cut in half. Serve immediately.

SPICY TUNA
FISH CAKES

SERVES: *4* | **PREP:** *15–20 mins* | **COOK:** *8–10 mins*

INGREDIENTS

*200 g/7 oz canned tuna in oil,
   drained*

2–3 tbsp curry paste

1 spring onion, finely chopped

1 egg, beaten

200 g/7 oz mashed potatoes

*4 tbsp plain flour, plus extra for
   dusting*

*sunflower oil or groundnut oil, for
   shallow-frying*

salt and pepper (optional)

rocket and lemon wedges, to serve

1. Place the tuna in a large mixing bowl. Add the curry paste, spring onion, egg and mashed potatoes. Season to taste with salt and pepper, if using, and mix together.

2. Divide the mixture into four portions and shape each portion into a ball. On a floured surface, flatten each ball slightly to make a patty shape of your preferred thickness. Season the flour to taste with salt and pepper, if using. Dust each patty in the flour.

3. Heat the oil in a large frying pan, add the patties and fry for 3–4 minutes on each side until crisp and golden. Serve immediately with rocket and lemon wedges.

FALAFEL PITTA POCKETS

SERVES: *4* | **PREP:** *30 mins* | **COOK:** *15–20 mins*

INGREDIENTS

4 pittas

1 shallot, quartered

2–3 garlic cloves

425 g/15 oz canned chickpeas,
drained and rinsed

25 g/1 oz fresh flat-leaf parsley
leaves

1 tsp ground coriander

1 tsp ground cumin

½ tsp salt

⅛ tsp cayenne pepper

2 tbsp olive oil

2 tbsp plain flour

½ tsp baking powder

rapeseed oil, for frying

shredded lettuce, tomato slices,
cucumber slices and Kalamata
olives, to serve

TAHINI DRESSING

2 tbsp tahini

juice of 1 lemon

2–3 tbsp water

½ tsp salt

⅛ tsp pepper

⅛ tsp cayenne pepper

1. Preheat the oven to 200°C/400°F/Gas Mark 6. Wrap the pittas in foil and place in the preheated oven to warm through.

2. Place the shallot and garlic in a food processor and pulse a few times to chop. Add the chickpeas, parsley, coriander, cumin, salt, cayenne pepper, olive oil and flour and process to a chunky purée. Add the baking powder and pulse once to incorporate.

3. To make the dressing, put all the ingredients in a small bowl and stir to combine.

4. Heat 5 mm/¼ inch rapeseed oil in a large frying pan. Make walnut-sized balls out of the chickpea mixture, then flatten the balls into 5-mm/¼-inch thick patties. Add several patties to the hot oil and fry for about 1½–2 minutes on each side until well browned. Transfer to a plate lined with kitchen paper to drain. Repeat until all the patties have been fried.

5. Remove the pittas from the oven and slice in half. Stuff each half pitta with 2–3 patties, drizzle with the dressing and fill with shredded lettuce, tomato slices and cucumber slices. Serve immediately with olives.

CHINESE VEGETABLE RICE

INGREDIENTS

350 g/12 oz long-grain rice

1 tsp ground turmeric

2 tbsp sunflower oil

225 g/8 oz courgettes, sliced

1 red pepper, deseeded and sliced

1 green pepper, deseeded and sliced

1 fresh green chilli, deseeded and finely chopped

1 carrot, coarsely grated

150 g/5½ oz fresh beansprouts

6 spring onions, sliced

2 tbsp soy sauce

salt (optional)

fresh coriander leaves, to garnish (optional)

lime wedges, to serve

1. Add a little salt, if using, to a saucepan of water, then add the rice and turmeric and bring to the boil. Reduce the heat and simmer for 8–10 minutes, or until the rice is just tender. Drain thoroughly and press out any excess water with a sheet of kitchen paper. Set aside until needed.

2. Heat a wok or large frying pan over a medium–high heat, then add the oil. Add the courgettes to the wok and stir-fry for about 2 minutes. Add the red and green peppers and chilli and stir-fry for 2–3 minutes.

3. Stir the cooked rice into the wok, a little at a time, tossing well after each addition. Add the carrot, beansprouts and spring onions and stir-fry for a further 2 minutes.

4. Drizzle over the soy sauce and stir well. Transfer to serving bowls and scatter over the coriander leaves, if using. Serve immediately. with lime wedges.

CHAPTER FOUR

DINNER

BLACK
SESAME TOFU

SERVES: *2* | **PREP:** *10 mins* | **COOK:** *15 mins*

INGREDIENTS

1 egg, beaten

1 tbsp tamari

1½ tbsp black sesame seeds

*250 g/9 oz firm tofu, cut into bite-
sized chunks*

70 g/2½ oz rice noodles

2 tbsp sesame oil

150 g/5½ oz small broccoli florets

1 large garlic clove, crushed

½ tbsp lemon juice

1 tsp chilli flakes

½ tsp pepper

1 tsp crushed coriander seeds

1 tsp clear honey

2 spring onions, sliced, to garnish

*2 tbsp fresh coriander leaves, to
garnish*

1. Combine the beaten egg with the tamari in a shallow dish. Place the black sesame seeds in a separate shallow dish. Coat the tofu chunks with the egg mixture and then dip each chunk into the sesame seeds.

2. Cook the noodles according to the packet instructions. Drain, cover and set aside.

3. Add half the sesame oil to a non-stick frying pan and place over a medium–high heat. Add the broccoli and stir-fry for 2–3 minutes, then add the garlic, lemon juice, chilli, pepper and coriander seeds. Stir for a further 1–2 minutes, or until the broccoli is just tender. Stir in the honey, cover the pan, remove from the heat and set aside.

4. Heat the remaining oil in a separate frying pan over a medium heat. Add the tofu chunks and fry them for 3 minutes, turning once or twice. Serve the tofu with the broccoli mixture and noodles and garnish with the sliced spring onions and coriander leaves.

VEGETABLE
RICE BOWL

SERVES: *4* | **PREP:** *20 mins, plus marinating* | **COOK:** *20 mins*

INGREDIENTS

*2–3 red chillies, deseeded and finely
  chopped*
3 garlic cloves, crushed
50 ml/2 fl oz white wine vinegar
2 tbsp caster sugar
4 tbsp sunflower oil
1 tbsp soy sauce
1 tbsp sesame oil
1 tsp clear honey
300 g/10½ oz tofu, cut into cubes
300 g/10½ oz basmati rice
*1 large carrot, peeled and sliced
  into thin strings*
*200 g/7 oz chestnut mushrooms,
  sliced*
55 g/2 oz mangetout, shredded
55 g/2 oz baby spinach leaves
4 eggs
1 tbsp black sesame seeds

1. Put the chillies, garlic, vinegar and sugar into a small saucepan and bring to the boil. Remove from the heat and leave to cool, then stir in 2 tablespoons of the sunflower oil. Set aside.

2. Combine the soy sauce, sesame oil and honey, place in a non-metallic bowl with the tofu and leave to marinate for 10 minutes.

3. Cook the rice according to the packet instructions, then drain. Meanwhile, heat 1 tablespoon of the remaining sunflower oil in a separate saucepan, add the carrots and mushrooms and cook for 4–5 minutes until soft. Transfer to a plate with a slotted spoon.

4. Put the rice in the pan with the chilli mixture, then add the marinated tofu, carrots, mushrooms, mangetout and spinach. Cover and cook for 2–3 minutes.

5. Meanwhile, heat the remaining sunflower oil in a frying pan, add the eggs and fry to your taste. Divide the mixture between four bowls. Top each portion with a fried egg and spoonful of chilli sauce, sprinkle with the sesame seeds and serve.

MACARONI CHEESE

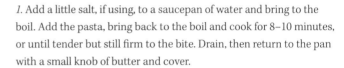

SERVES: *4* | **PREP:** *20 mins* | **COOK:** *30–40 mins*

INGREDIENTS

250 g/9 oz dried macaroni

55 g/2 oz butter, plus extra for cooking the pasta

55 g/2 oz plain flour

600 ml/1 pint warm milk

200 g/7 oz Cheddar cheese, grated

55 g/2 oz freshly grated Parmesan cheese

½ tsp freshly grated nutmeg

salt and pepper (optional)

1. Add a little salt, if using, to a saucepan of water and bring to the boil. Add the pasta, bring back to the boil and cook for 8–10 minutes, or until tender but still firm to the bite. Drain, then return to the pan with a small knob of butter and cover.

2. Meanwhile, melt the butter in a heavy-based saucepan over a low heat, then add the flour and stir to make a paste. Cook for 2 minutes. Add the milk a little at a time, whisking it into the paste, then cook for 10–15 minutes to make a loose, custard-style sauce.

3. Add three quarters of the Cheddar cheese and all the Parmesan cheese and stir through until melted. Season to taste with salt and pepper, if using, stir in the nutmeg and remove from the heat.

4. Preheat the grill to high. Put the macaroni into a shallow, ovenproof dish, then pour the sauce over. Scatter over the remaining Cheddar cheese and cook under the preheated grill until the cheese begins to brown. Serve immediately.

VEGETABLE
PIZZA

SERVES: *1* | **PREP:** *15–20 mins* | **COOK:** *12–15 mins*

INGREDIENTS

2 tbsp olive oil

30-cm/12-inch ready-made pizza base

3 tbsp tomato purée

1 onion, finely chopped

1 small green pepper, deseeded and thinly sliced

2 tomatoes, sliced

6 black olives, stoned and halved

100 g/3½ oz mozzarella cheese, torn into pieces

1 tbsp chopped fresh thyme

salt and pepper (optional)

1. Preheat the oven to 220°C/425°F/Gas Mark 7. Brush a large baking sheet with a little of the oil and place the pizza base on the sheet.

2. Spread the tomato purée over the pizza base to within 2 cm/ ¾ inch of the edge. Arrange the onion, green pepper and tomatoes over the pizza.

3. Scatter over the olives and cheese. Sprinkle with the thyme and season to taste with salt and pepper, if using, then drizzle with the remaining oil.

4. Bake in the preheated oven for 12–15 minutes, until bubbling and golden. Serve immediately.

VEGGIE
BURGER BOWL

SERVES: 4 | **PREP:** 25 mins, plus chilling | **COOK:** 35–40 mins

INGREDIENTS

2 red peppers, deseeded and
   chopped
2 yellow peppers, deseeded and
   chopped
2 red onions, cut into wedges
2 courgettes, thickly sliced
3 tbsp olive oil
400 g/14 oz canned chickpeas,
   drained and rinsed
200 g/7 oz frozen peas, thawed
200 g/7 oz frozen sweetcorn,
   thawed
15 g/½ oz fresh coriander
   (including stalks)
¼ tsp cumin
80 g/2¾ oz plain flour
1 tbsp sunflower seeds
1 tbsp sesame seeds
salt and pepper (optional)

DRESSING

1 avocado, stoned, peeled and
   chopped
200 g/7 oz natural yogurt
2 spring onions, chopped
1 garlic clove, crushed
1 tbsp lime juice
salt and pepper (optional)

1. Preheat the oven to 200°C/400°F/Gas Mark 6.

2. Place the red and yellow peppers, onions and courgettes in a roasting tin and drizzle with 1 tablespoon of the oil. Roast for 35–40 minutes until slightly charred at the edges.

3. Meanwhile, place the chickpeas, peas, sweetcorn, coriander, cumin and 70 g/2½ oz of the flour in a food processor and process to a thick paste. Add the sunflower seeds and sesame seeds, season with salt and pepper, if using, and process again until combined.

4. Using wet hands, divide the mixture into four portions and shape each portion into a patty. Dust the patties with the remaining flour and chill in the refrigerator for 20 minutes.

5. Meanwhile, to make the dressing, place the avocado, yogurt, spring onions, garlic and lime juice in a small blender and blend until smooth. Season to taste with salt and pepper, if using.

6. Heat the remaining oil in a frying pan, add the burgers and cook for 5–6 minutes on each side until cooked through.

7. Divide the roasted ratatouille between four warmed bowls, top each portion with a burger, then drizzle with the dressing and serve.

PAD THAI

SERVES: *4* | **PREP:** *20–25 mins* | **COOK:** *8–12 mins*

INGREDIENTS

225 g/8 oz thick rice noodles

2 tbsp groundnut oil or vegetable oil

4 spring onions, roughly chopped,
  plus extra to garnish

2 garlic cloves, crushed

2 fresh red chillies, deseeded and
  sliced

225 g/8 oz pork fillet, trimmed and
  thinly sliced

115 g/4 oz cooked, peeled large
  prawns

juice of 1 lime

2 tbsp Thai fish sauce

2 eggs, beaten

55 g/2 oz fresh beansprouts

handful of chopped fresh coriander

55 g/2 oz unsalted peanuts,
  chopped

1. Prepare the noodles according to the packet instructions. Drain and set aside.

2. Heat a wok or large frying pan over a medium–high heat, then add the oil. Add the spring onions, garlic and chillies and stir-fry for 1–2 minutes. Add the pork and stir-fry over a high heat for 1–2 minutes until cooked through.

3. Add the prawns, lime juice, fish sauce and eggs and stir-fry over a medium heat for 2–3 minutes until the eggs have set and the prawns are heated through.

4. Add the beansprouts, coriander, peanuts and noodles and stir-fry for 30 seconds until heated through. Garnish with spring onions and serve immediately.

STEAMED
SALMON

SERVES: *4* | **PREP:** *15–20 mins* | **COOK:** *22 mins*

INGREDIENTS

40 g/1½ oz butter, melted

*4 salmon fillets, about 140 g/5 oz
  each*

*juice and finely grated rind of
  1 lemon*

1 tbsp snipped fresh chives

1 tbsp chopped fresh parsley

salt and pepper (optional)

salad and crusty bread, to serve

1. Preheat the oven to 200°/400°F/Gas Mark 6. Cut out four 30-cm/12-inch squares of double thickness foil and brush with the melted butter.

2. Place a piece of salmon on each square and spoon over the lemon juice. Sprinkle with the lemon rind, chives, parsley, and salt and pepper to taste, if using.

3. Loosely wrap the foil over the salmon and seal firmly with the join on top.

4. Place the parcels on a baking sheet and bake in the preheated oven for 20 minutes, or until the fish flakes easily.

5. Transfer the salmon and juices to warmed serving plates and serve immediately with salad and crusty bread.

ONE-PAN SPICY CHICKEN

SERVES: *4* | **PREP:** *20 mins* | **COOK:** *30–35 mins*

INGREDIENTS

2 onions, peeled

100 g/3½ oz tomatoes, halved

3-cm/1¼-inch piece fresh ginger,
*   peeled and chopped*

3 garlic cloves, peeled

2 tbsp olive oil

4 x 150 g/5½ oz boneless, skinless
*   chicken breasts, cut into bite-*
*   sized pieces*

2 tsp ground cinnamon

1 tsp ground turmeric

2 tsp ground cumin

2 tsp ground coriander

1 large butternut squash, peeled,
*   deseeded and cut into large*
*   pieces*

50 g/1¾ oz dried apricots, halved

600 ml/1 pint chicken stock

175 g/6 oz red quinoa

125 g/4½ oz feta cheese, crumbled

salt and pepper (optional)

15 g/½ oz fresh mint leaves,
*   chopped, to garnish*

1. Chop 1 onion and place in a blender with the tomatoes, ginger and garlic. Blitz to a paste.

2. Heat the oil in a large, heavy-based saucepan or casserole, add the chicken and cook over a medium heat for 4–5 minutes until brown all over. Remove from the pan and set aside until needed.

3. Slice the remaining onion, add to the same pan and cook over a medium heat for 3–4 minutes, then stir in the spices and cook for a further 1 minute.

4. Stir the onion and tomato paste into the pan and cook for 2 minutes.

5. Return the chicken to the pan with the squash, apricots and stock. Simmer for 15–20 minutes until the chicken is cooked through. Season to taste with salt and pepper, if using.

6. Meanwhile, cook the quinoa according to the packet instructions.

7. Divide the chicken mixture and quinoa between four serving plates, sprinkle with cheese and garnish with mint to serve.

CAJUN CHICKEN

SERVES: *2* | **PREP:** *20 mins* | **COOK:** *30–35 mins*

INGREDIENTS

4 chicken drumsticks

4 chicken thighs

2 fresh sweetcorn cobs, husks and silks removed

85 g/3 oz butter, melted

sunflower oil, for cooking

SPICE MIX

2 tsp onion powder

2 tsp paprika

1½ tsp salt

1 tsp garlic powder

1 tsp dried thyme

1 tsp cayenne pepper

1 tsp black pepper

½ tsp white pepper

¼ tsp ground cumin

1. Using a sharp knife, make two to three diagonal slashes in the chicken drumsticks and thighs, then place them in a large dish. Add the corn cobs. To make the spice mix, mix all the ingredients together in a small bowl.

2. Brush the chicken and corn with the melted butter and sprinkle with the spice mix. Toss to coat well.

3. Heat the oil in a large griddle pan over a medium–high heat, add the chicken and cook, turning occasionally, for 15 minutes, then add the sweetcorn cobs and cook, turning occasionally, for a further 10–15 minutes, or until beginning to blacken slightly at the edges.

4. Check the chicken is tender and the juices run clear when a skewer is inserted into the thickest part of the meat. Transfer to a serving plate and serve.

CHICKEN & PEANUT CURRY

SERVES: *4* | **PREP:** *15 mins* | **COOK:** *20 mins*

INGREDIENTS

75 g/2¾ oz roasted, unsalted
*   peanuts*
4 chicken breast fillets
1 tbsp vegetable oil
1 shallot, diced
2-4 tbsp Thai red curry paste
400 ml/14 fl oz canned coconut
*   milk*
1 tbsp Thai fish sauce
1 tbsp soft light brown sugar
juice of 1 lime
25 g/1 oz chopped fresh coriander
*   leaves*
chopped fresh coriander, to garnish
*   (optional)*

1. Put the peanuts into a food processor and process for 2–3 minutes until smooth.

2. Line a large steamer basket with baking paper and place the chicken fillets on the paper. Place the steamer over boiling water, cover and steam for 10–12 minutes, until the chicken is tender and cooked through. Cut into the middle to check that the meat is no longer pink. Any juices that run out should be clear and piping hot with visible steam rising.

3. Meanwhile, heat the oil in a large frying pan and add the shallot. Cook, stirring frequently, for 5 minutes, or until soft. Add the curry paste and cook, stirring, for a further minute.

4. Open the can of coconut milk and scoop off the thick cream that has risen to the top. Add the cream to the pan and cook, stirring, until it begins to bubble. Add the remaining coconut milk along with the peanut butter, Thai fish sauce and sugar. Bring to the boil, then reduce the heat to low. Simmer for 5 minutes, or until the sauce thickens.

5. Stir in the lime juice and coriander. Serve the chicken fillets topped with a generous amount of the sauce and garnished with chopped coriander, if using.

CHICKEN PIE

INGREDIENTS

2 tbsp olive oil

450 g/1 lb chicken breast strips

175 g/6 oz baby button mushrooms

1 bunch of spring onions, chopped

115 g/4 oz crème fraîche

4 tbsp chicken stock

375 g/13 oz ready-rolled shortcrust pastry

beaten egg or milk, for glazing

salt and pepper (optional)

1. Preheat the oven to 220°C/425°F/Gas Mark 7. Place a baking sheet in the oven to preheat.

2. Heat the oil in a large frying pan over a high heat. Add the chicken and cook for 2–3 minutes, stirring frequently. Add the mushrooms and spring onions and cook for a further 2 minutes.

3. Add the crème fraîche, stock, and salt and pepper to taste, if using, then tip into a 1.4-litre/2½-pint shallow, ovenproof dish.

4. Lift the pastry on top, scrunching in the edges with your fingers to fit inside the rim of the dish. Make a small slit in the centre and brush with beaten egg to glaze.

5. Place the dish on the preheated baking sheet and bake for 20–25 minutes until the pastry is golden and firm. Divide the pie into four portions and serve immediately on warmed serving plates.

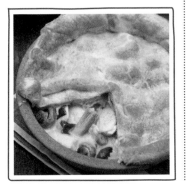

LEMON CHICKEN COURGETTI

SERVES: *4* | **PREP:** *10 mins* | **COOK:** *8 mins*

INGREDIENTS

2 green courgettes

2 yellow courgettes

2½ tbsp olive oil

2 large chicken breast fillets, cut crossways into 10 slices

1 tsp crushed coriander seeds

1 tsp crushed cumin seeds

½ tsp sea salt

½ tsp pepper

juice of 1 lemon

2 tbsp toasted pine nuts

3 tbsp fresh coriander leaves

1. Using a the side of a box grater, a vegetable peeler or a spiralizer, slice the courgettes into thin ribbons.

2. Add ½ tablespoon of the oil to a non-stick frying pan and place over a high heat. Add the chicken slices and fry, turning once or twice, for 1–2 minutes, or until lightly flecked with golden brown. Reduce the heat to medium and add half the remaining oil, the coriander seeds, cumin seeds, salt, pepper and half the lemon juice.

3. Cook, stirring occasionally, for 5 minutes, or until the chicken slices are cooked through. Check that the centre of the chicken is no longer pink.

4. Meanwhile, heat the remaining oil in a separate large frying pan, add the courgette ribbons and stir for 1–2 minutes, or until just tender and turning golden. Serve the chicken on the courgetti and scatter over the remaining lemon juice, the pine nuts and the fresh coriander leaves.

TURKEY WITH CORIANDER PESTO & SOBA NOODLES

SERVES: *6–8* | **PREP:** *10 mins, plus marinating* | **COOK:** *20 mins, plus resting*

INGREDIENTS

4 tbsp reduced-salt soy sauce

2 tsp chilli paste

3 garlic cloves, sliced

1 boneless, skinless turkey breast
about 1.3–1.8 kg/3–4 lb

450 g/1 lb dried soba noodles

PESTO

85 g/3 oz fresh coriander, chopped

125 ml/4 fl oz vegetable oil

50 g/1¾ oz sugar

4 garlic cloves

2 tbsp finely chopped fresh ginger

2 tsp chilli paste

juice of 1 lime

2 tsp salt

1. Combine the soy sauce, chilli paste and garlic in a bowl large enough to hold the turkey breast. Add the turkey breast and turn to coat. Cover and marinate in the refrigerator for at least 2 hours or overnight.

2. To cook the turkey, allow it to come to room temperature and preheat the grill to high. Grill for about 10 minutes on each side. Check the turkey is tender and the juices run clear when a skewer is inserted into the thickest part of the meat.

3. Meanwhile, cook the noodles according to the packet instructions. Drain and set aside.

4. To make the pesto, combine the coriander, oil, sugar, garlic, ginger, chilli paste, lime juice and salt in a food processor and process until well combined.

5. Remove the cooked turkey from the grill, loosely cover with foil and leave to rest for at least 5 minutes before slicing.

6. Toss the noodles with the pesto and slice the turkey into 5-mm/¼-inch slices. Serve immediately with the noodles.

TURKEY, SESAME
& GINGER NOODLES

SERVES: *4* | **PREP:** *10 mins* | **COOK:** *12 mins*

INGREDIENTS

150 g/5½ oz egg noodles
1 tbsp olive oil, for frying
2 garlic cloves, crushed
3-cm/1¼-inch piece fresh ginger,
  peeled and diced
400 g/14 oz turkey breast, cut
  into strips
125 g/4½ oz mangetout
100 g/3½ oz broccoli florets
1 red pepper, deseeded and sliced
2 spring onions, trimmed and sliced
150 g/5½ oz beansprouts
1 tbsp sesame oil
1 tbsp soy sauce
1 tbsp sweet chilli sauce
juice of ½ lime
100 g/3½ oz smooth peanut butter
100 g/3½ oz roasted peanuts,
  chopped
fresh coriander leaves, to garnish

1. Cook the egg noodles according to the packet instructions.

2. Heat the olive oil in a wok or large frying pan and add the garlic, ginger and turkey. Stir-fry over a medium heat for 3–4 minutes until the turkey is cooked through. Remove from the pan and set aside.

3. Add the mangetout, broccoli and red pepper to the wok and stir-fry over a medium heat for 4–5 minutes. Add the spring onions and beansprouts and cook for a further 1 minute.

4. Whisk together the sesame oil, soy sauce, chilli sauce, lime juice and peanut butter in a small bowl and add to the wok along with the turkey and noodles. Toss well together.

5. Divide the turkey and noodles between four warmed serving bowls, top with the peanuts and garnish with coriander to serve.

SPAGHETTI CARBONARA

SERVES: *4* | **PREP:** *20 mins* | **COOK:** *15 mins*

INGREDIENTS

450 g/1 lb dried spaghetti

1 tbsp olive oil

*225 g/8 oz rindless pancetta or
    streaky bacon, chopped*

4 eggs

5 tbsp single cream

*2 tbsp freshly grated Parmesan
    cheese*

salt and pepper (optional)

1. Add a little salt, if using, to a large, heavy-based saucepan of water and bring to the boil. Add the pasta, bring back to the boil and cook for 8–10 minutes, or until tender but still firm to the bite.

2. Meanwhile, heat the oil in a heavy-based frying pan. Add the pancetta and cook over a medium heat, stirring frequently, for 8–10 minutes until crisp.

3. Beat the eggs with the cream in a small bowl and season to taste with salt and pepper, if using.

4. Drain the pasta and return to the pan. Tip in the pancetta, then add the egg mixture and half the cheese. Stir well, then transfer the spaghetti to a warmed serving dish.

5. Sprinkle with the remaining cheese and serve immediately.

SPAGHETTI & MEATBALLS

SERVES: *4* | **PREP:** *25–30 mins* | **COOK:** *50 mins*

INGREDIENTS

*50 g/1¾ oz fresh white
    breadcrumbs*
50 ml/1¾ fl oz skimmed milk
*400 g/14 oz fresh lean pork mince
    (10 per cent fat)*
1 onion, very finely chopped
2 garlic cloves, crushed
2 tbsp chopped fresh parsley
2 tsp crushed fennel seeds
1 tbsp olive oil
1–2 tsp salt
*300 g/10½ oz dried wholegrain
    spelt spaghetti, or wholemeal
    spaghetti*
salt and pepper (optional)
fresh basil leaves, to garnish

SAUCE

*125 g/4½ oz courgettes, coarsely
    grated*
3 garlic cloves, finely grated
*800 g/1 lb canned chopped
    tomatoes*
1 tbsp tomato purée
1 tsp maple syrup
1 tsp red wine vinegar

1. Mix the breadcrumbs with the milk and leave to soak for a few minutes, then transfer to a mixing bowl and add the pork, onion, garlic, parsley, fennel seeds, and salt and pepper, if using. Combine well, then shape into 16 meatballs, transferring each to a plate as you shape it.

2. Heat the oil in a large frying pan with a lid. Add the meatballs and cook, uncovered, over a medium–high heat for a few minutes, turning occasionally, until slightly brown all over. Transfer to a plate with a slotted spoon, cover and set aside.

3. To make the sauce, reduce the heat to medium and add the courgettes to the pan. Cook for 1–2 minutes, then add the garlic and cook for a few seconds.

4. Add the tomatoes, tomato purée, maple syrup and vinegar, mix thoroughly and bring to a gentle simmer. Cover and cook for 15 minutes, then remove the lid and cook, stirring occasionally, for a further 10 minutes.

5. Return the meatballs to the pan and stir to coat in the sauce, then cook for a further 10 minutes, or until about half the liquid has evaporated and you have a rich sauce.

6. Meanwhile, add 1–2 teaspoons of salt to a large saucepan of water and bring to the boil. Add the spaghetti and cook for 8–10 minutes, until tender but still firm to the bite. Drain the spaghetti, transfer to a serving platter and spoon the tomato sauce and meatballs on top. Garnish with basil leaves and serve immediately.

CHILLI CON CARNE

INGREDIENTS

200 g/7 oz basmati rice

2 tbsp olive oil

1 large onion, sliced

500 g/1 lb 2 oz fresh lean beef mince

1 garlic clove, crushed

400 g/14 oz canned chopped
tomatoes

400 g/14 oz canned red kidney
beans, drained and rinsed

200 ml/7 fl oz beef stock

2 tbsp tomato purée

2 tsp crushed dried chillies

salt and pepper (optional)

1. Add a little salt, if using, to a saucepan of water, then add the rice and cook for 10–12 minutes until tender. Drain.

2. Meanwhile, heat the oil in a large saucepan over a high heat, add the onion and beef and fry, stirring frequently and breaking up the beef with a wooden spoon, until the beef is brown all over.

3. Stir in the garlic, then add the tomatoes, beans, stock, tomato purée and chillies. Stir until boiling, then reduce the heat, cover and simmer, stirring occasionally, for 15 minutes. Season to taste with salt and pepper, if using.

4. Serve immediately with the rice.

DOUBLE-DECKER BURGERS

SERVES: *4* | **PREP:** *20 mins* | **COOK:** *10 mins*

INGREDIENTS

900 g/2 lb fresh beef mince

2 tsp salt

½ tsp pepper

vegetable oil, for frying

8 Cheddar cheese slices

TO SERVE

4 soft burger buns, split

lettuce leaves

tomato slices

red onion slices

gherkins, halved lengthways

1. Place the beef in a medium-sized bowl with the salt and pepper and gently mix to combine. Divide into eight equal-sized portions, then shape each portion into a patty no thicker than 1 cm/½ inch – the thinner the better.

2. Place a large griddle pan over a medium–high heat. Add enough oil to coat the base of the pan. Add the patties and cook for about 4 minutes, without moving, until the burgers are brown and release easily from the pan. Turn and cook on the other side for 2 minutes, then put a slice of cheese on top of each burger and cook for a further 2 minutes, or until cooked to your liking.

3. To serve, place a burger on each bun base, then place a second burger on top. Add the lettuce leaves, tomato slices, onion slices and gherkins. Finish with the bun tops and serve immediately.

POT ROAST

SERVES: *6* | **PREP:** *30 mins* | **COOK:** *3 hours 45 mins*

INGREDIENTS

2½ tbsp plain flour

1 rolled brisket joint, weighing
1.6 kg/3 lb 8 oz

2 tbsp vegetable oil

25 g/1 oz butter

1 onion, finely chopped

2 celery sticks, diced

2 carrots, diced

1 tsp dill seed

1 tsp dried thyme

350 ml/12 fl oz red wine

150–225 ml/5–8 fl oz beef stock

4–5 potatoes, cut into large chunks
and parboiled for 5 minutes

salt and pepper (optional)

chopped fresh dill, to garnish

1. Preheat the oven to 140°C/275°F/Gas Mark 1. Mix 2 tablespoons of the flour with 1 teaspoon salt and ¼ teaspoon pepper, if using, in a large shallow dish. Dip the meat in the flour to coat.

2. Heat the oil in a flameproof casserole over a medium heat, add the meat and and cook, turning frequently, until brown all over. Transfer to a plate. Add half the butter to the casserole, then add the onion, celery, carrots, dill seed and thyme and cook for 5 minutes.

3. Return the meat and juices to the casserole. Pour in the wine and enough stock to reach one third of the way up the meat, then bring to the boil.

4. Cover, transfer to the preheated oven and cook for 3 hours, turning the meat every 30 minutes. Add the potatoes and more stock after 2 hours, if necessary.

5. Transfer the meat and vegetables to a warmed serving dish. Strain the cooking liquid to remove any solids, then return the liquid to the casserole. Bring the cooking liquid to the boil over a medium–high heat. Mix the remaining butter and flour to a paste, then add small pieces of the paste to the cooking liquid, whisking constantly until smooth. Pour the sauce over the meat and vegetables. Sprinkle with dill and serve.

QUICK BEEF STEW

SERVES: *4* | **PREP:** *20 mins* | **COOK:** *35 mins*

INGREDIENTS

900 g/2 lb sliced stir-fry beef
3 tbsp plain flour
2 tbsp olive oil
1 large onion, diced
2 garlic cloves, finely chopped
225 ml/8 fl oz red wine
450 g/1 lb button mushrooms,
*   quartered*
450 g/1 lb new potatoes, diced
4 carrots, diced
2 celery sticks, diced
700 ml/1¼ pints beef stock
3 tbsp tomato purée
1 tbsp finely chopped fresh thyme
*   leaves*
2 tbsp finely chopped fresh parsley
salt and pepper (optional)

1. Season the beef with ½ teaspoon salt and ½ teaspoon pepper, if using, then toss it in the flour.

2. Heat the oil in a large, heavy-based saucepan over a medium–high heat. Add the meat and cook, stirring frequently, for about 4 minutes until brown all over. Add the onion and garlic to the pan and cook for 2–3 minutes until the onion begins to soften. Add the wine and bring to the boil, scraping up any sediment from the base of the pan.

3. Add the vegetables to the pan with 1 teaspoon salt, ½ teaspoon pepper, if using, the stock, tomato purée and thyme. Bring to the boil, then reduce the heat to low, cover and simmer for about 15 minutes until the vegetables are tender.

4. Remove the lid of the pan and continue to simmer for a further 5 minutes until the sauce is slightly thickened. Stir in the parsley and add salt and pepper to taste, if using. Serve hot.

SLICED BEEF IN
BLACK BEAN SAUCE

SERVES: *4* | **PREP:** *15 mins* | **COOK:** *10–12 mins*

INGREDIENTS

3 tbsp groundnut oil

450 g/1 lb sirloin steak, thinly sliced

*1 red pepper, deseeded and thinly
  sliced*

*1 green pepper, deseeded and thinly
  sliced*

1 bunch of spring onions, sliced

2 garlic cloves, crushed

1 tbsp grated fresh ginger

2 tbsp black bean sauce

1 tbsp sherry

1 tbsp soy sauce

1. Preheat a wok or large frying pan over a high heat. Add 2 tablespoons of the oil and heat until very hot. Add the beef and stir-fry until beginning to brown. Remove and set aside.

2. Add the remaining oil and the red and green peppers and stir-fry for 2 minutes.

3. Add the spring onions, garlic and ginger and stir-fry for 30 seconds.

4. Add the black bean sauce, sherry and soy sauce, then stir in the beef and heat until bubbling. Serve immediately.

CHAPTER FIVE

DESSERTS
& DRINKS

COCONUT MILK, STRAWBERRY & HONEY ICE CREAM

SERVES: 6 | **PREP:** *30 mins, plus freezing* | **COOK:** *No cooking*

INGREDIENTS

*450 g/1 lb strawberries, hulled and
   halved*
*400 ml/14 fl oz canned full-fat
   coconut milk*
85 g/3 oz clear honey

1. Purée the strawberries in a food processor or liquidizer, then press through a sieve set over a mixing bowl to remove the seeds.

2. Add the coconut milk and honey to the strawberry purée and whisk together.

3. Pour the mixture into a large roasting tin to a depth of 2 cm/¾ inch, cover the top of the tin with clingfilm, then freeze for about 2 hours until just set.

4. Scoop back into the food processor or liquidizer and blitz again until smooth to break down the ice crystals. Pour into a plastic container or 900-g/2-lb loaf tin lined with non-stick baking paper. Place the lid on the plastic container or fold the paper over the ice cream in the loaf tin. Return to the freezer for 3–4 hours, or until firm enough to scoop.

5. Serve immediately or leave in the freezer overnight or until needed. Thaw at room temperature for 15 minutes to soften slightly, then scoop into individual dishes to serve.

CHOCOLATE YOGURT POPS

MAKES: *10 pops* | **PREP:** *20 mins, plus freezing* | **COOK:** *No cooking*

INGREDIENTS

325 g/11½ oz Greek-style yogurt
2 bananas, peeled and mashed
4 tsp honey
300 g /10½ oz dark chocolate, chopped
100 g/3½ oz coconut oil
100 g/3½ oz milk chocolate, chopped
100 g/3½ oz white chocolate, chopped
1 tbsp pistachio nuts, chopped

YOU WILL ALSO NEED:

10 x 100 ml/3½ fl oz ice lolly moulds
10 ice lolly sticks

1. Place the yogurt in a bowl with the mashed banana and honey. Mix well.

2. Pour the yogurt mixture into 10 x 100 ml/3½ fl oz lolly moulds. Insert the ice lolly sticks and freeze for at least 2 hours.

3. Gently melt the dark chocolate and coconut oil in a heatproof bowl suspended over a pan of simmering water. Don't let the bowl touch the water.

4. Melt the milk chocolate in the same way as the dark chocolate.

5. Remove the lollies from their moulds and dip into the melted dark chocolate and coconut oil, then return to the freezer for a couple of minutes to set.

6. To decorate the lollies, swirl milk chocolate around each one with a fork, then sprinkle with white chocolate and pistachio nuts. Return to the freezer to set.

MINI APPLE CRUMBLES

SERVES: *4* | **PREP:** *15 mins* | **COOK:** *20 mins*

INGREDIENTS

2 large Bramley apples, peeled,
cored and chopped
3 tbsp maple syrup
juice of ½ lemon
½ tsp ground allspice
55 g/2 oz unsalted butter
100 g/3½ oz rolled oats
40 g/1½ oz light muscovado sugar

1. Preheat the oven to 220°C/425°F/Gas Mark 7. Place a baking sheet in the oven to heat. Put the apples into a saucepan and stir in the maple syrup, lemon juice and allspice.

2. Bring to the boil over a high heat, then reduce the heat to medium, cover the pan and cook for 5 minutes, or until almost tender.

3. Meanwhile, melt the butter in a separate saucepan, then remove from the heat and stir in the oats and sugar.

4. Divide the apples between four 200-ml/7-fl oz ovenproof dishes. Sprinkle over the oat mixture. Place in the oven on the preheated baking sheet and bake for 10 minutes until lightly browned and bubbling. Serve warm.

GRILLED STONE FRUIT POTS

SERVES: 6 | **PREP:** 10 mins | **COOK:** 5–10 mins

INGREDIENTS

375 g/13 oz low-fat ricotta cheese

2 tsp freshly grated orange rind

3 firm, ripe peaches, stoned and quartered

3 firm, ripe nectarines, stoned and quartered

3 ripe plums, apricots or figs, stoned and halved or quartered

2 tbsp honey

2 tbsp flaked almonds

1. In a medium-size bowl, stir together the ricotta and orange rind.

2. Preheat the grill to medium–high and grill the fruit, cut side down, turning once or twice, for about 5 minutes or until they are softened and beginning to caramelize.

3. To serve, spoon the ricotta into six small dessert bowls or cups. Top each with some grilled fruit, drizzle with the honey and sprinkle the almonds over the top. Serve immediately.

CRUNCH-TOPPED
ROAST PEARS

SERVES: *4* | **PREP:** *10 mins* | **COOK:** *20 mins*

INGREDIENTS

4 dessert pears, such as Comice or
Bartlett, each weighing about
150 g/5½ oz
200 ml/7 fl oz medium white wine
1 tbsp demerara sugar
½ tsp mixed spice
25 g/1 oz mixed nuts, toasted and
chopped
15 g/ ½ oz rolled oats
2 tbsp wholemeal breadcrumbs
2 tbsp sunflower seeds
8 sprays of cooking oil spray

1. Preheat the oven to 190°C/375°F/Gas Mark 5.

2. Cut the pears in half lengthways and remove the cores. Place in a large shallow baking dish. Pour the white wine around the pears and bake in the preheated oven for 10 minutes.

3. Meanwhile, combine the sugar, spice, nuts, oats, breadcrumbs and sunflower seeds in a bowl.

4. Remove the pears from the oven, top each with some of the nut mixture, then spray with cooking oil spray. Return to the oven for 7–8 minutes, or until the topping is golden. Serve drizzled with any juice left in the dish.

CHOCOLATE, CINNAMON & VANILLA CUSTARD POTS

MAKES: *8 pots* | **PREP:** *20 mins* | **COOK:** *50 mins, plus chilling*

INGREDIENTS

450 ml/15 fl oz semi-skimmed milk

200 g/7 oz 70% plain chocolate, broken into pieces, plus 1 tbsp finely grated plain chocolate to decorate

1 tsp vanilla extract

¼ tsp ground cinnamon

4 tbsp runny honey

2 eggs, plus 2 egg yolks

90 g/3¼ oz 0% fat Greek-style natural yogurt, to decorate

1. Preheat the oven to 150°C/300°F/Gas Mark 2. Pour the milk into a heavy-bottomed saucepan, bring just to the boil, then take off the heat and stir in the chocolate pieces, vanilla extract, cinnamon and 3 tablespoons of honey. Set aside for 5 minutes, or until the chocolate has melted. Stir until the milk is an even dark chocolate colour.

2. Put the eggs and egg yolks in a large jug and beat lightly with a fork. Gradually pour in the warm chocolate milk, beating all the time with a wooden spoon, until smooth. Strain back into the saucepan through a sieve, then press any remaining chocolate through the sieve using the back of the wooden spoon.

3. Put six 175-ml/6-fl oz ovenproof cups or ramekins in a roasting tin. Fill the cups with the chocolate milk, then pour hot water into the roasting tin to reach halfway up the cups. Cover the cups with foil, then bake for 40–45 minutes, or until the custards are just set, with a slight wobble in the centre.

4. Using oven gloves, lift the cups out of the roasting tin and leave to cool, then cover with clingfilm and chill in the refrigerator for 4–5 hours.

5. Place the cups on a serving platter, remove the clingfilm and top each with a spoonful of yogurt, a drizzle of the remaining honey and a little grated chocolate.

NO-BAKE BERRY CHEESECAKE

SERVES: *8* | **PREP:** *20 mins, plus chilling* | **COOK:** *No cooking*

INGREDIENTS

2 tbsp melted coconut oil
50 g/1¾ oz walnuts
60 g/2¼ oz ground almonds
200 g/7 oz Medjool dates, stoned

FILLING

600 g/1 lb 5 oz cream cheese
grated zest of 2 lemons
100 g/3½ oz icing sugar
100 ml/3½ fl oz double cream
200 g/7 oz Greek-style natural
*   yogurt*

TOPPING

100 g/3½ oz blueberries
100 g/3½ oz raspberries
100 g/3½ oz strawberries
cacao nibs and fresh mint leaves, to
*   decorate*

1. Lightly oil a 23-cm/9-inch springform tin with 1 tablespoon of the coconut oil.

2. Place the walnuts, ground almonds and dates in a food processor and blitz until they are broken down to fine crumbs. With the machine running, pour in the remaining coconut oil.

3. Press the mixture into the base of the prepared tin.

4. To make the filling, place the cream cheese, lemon zest and icing sugar in a bowl and whisk until smooth. Add the cream and yogurt, and continue to whisk until the mixture is combined and stiff.

5. Spoon the cream cheese filling onto the base and chill in the refrigerator for at least 3 hours.

6. Remove the cheesecake from the tin and place on a serving plate. Sprinkle over the blueberries and raspberries.

7. Purée the strawberries in a blender and drizzle over the top of the cheesecake. Decorate with cacao nibs and mint leaves to serve.

COCONUT ICE

MAKES: *approx. 50 pieces* | **PREP:** *25 mins, plus setting* | **COOK:** *No cooking*

INGREDIENTS

sunflower oil, for oiling
400 g/14 oz canned condensed milk
1 tsp vanilla extract
300 g/10½ oz desiccated coconut
300 g/10½ oz icing sugar
3 tbsp cocoa powder, sifted
few drops of red or pink food
*   colouring (optional)*

1. Oil the base of a shallow 18-cm/7-inch square cake tin and line with baking paper. Mix the condensed milk and vanilla extract together in a large bowl. Add the coconut and icing sugar. Stir with a wooden spoon until the mixture becomes very stiff.

2. Transfer half of the mixture to a separate bowl. Add the cocoa powder and mix well until it is an even colour. Spread over the base of the prepared tin and press down with the back of a spoon.

3. If using food colouring, mix a few drops into the remaining bowl of mixture until evenly pink in colour. Spread over the chocolate layer and smooth the top. Leave to set overnight before turning out and cutting into squares.

CHOCOLATE ORANGE MUG CAKE

SERVES: *1* | **PREP:** *3 mins* | **COOK:** *2 mins*

INGREDIENTS

20 g/¾ oz almond butter
1 heaped tbsp gram flour
1 heaped tbsp cocoa powder
½ tsp baking powder
2 tsp caster sugar
1 large egg
grated zest of 1 orange
Greek-style natural yogurt, to serve

1. Place the almond butter, flour, cocoa powder, baking powder, sugar, egg and half the orange zest in a large microwave-proof mug and mix well together with a teaspoon.

2. Bake in the microwave on Medium for 2 minutes until risen and cooked through.

3. Serve the mug cake with a dollop of yogurt, sprinkled with the remaining orange zest.

CHURROS

MAKES: *16 churros* | **PREP:** *30 mins, plus cooling* | **COOK:** *25–30 mins*

INGREDIENTS

225 ml/8 fl oz water

85 g/3 oz butter or lard, diced

2 tbsp dark muscovado sugar

*finely grated rind of 1 small orange
   (optional)*

pinch of salt

175 g/6 oz plain flour, sifted

*1 tsp ground cinnamon, plus extra
   for dusting*

1 tsp vanilla extract

2 eggs

groundnut oil, for deep-frying

caster sugar, for dusting

1. Heat the water, butter, muscovado sugar, orange rind, if using, and salt in a heavy-based saucepan over a medium heat until the butter has melted. Add the flour, cinnamon and vanilla extract, then remove from the heat and beat rapidly until the mixture pulls away from the side of the pan.

2. Leave to cool slightly, then beat in the eggs, one at a time, beating well after each addition, until the mixture is thick and smooth. Spoon into a piping bag fitted with a wide star nozzle.

3. Heat enough oil for deep-frying in a large saucepan or deep-fryer to 180–190°C/350–375°F, or until a cube of bread browns in 30 seconds. Pipe 13-cm/5-inch lengths about 7.5 cm/3 inches apart into the hot oil. Fry for 2–3 minutes, turning frequently, until crisp and golden. Remove with a slotted spoon and drain on kitchen paper. Keep the cooked churros warm while frying the remaining mixture.

4. Dust with caster sugar and cinnamon to serve.

PIÑA COLADA LOLLIES

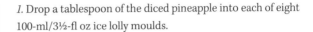

MAKES: *8 lollies* | **PREP:** *25 mins, plus freezing* | **COOK:** *No cooking*

INGREDIENTS

600 g/1 lb 5 oz pineapple flesh,
finely diced
200 ml/7 fl oz coconut milk
6 tbsp caster sugar
2 tbsp coconut-flavoured white rum

YOU WILL ALSO NEED:

8 x 100 ml/3½ fl oz ice lolly moulds
8 ice lolly sticks

1. Drop a tablespoon of the diced pineapple into each of eight 100-ml/3½-fl oz ice lolly moulds.

2. Put the remaining pineapple in a blender with the coconut milk, sugar and rum and whizz until smooth.

3. Strain through a fine metal sieve, pressing down to extract all the juice. Discard the solids. Pour the mixture into the ice lolly moulds. Insert the ice lolly sticks and freeze for 6–8 hours, or until firm.

4. To unmould the lollies, dip the frozen moulds into warm water for a few seconds and gently release the lollies while holding the sticks.

BEERAMISU

SERVES: *8* | **PREP:** *20–25 mins, plus chilling* | **COOK:** *No cooking*

INGREDIENTS

750 g/1 lb 10 oz mascarpone cheese
600 ml/1 pint double cream
300 g/10½ oz caster sugar
450 ml/16 fl oz stout
1 tbsp vanilla extract
50 sponge fingers
2 double shots espresso
400 ml/14 fl oz Irish cream liqueur
cocoa powder, for dusting

1. In a large bowl beat together the mascarpone cheese, cream and sugar until combined. Gradually add the stout and vanilla extract and beat until the mixture resembles a thick cream.

2. In a medium-sized bowl soak the sponge fingers in the espresso and Irish cream liqueur for around 10 seconds, then break up the softened biscuits using a spoon.

3. In a large bowl layer the mascarpone mixture and then the soaked biscuit mixture alternately until there are two layers of each mixture. Finish off with a final layer of the mascarpone mixture.

4. Chill in the refrigerator for at least 3 hours, or until ready to serve. To serve, remove from the refrigerator and dust with cocoa powder.

GRAPEFRUIT & CHERRY GIN & TONIC

SERVES: *1* | **PREP:** *5 mins* | **COOK:** *No cooking*

INGREDIENTS

1 slice grapefruit

4 cherries, stoned

2 measures gin

ice cubes

175 ml/6 fl oz tonic water

2 cherries, stoned, to decorate

1. Cut the grapefruit slice into chunks.

2. Place the grapefruit and cherries into a cocktail shaker.

3. Using a muddler, crush the grapefruit and cherries for about 30 seconds to release the flavour and oils.

4. Add the gin to the cocktail shaker and stir. Pour the mixture into a Collins or highball glass.

5. Add some ice cubes to the glass and top up with tonic water.

6. Decorate with cherries on top and serve immediately.

CLUB MOJITO

SERVES: *1* | **PREP:** *10 mins* | **COOK:** *No cooking*

INGREDIENTS

1 tsp sugar syrup

6 fresh mint leaves, plus extra to garnish

juice of ½ lime

4–6 cracked ice cubes

2 measures Jamaican rum

soda water

dash Angostura bitters

1. Put the sugar syrup, mint leaves and lime juice into a chilled glass.

2. Muddle the mint leaves, then add the cracked ice cubes and rum.

3. Top up with soda water and finish with the Angostura bitters. Garnish with the extra mint leaves and serve immediately.

FROZEN STRAWBERRY DAIQUIRIS

SERVES: *2* | **PREP:** *12–15 mins, plus cooling* | **COOK:** *5 mins*

INGREDIENTS

400 g/14 oz strawberries

8 ice cubes

100 ml/3½ fl oz white rum

50 ml/2 fl oz lime juice

SUGAR SYRUP

55 g/2 oz caster sugar

75 ml/2½ fl oz water

1. To make the sugar syrup, put the sugar and water in a saucepan and heat gently, stirring, until the sugar has dissolved. Bring to the boil, then cook over a medium heat, without stirring, for 2 minutes. Remove from the heat and leave to cool slightly.

2. Hull and slice the strawberries, leaving two whole for decoration.

3. Crush the ice in a blender. Add 2 teaspoons of the cooled sugar syrup to the ice (you can store the remaining sugar syrup in the refrigerator for several weeks).

4. Add the rum, lime juice and sliced strawberries. Blend until slushy, then pour into chilled cocktail glasses. Decorate the sides of the glasses with whole strawberries.

CIDER & RASPBERRY SLUSHIE

SERVES: *1* | **PREP:** *10 mins, plus freezing* | **COOK:** *No cooking*

INGREDIENTS

500 ml/18 fl oz cider
150 g/5½ oz fresh raspberries
2 fresh raspberries, to decorate

1. Pour the cider into a freezerproof plastic container with a lid.

2. Secure the lid and place in the freezer for 3 hours, or until the cider has frozen.

3. Remove the cider from the freezer and break up with a fork until you have small chunks.

4. Put the raspberries in a blender with the cider chunks and blend until slushy.

5. Serve immediately in a pint glass with a straw and decorate with the fresh raspberries.

PEACH & BASIL
GIN FIX

SERVES: *1* | **PREP:** *15 mins, plus cooling* | **COOK:** *5 mins*

INGREDIENTS

1 ripe peach, cut into thin slices
125 ml/4 fl oz water
100 g/3½ oz caster sugar
12 fresh basil leaves
crushed ice
2 measures gin
¾ measure lemon juice
peach slices, to decorate (optional)
fresh basil leaves, to decorate
  (optional)

1. Place the peach slices, water and sugar into a saucepan and bring to the boil over a high heat. Add the basil leaves then remove from the heat and leave to cool. Once cooled, strain the liquid through a fine sieve and store in a sterilized, sealable jar.

2. Fill a lowball glass with crushed ice. Add 1 measure of the peach-infused syrup to the glass and then add the gin and lemon juice. Any remaining syrup should be stored in the refrigerator and used within 1 week.

3. Stir well and decorate the glass with the peach slices and basil leaves, if using. Serve immediately.

BLACKBERRY MARGARITA

SERVES: *4* | **PREP:** *15 mins* | **COOK:** *No cooking*

INGREDIENTS

200 g/7 oz blackberries
handful ice cubes
1 tbsp caster sugar
8 measures tequila
4 measures triple sec
2 measures lime juice
1 lime wedge
1 tbsp sea salt
4 blackberries, to decorate
4 mint sprigs, to decorate

1. Place the blackberries, ice cubes, caster sugar, tequila, triple sec and lime juice into a blender.

2. Blend the mixture for about 1 minute, or until completely smooth.

3. Rub the rims of four chilled margarita glasses with the lime wedge. Place the sea salt on a small plate and roll the rims in the salt.

4. Divide the cocktail carefully between the four glasses.

5. Decorate with the blackberries and mint and serve immediately.

BEETROOT
VIRGIN MARY

SERVES: *1* | **PREP:** *10 mins* | **COOK:** *No cooking*

INGREDIENTS

30 g/1 oz raw beetroot, peeled
175 ml/6 fl oz tomato juice
1 tsp Worcestershire sauce
¼ tsp celery salt
¼ tsp pepper
1 tsp freshly grated horseradish
½ tsp hot pepper sauce
ice cubes
1 lemon slice, to decorate
1 celery stick, to decorate

1. Cut the beetroot into small pieces. Place in a cocktail shaker and crush thoroughly with a muddler or pestle to release the colour and flavour.

2. Add the tomato juice, Worcestershire sauce, celery salt, pepper, horseradish and hot pepper sauce. Stir well with a bar spoon.

3. Pour the mixture into a Collins or highball glass.

4. Add some ice cubes and stir again.

5. Decorate the drink with the lemon slice and celery stick. Serve immediately.

KIWI & CUCUMBER INFUSED WATER

MAKES: *1.5 litres/ 2¾ pints* | **PREP:** *20 mins, plus freezing* | **COOK:** *No Cooking*

INGREDIENTS

½ cucumber

2 kiwis, peeled and thickly sliced

1 litre/1¾ pints chilled water

LEMON ICE CUBES

zest of 1 lemon

water to fill an ice-cube tray

1. Make your lemon ice cubes at least 4 hours before they are needed. Cut the lemon zest into pieces that will sit neatly in the holes of an ice-cube tray. Place the zest pieces in the holes of the tray and fill the holes with water. Freeze for at least 4–6 hours, or until needed.

2. When ready to serve, peel ribbons from a cucumber using a vegetable peeler. Place the ribbons in the bottom of a jug, along with the fresh kiwi slices.

3. Add the lemon zest ice cubes to the jug and top up with the chilled water. Serve immediately.

INDEX

..... ✕ .....

This edition published by Parragon Books Ltd in 2017
LOVE FOOD is an imprint of Parragon Books Ltd

Parragon Books Ltd
Chartist House
15–17 Trim Street
Bath BA1 1HA, UK
www.parragon.com/lovefood

Copyright © Parragon Books Ltd 2017

LOVE FOOD and the accompanying heart device is a
registered trademark of Parragon Books Ltd in Australia,
the UK, USA, India and the EU.

All rights reserved. No part of this publication may be
reproduced, stored in a retrieval system or transmitted,
in any form or by any means, electronic, mechanical,
photocopying, recording or otherwise, without the prior
permission of the copyright holder.

ISBN 978-1-4748-6890-7

Printed in China

Edited by Fiona Biggs
Cover photography by Al Richardson

The cover shot shows the Pad Thai on page 126.

.... *Notes for the Reader* ....

This book uses both metric and imperial measurements.
Follow the same units of measurement throughout;
do not mix metric and imperial. All spoon measurements
are level: teaspoons are assumed to be 5 ml, and tablespoons
are assumed to be 15 ml. Unless otherwise stated, milk
is assumed to be full fat, eggs and individual fruits and
vegetables are medium, pepper is freshly ground black
pepper and salt is table salt. Unless otherwise stated,
all root vegetables should be peeled prior to using.

The times given are an approximate guide only.
Preparation times differ according to the techniques used
by different people and the cooking times may also vary
from those given. Please consume alcohol responsibly.